David G. Richards

# Georg Büchner's *Woyzeck*

## A History of Its Criticism

CAMDEN HOUSE

First published 2001
by Camden House

Camden House is an imprint of Boydell & Brewer Inc.
PO Box 41026, Rochester, NY 14604–4126 USA
and of Boydell & Brewer Limited
PO Box 9, Woodbridge, Suffolk IP12 3DF, UK

ISBN: 1–57113–220–1

**Library of Congress Cataloging-in-Publication Data**

Richards, David G., 1935–
 Georg Büchner's Woyzeck: A history of its criticism / David G. Richards.
  p. cm. — (Studies in German literature, linguistics, and culture. Literary
criticism in perspective).
 Includes bibliographical references and index.
 ISBN 1–57113–220–1 (alk. paper)
 1. Büchner, Georg, 1813–1837. Woyzeck. I. Title. II. Studies in German literature, linguistics, and culture (Unnumbered). Literary criticism in perspective.

PT1828.B6 R52 2001
832'.7—dc21

                                                                00–067460

A catalogue record for this title is available from the British Library.

This publication is printed on acid-free paper.
Printed in the United States of America

*For Friederike*

# Contents

# Acknowledgments

I AM GRATEFUL TO Dean Kerry S. Grant of the College of Arts and Sciences, University at Buffalo, for support from the College's Research Initiative Fund, to my wife Friederike for her patience and helpful suggestions, to Jim Hardin for his critique of my manuscript, and especially to Jim Walker for his careful and expert copyediting and editorial assistance.

D. G. R.
September 2000

# Introduction

ALTHOUGH GEORG BÜCHNER'S DRAMA WOYZECK was never completed by the author and exists only in drafts or fragments of drafts, its influence on German drama of the twentieth century, and perhaps on European drama as well, is without equal. Georg Steiner writes that it "poses in a new way the entire problem of modern tragedy" (1963, 271). According to Walter Höllerer: "The psychological, the social-critical, the realistic, the naturalistic, the expressive, the surreal, the epic, the lyrical, and the 'gestic' (Beckett, Ionesco, Adamov) theater can refer to Georg Büchner as a source, and do refer to him" (1958, 66). *Woyzeck* is one of the few plays Antonin Artaud wanted to stage as part of his program for the "Theater of Cruelty." Büchner's works have served as models for the documentary theater of Peter Weiss, Rolf Hochhuth, and Heinar Kipphardt, and they have been admired and imitated by such German dramatists as Gerhart Hauptmann, Frank Wedekind, Georg Kaiser, Ernst Toller, Ödön von Horváth, Bertolt Brecht, Max Frisch, and Heiner Müller. Max Reinhardt, the preeminent theater director of his time, told Bertolt Brecht that *Woyzeck* was the "strongest drama of German literature" (Hartung 1988, 1102). In Alban Berg's adaptation it has also become the text of one of the century's greatest operas, *Wozzeck*.

The rise to this kind of stature and recognition by an author whose literary works were created in the hours stolen from his study of anatomy and other medical disciplines and who died at the age of twenty-three, an author whose literary output consists of one work published during his lifetime (*Dantons Tod*), another one ready for publication (*Leonce und Lena*) and two unfinished manuscripts (*Lenz* and *Woyzeck*) surely provides one of the most remarkable and fascinating subjects in the history of the reception of literary works. During his lifetime Büchner attracted very little attention, and that primarily from other writers who recognized his potential more than his actual accomplishment. In words written by Georg Herwegh in commemoration of Büchner and inscribed on his tombstone: "Ein unvollendet Lied sinkt er ins Grab, / Der Verse schönste nimmt er mit hinab" (He sinks as an uncompleted song into his grave / Taking his most beautiful verses with him). And again, it was primarily other writers, including Karl Emil Franzos, the first editor of *Woyzeck*, who led the way in Büchner's rediscovery at the end of the nineteenth century. Gerhart Hauptmann discovered him for naturalism, Frank Wedekind and Georg Kaiser for expressionism, Bertolt Brecht for the epic theater, and so on.

Except for numerous essays published by Franzos, criticism on Büchner in the nineteenth century was limited to brief entries in literary histories. Then, following the lead of Hauptmann, Wedekind, and other representatives of the new literary movements, critics after the turn of the century began to pay serious attention to Büchner's works. In keeping with the tendencies of the time, this early criticism dealt primarily with the works in the context of the author's biography and with his relationship to contemporary literary movements and other intellectual currents. After coming to a standstill during the Third Reich, criticism resumed with the comprehensive and complementary studies by Hans Mayer and Karl Viëtor in the fifties which were followed by what may be seen as the most fruitful period of Büchner-scholarship, a period that includes close and thorough investigation of the language, form, and content of the works, the publication of several new editions, and, in the case of *Woyzeck*, a lively controversy with regard to the construction of an editorially sound and valid reading and acting text from the fragments of this unfinished work.

Following more than two decades of close analysis of the language and form of the works, criticism of the eighties and nineties opened up to include greater emphasis on the content of the works in a variety of contexts such as the political, social, and scientific conditions of the time in which they take place and in which they were written. Seen as relevant for a full understanding of *Woyzeck*, for example, is the situation of soldiers, the state of medical knowledge as it pertained to the evaluation of the historical Woyzeck's behavior, the implications his mental disturbances and the court's evaluations of them had on the judgment of his criminal act, and the relationship of these factors to the social and political situation of his time. Other trends of recent criticism have been to explore in greater depth the themes, motifs, and other elements identified by earlier interpreters and to apply new methodologies to the analysis of the play: feminist critics, for example, have placed greater emphasis on Marie and her fate as it unfolds in a patriarchal society.

Since *Woyzeck's* belated publication by the novelist and amateur editor, Karl Emil Franzos, interpreters and critics have had to rely on versions of the text put together with varying degrees of editorial expertise and objectivity. Hence the history and problematics of editing have become an integral and unavoidable part of the criticism of the play. Some discussion of and reference to editions is spread throughout the following text, but for the most part I have dealt with the topic separately in chapter three.

While not meant to be complete, my review of the criticism on *Woyzeck* includes most of the works that have been repeatedly cited by subsequent critics and that in my view contribute to a better understanding of the text. Listed in the bibliography are all works cited but by no means all the works I have read. Not included, for example, are studies comparing *Woyzeck* and works by other authors and discussions of possible influence, unless such studies open a new perspective or shed new light on Büchner's play. Similarly, the findings of more recent investigations of the historical, scientific, and sociological situation of Woyzeck's time have been included only in so far as they relate to Büchner's drama.

The goal of the present study, then, is to bring together in one place the most important and relevant findings from a century of critical writing on Büchner's *Woyzeck*. The magnitude of the task faced by someone wanting to gain familiarity with criticism on Büchner can be suggested by reference to Werner Schlick's bibliography of writings on Büchner up to 1965 (*Das Georg Büchner-Schrifttum bis 1965: Eine Internationale Bibliographie*, 1968), a terminus that immediately precedes the true explosion of writings on Büchner. Schlick's bibliography contains just under eight hundred items. No complete bibliography has been published subsequent to Schlick's. For updates readers must consult the reviews of scholarship by Gerhard Knapp (1975, 1977, and 1984), the bibliographies contained in critical works, and those published in the *Georg Büchner Jahrbuch*. No review of Büchner scholarship exists in English, and none of the *Forschungsberichte* in German, such as Knapp's, contains anything like the detail of the current study. (Knapp's review of scholarship on *Woyzeck* consists of twenty-four pages, including three of bibliography.)

Quotations from Büchner's works are from Werner R. Lehmann's Hamburg edition. Citations from works other than *Woyzeck* are indicated by volume and page numbers, those from *Woyzeck*, by draft and scene, for example, H4,7, with the addition in most cases of the scene's title or some other means of identification. Editors now agree that Büchner worked on *Woyzeck* in three phases. At the time of his death he was in the process of writing out a final, complete version (H4 in Lehmann's designation) from two earlier drafts or compositional stages. The first stage, designated H1 by Lehmann, consists of two or three scenes taking place at a fair followed by a sequence of scenes leading up to and including the murder and its aftermath. In the second draft or group of scenes, H2, Büchner adds the Captain and the

Doctor, deepens the characterization of Woyzeck and Marie, and expands the horizons of their world. Two additional scenes exist apart from these three major scenic groups and are designated H3 by Lehmann. There is no clear evidence as to when they were written or how they relate to the other groups of scenes. (See the appendix for a complete list of scenes.)

# Works Cited

Franzos, Karl Emil, ed. *Sämmtliche Werke und handschriftlicher Nachlaß: Erste kritische Gesammt-Ausgabe.* Frankfurt: J. D. Sauerländer, 1879.

Hartung, Günter. "Woyzecks Wahn." *Weimarer Beiträge* 34 (1988): 1102–17.

Höllerer, Walter. "Georg Büchner." Chap. in *Zwischen Klassik und Moderne. Lachen und Weinen in der Dichtung einer Übergangszeit*, 100–142. Stuttgart: Ernst Klett Verlag, 1958.

Knapp, Gerhard P. *Georg Büchner.* Stuttgart: Sammlung Metzler, 1977. 2nd ed., 1985.

Knapp, Gerhard P. *Georg Büchner: Eine kritische Einführung in die Forschung.* Frankfurt: Fischer Athenäum Taschenbücher, 1975.

Lehmann, Werner R. *Georg Büchner: Sämtliche Werke und Briefe. Vol. 1, Dichtungen und Übersetzungen mit Dokumentation zur Stoffgeschichte.* Hamburg: Christian Wegner Verlag, 1967.

Schlick, Werner. *Das Georg Büchner-Schrifttum bis 1965: Eine Internationale Bibliographie.* Hildesheim: Georg Olms Verlagsbuchhandlung, 1968.

Steiner, George. *The Death of Tragedy.* New York: Hill and Wang, 1963.

# 1: Criticism to 1945

B ETWEEN JANUARY 1835 AND HIS DEATH IN FEBRUARY 1837 at the age of twenty-three, Georg Büchner dashed off four literary works of such power and originality that they have gained secure places in the literary canon. And even though his final two works, *Lenz* and *Woyzeck*, remained unfinished, they have become recognized as precursors of modern prose and drama and have had an extraordinary influence on twentieth-century literature. During this brief period of literary activity Büchner also carried out the meticulous research for and wrote a doctoral dissertation on the nervous system of a fish, the barbel, and translated two plays by Victor Hugo. Before writing his first literary work, he had already made a name for himself as the author of one of the most radical and revolutionary political pamphlets of the century, "Der hessische Landbote" (The Hessian Courier), as a consequence of which he was forced to seek safety in exile, first in Strasbourg and then in Zurich, where his life and promising career as a professor at the university of Zurich were cut short by typhoid fever.

The only one of his literary works to be published during Büchner's lifetime was *Dantons Tod* (Danton's Death), which had been recommended to the publisher by the writer and critic Karl Gutzkow. Efforts on the part of Gutzkow and Büchner's family to publish Büchner's literary remains came to naught because of petty bickering over royalties and the lack of cooperation of Büchner's fiancée Minna Jaeglé, who had come into conflict with members of the Büchner family. The ultimate consequence of this conflict was the loss to posterity of Büchner's journal, a significant part of his correspondence, and possibly a play about Pietro Aretino, all of which were destroyed by Minna in a misguided attempt to protect his memory and reputation. The family too can be faulted for its careless disregard of Büchner's manuscripts, which they did not protect from being damaged by water and mice.

Fortunately, Gutzkow published *Leonce und Lena* and *Lenz* in the periodical *Telegraph für Deutschland* in 1838 and 1839 respectively and again in 1842 in a collection of diverse short works he edited. In 1850 Büchner's brother Ludwig brought together the previously published works with excerpts from Büchner's letters in an edition of his *Nachgelassene Schriften* (Literary Remains). Lacking appreciation for his art and in an effort to make his brother appear less radical, Ludwig took considerable liberty in altering the texts. And, although he knew it to be his brother's favorite work, he did not make an effort to include *Woyzeck*, allegedly because of the difficulty in deciphering his brother's handwriting and of deriving a coherent text from drafts representing different stages of composition, but also, as he later admitted to Karl Emil Franzos, because of the "cynicism" of that work.

It was not until more than four decades after Büchner's death that *Woyzeck* was made public by Franzos, a journalist and novelist, whose edition of the text first appeared in 1875 in *Die Neue Freie Presse*, a Viennese newspaper, then again in 1877 in a Berlin weekly, *Mehr Licht*, and finally in his 1879 edition of Büchner's *Sämmtliche Werke und handschriftlicher Nachlaß* (Collected Works and Literary Remains). The volume claims in a subtitle to be the first "critical" edition, but in fact Franzos was an amateur editor, whose edition, especially in the case of *Woyzeck* (or *Wozzeck* as he read it), is anything but critical. Despite the shortcomings of his text, however, the importance of Franzos's contribution to the rediscovery of Büchner should not be underestimated, for there is no telling what might have happened to Büchner's manuscripts had he not taken a passionate interest in them.

Franzos was later severely criticized by Georg Witkowski, who in the second decade of the twentieth century received the task of editing the newly acquired manuscripts for the Insel publishing house. Witkowski complained that Franzos had mishandled the manuscripts of *Woyzeck* in a "barbaric" fashion by treating them with chemicals in order to be able to decipher them, and that his construction and editing of the text was arbitrary and indefensible. From 1879 until the publication of Witkowski's edition in 1920, the only available texts of *Woyzeck* were Franzos's and constructions largely based on his which were included in the collected works edited by Paul Landau (1909), Rudolf Franz (1912), and Wilhelm Hausenstein (1916). Because of the problem of editing the text and of attempting to assemble a sequence of scenes that is sufficiently complete to be performed in the theater or read as a play, the earliest criticism of *Woyzeck* is textual criticism.

Franzos's work first became suspect in 1914 when Hugo Bieber revealed his discovery of documents relating to the accountability of one Johann Christian Woyzeck (not Wozzeck), who had been tried and found guilty for the murder of his mistress. Bieber refers to the evaluation of Woyzeck's mental state that was published by the court appointed doctor, Johann Christian Clarus, to the ensuing controversy between experts contesting and disagreeing with Clarus's findings, and to Clarus's second evaluation, in which he found no reason to disagree with his initial findings and in consequence of which Woyzeck was publicly executed in Leipzig on 27 August 1824.

Based on Bieber's findings and his study of the original manuscripts, Hausenstein opts for the spelling "Woyzeck" for his Insel edition of 1916, a reading also accepted by Witkowski. Büchner clearly writes "Woyzeck" whenever he uses the entire name; otherwise he uses a variety of abbreviations such as "Wozeck" and "Wozek." (Büchner always wrote in haste and had a tendency to abbreviate.) Long after "Woyzeck" had been accepted as the correct reading, however, the play continued to be known as "Wozzeck," in large part because of Alban Berg's masterful opera by that name, which is based on Franzos's text.

Much more egregious than his misreading of the name, however, is Franzos's claim to have accurately reproduced the text of the manuscript, when in fact he added material of his own, made cuts and changes in Büchner's text, and transposed passages: "If a passage was so illegible that I could only conjecture its content, not ascertain it with certainty," he wrote,

> then I preferred to omit it completely, instead of writing down my supposition. For the scenes that were contained in both the first and second version I used the text of the latter, with the exception of just one scene that was incomparably stronger and more colorful in the older version. . . . As far as the sequence of scenes is concerned, this was naturally a difficult matter, since no indication for that is contained in the manuscripts. Besides the necessary concern for the content I was also governed by another, aesthetic consideration in determining this sequence. It was my effort to arrange the two elements which constitute "Wozzek," the grotesque and the tragic, so that the effect of the latter would not be weakened by the former.
>
> Not a syllable has been omitted. Where all-too-coarse expressions were simply indicated by initial letters and dashes, the poet had already done the same. (Franzos, 204)

According to Witkowski, however, Büchner does not refrain from writing out coarse words, and Franzos does in fact omit extensive passages without justification. He also gives false information about the manuscript itself and the degree of its illegibility, and he fails to recognize the coherent sequences of scenes constituting different stages of composition (24–25; see Franzos, 203). Witkowski concludes that Franzos had no understanding for Büchner's art, which was foreign to his time. In the same way that painting used to be restored according to the stylistic principles current at the time of restoration, Franzos distorted the grand conception of Büchner's work and severely diminished his artistry by presenting a text that is a poor copy of the original (30–31).

The sequence of scenes in Franzos's edition had already been criticized and altered by Paul Landau in his 1909 edition of Büchner's works, an edition noteworthy for its fine biographical and historical introduction. To strengthen the exposition and remove some of the "gaps and deficiencies of incompleteness" in Franzos's text (149), Landau rearranges some of the first nine scenes. He begins with a group of scenes that introduce Woyzeck and the various activities he is engaged in to earn money, that is, the scenes with the Captain and the Doctor (H4,5; H4,1; H4,2; and H4,8). These are followed by a sequence of scenes dealing with Marie's betrayal and Woyzeck's growing jealousy (H4,3 [=H2,3 and H1,2]; H4,6; H3,1; H4,4; H2,7; H2,8). Landau deletes the scene in which the Drum Major brags about his manliness (H4,14), because it disturbs the rapid development of the plot (149–52).

Max Zobel von Zabeltitz accepts Landau's construction, except for his omission of the Drum Major scene (1915, 76). Like Landau, Zabeltitz bases his argument on traditional or classical concepts of plot construction, not on the evidence of the manuscripts, which neither he nor Landau consulted. Furthermore, neither writer makes mention of any scientific principles or procedures for editing. In each case the guiding principles are the editors' preconceived notions about dramatic form and structure and their subjective, aesthetic sense of what constitutes a strong and convincing development of plot. While both Landau and Zabeltitz mention Büchner's proximity and indebtedness to Shakespeare and to Lenz and other dramatists of the Sturm und Drang including the young Goethe, neither author makes an attempt to discover the peculiar stylistic elements of those works that are also found in *Woyzeck*. According to Landau, *Woyzeck* goes beyond *Dantons Tod* in the maturity of construction and the sureness of technique, but it is nevertheless a torso in which the lack of a "completing, forming hand" is everywhere visible. Some things are only suggested; some motifs are doubled. But these deficiencies disappear before the magnitude of the whole. Like Goethe's *Urfaust*, *Woyzeck* is a "chaos out of which emerges a powerful, unified work" (72, 76) — with a little help from the editor, we must assume.

In his disagreement with Landau and Zabeltitz, Walter Kupsch, writing in 1920, maintains that *Woyzeck* is not a fragment. And, though he admits to not having been able to see the manuscripts, he disagrees with Franzos's claim that the arrangement of scenes is arbitrary. His goal is to establish the "logically and psychologically developing unity" in the sequence of scenes that is missing in Franzos's edition. Neither Landau nor Zabeltitz properly understand the play, Kupsch claims, hence their work is in need of "completion and correction" (8), but the modifications he suggests are minimal. By moving H4,8 (At the Doctor's) to second position, for example, and by placing H4,4 (Marie's

Room [Marie with earrings]) after H2,7 (The Captain. The Doctor), Kupsch claims to have tightened the chronological development from five to three days and to have strengthened the causal connection between the scenes. These and a few other minor transpositions are based on psychoanalytic considerations, he claims, and result in a more convincing psychological development of the characters and an improvement in the development of the plot from exposition through intensification (*Steigerung*) to the high point and peripety of Woyzeck's discovery of Marie with her new earrings, which betray her infidelity (41–44).

While he attempts on the one hand to tighten the play's chronology, causality, and traditional line of plot development, Kupsch recognizes on the other that Büchner's principle of form is unique in his time (72). "The individual scenes stand to a certain extent as particular works of art within a total work of art (*Sonderwerk im Gesamtkunstwerk*)" and take their meaning from the meaning of the whole. In the relationship of the parts to the whole that reflects the world in its totality, Büchner's works represent the "first consistently realistic literature in Germany," a literature that differs from Naturalism's slavish imitation of a segment of reality independent of its connection to the whole. Like Landau and Zabeltitz, Kupsch notes the influence of Shakespeare and Lenz's *Soldaten*. But whereas Lenz's figures are driven by external fate and therefore lack moral responsibility for their actions, Büchner's Woyzeck is a true tragic Shakespearean hero (74–75, 77–79).

Seemingly inconsistent with the connection to Shakespeare is Kupsch's conjecture that the commedia dell'arte was an influence on Büchner, a conclusion suggested to him by the jerkiness (*Sprunghaftigkeit*) in some of the scenes (as constructed by Franzos, it may be added). According to Kupsch, the dashes, which Franzos and others interpreted as a sign of fragmentariness, should be filled with extemporaneous motion and gesture to enliven the scene. (In fact, Franzos added dashes where he considered the text to be incomplete, that is, where he assumed that Büchner would have made additions or corrections.) Kupsch wrote out two scenes with added stage instructions to indicate how this could work (80–84). What he added is indeed effective, but it is also the kind of action directors and actors would naturally add on their own.

Kupsch found evidence for his argument in the fact that only five of twenty-seven figures with speaking parts in *Woyzeck* have names; the others have designations pointing to types which can be identified with types from the commedia dell'arte: the Captain = Capitano or Scaramuccia; the Doctor = Dottore; the Drum Major = Spaviento or the *miles gloriosus*; Andres = Pierrot; Marie = Colombine; and so forth. Considering the problematic and complex nature of Büchner's caricatures of the Doctor and especially the Captain, Kupsch's comparison of them to the stock types of the commedia is of questionable validity, whether or not Büchner was familiar with the genre either directly or indirectly, and has not found favor with subsequent critics.

Both Kupsch and Zabeltitz discuss the documentary material discovered by Bieber, especially Clarus's evaluations of the historical Woyzeck, and compare Büchner's Woyzeck with the historical source. Writing at the same time as Kupsch, Fritz Bergemann, the subsequent editor of Büchner's works for Insel, published an article in which he too compares the two figures. What each of these comparisons reveals is that Büchner's portrayal of Woyzeck refutes and reverses Clarus's conclusions about Woyzeck's accountability and guilt by revealing the social circumstances and psychological condition that extenuate Woyzeck's crime. As represented by the socialist Büchner, Bergemann concludes, Woyzeck is a victim of his class and his desperate poverty: in order to support his woman and child, he allows himself to be used like a guinea pig for medical experiments, and he further undermines his health by taking on a variety of odd jobs. When his mind breaks down under the strain, he feels compelled by seemingly exterior forces to kill the woman he loves and to take his own life (1920, 248–49). (In these early editions Woyzeck drowns himself.)

The first attempt since Franzos's to work from Büchner's manuscripts was undertaken by Georg Witkowski in 1920 for an Insel edition of *Woyzeck*. Unlike Franzos, Witkowski endeavored to decipher and reproduce the texts as precisely as possible. Some new and better variant readings were subsequently proposed by Walter Hoyer, a student of Witkowski's, in his 1922 dissertation "Stoff und Gestalt bei Georg Büchner" (Material and Form in the Works of Georg Büchner) and by Fritz Bergemann in 1922. Furthermore, where Witkowski finds no particular order of scenes in the preliminary drafts, Hoyer identifies two versions and two separate scenes (H3,1 and 2), which he considers to have been written subsequent to the completion of the drafts.

In his 1922 edition for Insel, *Georg Büchners Sämtliche Werke und Briefe* (Georg Büchner's Complete Works and Letters), Bergemann goes beyond Witkowski and Hoyer to discover a division of manuscripts and sequence of scenes that, with minor exceptions, appears to be beyond dispute. He identifies two preliminary drafts, H1 and H2, a final uncompleted version, H4, and a sheet containing two scenes, H3, which he assumes were written between the drafts and the final version. His findings are based on the characteristics of the manuscripts, the presumed order of the manuscript pages, and internal evidence: the first versions are contained on five gray folio sheets, the final version on six quarto sheets, and the two separate scenes on one quarto sheet. Problematic in this division is only the placement of a fragmentary scene with the heading "Gerichtsdiener. Barbier. Arzt. Richter" (Court Clerk. Barber. Doctor. Judge), which may be the final scene of the first draft (H1) or the first scene of the second (H2). Bergemann places it at the beginning of H2 but recognizes that it may be the end of H1, which would provide further evidence for the sequence H1 and H2, or it may be the author's notation for the goal to be reached in H2 (699–705).

Bergemann follows sound editorial principles in his separation of the final manuscript from the preceding drafts, which he includes in an appendix under the heading "Lesarten" (variants). In general he does not consider it appropriate to contaminate H4 by the addition of scenes from the earlier drafts, but he makes two well-founded exceptions: where Büchner left a page and a half blank under the title "Buden. Lichter. Volk" (Booths. Lights. People), Bergemann adds material from both earlier drafts, and where the final manuscript breaks off after the scene in the barracks, the so-called testament scene (H4,17), he adds the scenes from H1 that portray the catastrophe of the murder, Woyzeck's return to the scene of the crime, and the arrival of people, who hear strange sounds coming from the water (H1,15, 19, 20, 16). In both cases, Bergemann sets the additions off from the rest of the text by using a different typeface (705).

Unfortunately, Bergemann departed from this nearly ideal solution in subsequent editions by adding further contaminations to the final version, including even a shift in the sequence of scenes in H4 itself, a practice he criticized in the edition by Franzos. To explain his departure from the sequence he had previously established, he now identifies H4 as a fragment which lacks the final dramatic arrangement: "Its sequence of scenes has long since and everywhere been given up as impossible" (1958, 484). Apparently he was unaware of Hans Winkler's sound argument based on internal and external evidence for precisely the sequence of scenes Bergemann now considered to be impossible (see below). Bergemann shifts the scene in which Woyzeck shaves the Captain from the fifth to the first position, and he contaminates H4,9 (The Captain. The Doctor) by restoring Woyzeck's appearance from H2,7. He now places the superfluous "Doctor's Courtyard" (H3,1), and an additional barracks scene (H1,8), immediately following the scene "Open Field" (H4,12), in which Woyzeck receives the command to kill Marie, thereby interrupting and retarding the forward thrust of the plot action (1958, 508–509, 619–22). Only by means of notes in the appendix is it possible for users of the editions after 1922 to reconstruct the sequence of scenes as contained in the manuscripts. With few exceptions, Bergemann's text and construction remained unquestioned and unchallenged until 1967.

Before critics and literary historians began taking Büchner seriously, and before the plays reached the stage and a broader audience, the primary appeal of his works was to readers with a socialist orientation and the desire to change society. For example, in an attempt to demonstrate the similarity of Büchner's views with those of the new social-democratic movement and thereby to identify him as a precursor, the *Neue Welt*, a socialist newspaper edited by Wilhelm Liebknecht, published in 1879 an article in seven installments dealing with Büchner's biography and works. In 1891 the editor of the *Volksstimme* in Leipzig was sentenced to four months in jail for printing *Dantons Tod* (Goltschnigg 1975, 43–44). "Der hessische Landbote" (The Hessian Courier) was celebrated as Germany's first socialist pamphlet.

Büchner's discovery and reception by writers began with the naturalists, who were closely allied with the socialist movement. Gerhart Hauptmann lectured on him to the members of the literary organization "Durch" in June 1887. According to Hauptmann, Büchner's works had a "tremendous impact" on him, and he admits to having made Büchner into a cult figure and to having undertaken several pilgrimages to his grave in Zurich (Johann 1958, 166). A number of Hauptmann's works, especially "Bahnwärter Thiel" and "Der Apostel," clearly reveal Büchner's influence. In the founding meeting of the Freie Volksbühne (Free Peoples' Theater) in 1890, Bruno Wille recommended the performance of *Dantons Tod* along with naturalist plays. Although the suggestion was accepted by the theater's director, Otto Brahm, twelve years elapsed before its premiere performance by the Neue Freie Volksbühne on 5 January 1902 in Berlin's Belle-Alliance Theater.

Expressionist writers, too, were passionate admirers of Büchner's works, especially *Woyzeck*. Frank Wedekind is reported to have said that his *Frühlings Erwachen* (Spring's Awakening) would not have been written without *Woyzeck* (Goltschnigg 1975, 164). Georg Heym discovered in Büchner "a new God" to be placed next to Grabbe on his altar (Goltschnigg 170). Like the naturalists, the expressionists admired Büchner as a revolutionary, but they also discovered new aspects of his art. The innovations of these movements helped critics to discover elements of Büchner's modernity for themselves, for example, his use of grotesque language and the open or episodic structure of his plays. And the works of these playwrights prepared the way for the premiere performance of *Woyzeck* in November 1913 in Munich's Residenz Theater. Seventy-six years after it was written, Büchner's masterpiece reached the stage and has remained a mainstay of German theater.

As might be expected, the emphasis on Büchner as a revolutionary and socially critical thinker and artist did not make him popular among academic critics, who were generally conservative and nationalistic. As new editions of his works were published and sales increased, however, and as his plays were performed more and more in the theaters, his stature as a major German writer became sufficiently apparent to attract serious attention from academicians. Beginning in the twenties, attempts were made to de-emphasize and even deny the socially critical and revolutionary content of Büchner's works by pointing to the despair he experienced after the failure of his revolutionary activities and his supposed renunciation of the possibility of revolution, or by connecting him to German Romanticism and considering him to be a myth-maker, or by identifying him as a pessimist or nihilist. Such approaches predominated during Hitler's Third Reich and have been considered by critics, especially those on the political left, as pre-fascist or fascist, as an attempt at the *Gleichschaltung* (coordination, leveling) that made it possible to retain Büchner in the canon of acceptable authors during this period.

Two major studies attempting to establish Büchner's relationship and indebtedness to Romanticism were published in the early twenties, Heinz Lipmann's *Georg Büchner und die Romantik* (1923) and Armin Renker's *Georg Büchner und das Lustspiel der Romantik: Eine Studie über "Leonce und Lena"* (Georg Büchner and the Comedy of Romanticism: A Study of *Leonce and Lena*, 1924). In the case of *Leonce und Lena*, which parodies Romantic sensibility and a number of Romantic themes, finding sources and parallels in works by Romantic authors is not unrewarding, but the relevance of Romanticism for *Woyzeck* is questionable and was soon criticized and rejected by Hans Winkler.

In Lipmann's view, *Woyzeck* answers Lena's question whether we must redeem ourselves through our pain. Woyzeck is a symbol of the unredeemed world. He becomes a revolutionary against God and against his tormentors. Woyzeck represents the "most simple and pure nature" of which Lenz speaks, and nature gives him the solution to his intolerable situation: he is to kill Marie and then become a part of nature by disappearing into the water, by returning to the "Urgrund," to the elements. (Lipmann's interpretation is based on Franzos's edition, in which Woyzeck drowns; it is undermined, as Winkler later points out [168–69], if one assumes that he does not drown.) Lipmann considers this fate to be the realization of a Dionysian myth and therefore the fulfillment of a Romantic longing. The myth is Greek in its affirmation of life, nature, and Epicureanism, and it is Christian in its symbolism, in the passion Woyzeck suffers, and in his desire for salvation. Furthermore, Lipmann continues, the myth of the people (*Volk*) is realized in and through Woyzeck; the myth of the simple man is the myth of all people. The same concept of life dominates and fills every individual (37–40, 132–33).

The most extensive, balanced, and by far the best early investigation of *Woyzeck* is the 1925 dissertation and book by Hans Winkler: *Georg Büchners "Woyzeck."* Winkler divides his study into three main parts: in the first he deals with the text and Büchner's sources, in the second with the play's content, and in the third with its style. Following a brief review of the history of the text, Winkler concludes that Witkowski and Bergemann have succeeded in finally deciphering the text and that the sequence of drafts and the order of scenes established by Bergemann are convincing. But whereas Bergemann's findings are based primarily on careful study of the manuscripts, Winkler sets out to test their validity by analyzing the content of the scenes as they relate to the development of plot.

In a scene-by-scene analysis of the presumed first draft, Winkler demonstrates how the order and sequence of scenes constitutes a clear and consistent development of the plot, with events taking place on three consecutive evenings, which is not to say that the composition is uniform and entirely clear and consistent. There are indications already in the first draft, Winkler claims, that Büchner had somewhat changed his plan during its composition. This is apparent, for example, in two different sequences dealing with Woyzeck's acquisition of a knife and his plan to kill Marie (20–30). Analysis of the second draft yields similar results: "all the scenes are directly linked and stand in a definite sequence," and the action takes place in an afternoon and evening and the early part of the following day. Winkler rightly disagrees with Hoyer and Witkowski, who consider the arrangement of scenes in these drafts to be entirely arbitrary. By comparing the drafts in their entirety, and by comparing scenes that are duplicated in the two drafts, he demonstrates that H2 clearly follows H1 and represents a later stage of development in terms both of the clearer development of the plot and of the more concise and refined artistic execution. It is thus parallel to and different from H1, not part of a single stage of development as assumed by Witkowski and Hoyer, and implicitly also by Bergemann in his inclusion of material from H1 and H2 to construct the fair scene (H4,4) for his stage version (42–52).

Winkler disagrees with Bergemann's placement of H3 between H2 and H4 and with Hoyer's assumption that these two scenes were the last composed by Büchner. In Winkler's view, they were written between H1 and H2. The first one, "Der Hof des Professors" (The Professor's Courtyard), breaks off in mid-scene and appears to have been dashed off in a moment of high spirits. It contains personal, satirical references of the sort Büchner reduced or eliminated during the progression of the work. It is similar to the "Woyzeck. Doctor" scene in H2, which was reworked for H4. Since both scenes deal with the same material, it is unlikely that Büchner would have included both in the same draft (52–55).

The second scene in H3, "Der Idiot. Das Kind. Woyzeck," must follow the murder, Winkler assumes, because Woyzeck's clothes are wet, indicating that he has just come from the pond. Hence the scene appears to follow the events of H1, which ends with Woyzeck in the pond, or possibly with the fragmentary "Court Clerk. Barber. Doctor. Judge," which Winkler considers the first scene of H2. Winkler's otherwise sound analysis falters here: although he recognizes that the references to water in H3,2 are part of a child's counting game, he nevertheless interprets them as also applying to Woyzeck, who, we are to presume, has just returned wet from the pond (54). While it is not justified to indicate that Woyzeck drowns at the end, as did Franzos and the editors who follow his lead, it is also not justifiable to preclude that possibility by placing this scene after Woyzeck's entry into the pond.

Through a scene-by-scene analysis and interpretation, Winkler attempts to provide justification based on content for the sequence of scenes in H4 established by Bergemann. Of primary importance for the construction of a text suitable for performance are the gaps left by Büchner in his final extant manuscript. The first of these consists of one and one-half pages under the title "Buden. Lichter. Volk" (Fair Booths. Lights. People). It is clear from the inclusion of a title and the size of this space, and it is strongly suggested by the material for the scene in both H1 and H2, that Büchner intended to fill in this space. We cannot know, however, why he left the space blank. Did he consider the scene to be sufficiently complete in the earlier drafts that he simply did not take the time to recopy it into this space? Or was he not satisfied with the earlier drafts, and did he plan a complete reworking of this material? Winkler makes a sound argument for considering H2,3 and 5 as the basis for filling the gap, not H1,1 and 2, which Bergemann, Hoyer, and Ernst Hardt use for their stage versions. Winkler claims that the scenes in H2 include the essential elements from H1 in a tighter, more concentrated composition and with less obvious satire, which is in keeping with the general development from the early to the late stage of composition. Furthermore, the scenes from H1 require a change of place which is avoided in H2 (46–50). There is much to recommend Winkler's argument, which is based both on sound editorial principles and internal evidence.

Winkler's solution for H4,9 (Captain. Doctor) is also persuasive. Despite the space left blank following this scene, he accepts it as it stands and argues against the addition of material from the earlier version in which Woyzeck appears (H2,7). The purpose of the earlier version is to make Woyzeck aware of Marie's relationship with the Drum Major. This is made superfluous by a shift in plan in the final manuscript, according to which Woyzeck's suspicion has already been aroused by evidence far stronger than that presented by the Captain's allusions in H2,7. After having made three attempts to write it, Büchner could not bring himself to cut this scene entirely, Winkler conjectures, so he included it as an episode, a fragment, which has no meaning for the development of the plot. It is a witty interlude, in Winkler's opinion, whose effect is somewhat forced (60, 75–77).

Winkler concludes that H4 represents a unified plan with a tight and clear development of plot. It closely follows H2 in the sequence of scenes and incorporates all scenes from H2 with only one change in sequence. By comparing the scenes from H4 with those from the earlier version, Winkler demonstrates a consistent development in form and content, as seen in the above analysis of H4,9 and its predecessor H2,7. As Winkler observes, Büchner moves in the direction of greater concision and compression, increased emotional impact, and a more intense and mysterious atmosphere or mood. Where verbal expressiveness is reduced, the importance of mime and gesture is increased. Description is transformed into action or into more graphic images. The collective evidence of these changes makes a strong and convincing case for Bergemann's sequence of manuscripts (67–69).

In the second part of his study Winkler lists and discusses the known and possible sources for Büchner's play, namely, Clarus's report and the accounts of several similar cases from the time. Winkler notes that considerable attention was given in the early part of the nineteenth century to criminals of various kinds and to the questions of accountability and punishment. Winkler writes that some authorities went so far as to argue that all criminals were victims of extenuating circumstances and should therefore not be held accountable or punished for their crimes (91–94).

Winkler's extensive comparison of *Woyzeck* with Clarus's report demonstrates Büchner's reliance on this source, but it also reveals how he emphasized the shy and introspective part of Woyzeck's character and almost completely eliminated his unsavory and violent side (97–108). Likewise, Marie has little in common with the three women in

Woyzeck's life. Thus, rather than copying nature, Winkler concludes, Büchner tried to discover the essence and the meaning of a man who may be seen to embody the elemental simplicity of the common people. He captures the soul, the inner development, and the fate of an ordinary man, thereby fulfilling the program he describes in *Lenz*:

> I demand in everything — life, the possibility of existence, and then it's good; we needn't ask then whether it is beautiful or ugly. The feeling that what has been created has life stands above such considerations and is the only criterion in matters of art. . . . One must love mankind in order to be able to penetrate into the peculiar essence of each individual. No one may be considered too lowly or too ugly; only then can he be understood. The least distinguished face makes a deeper impression than the mere perception of beauty. And one can cause the figures to emerge from themselves without copying anything into them from outside where no life, no muscles, no pulse are felt to swell and throb. (I.87)

Woyzeck's tragedy, according to Winkler, is the tragedy of the *Volk* in general, a connection that is reinforced by the inclusion in the play of folk songs and fairy-tale motifs, which Winkler discusses in some detail (127–33). The songs were collected by Büchner himself, and some are recorded here for the first time. (Landau and others had previously noted that *Woyzeck* is characterized by the sober simplicity of folk literature and is especially close to the ballad in form and content [Landau 78].)

Through his discussion of the manuscripts and sources, Winkler carefully and thoroughly lays the foundation for his analysis of the play's content and "idea" or meaning. He concludes that Woyzeck's fate is determined by a transcendent force of nature rather than by the three immanent forces identified by Kupsch, namely, Woyzeck's social distress, his passion, and the sexual drive of the subplot (Kupsch 94). It is this force of nature that compels Woyzeck to murder Marie, that uses him as an instrument or puppet, and to which he submits in religious devotion. It is the same force that creates the underlying mood of many folk songs and allows us to perceive *Woyzeck* as a dramatized folk song. This "transcendent, almost demonic principle" is concentrated in the "mythic fairy-tale" told by the Grandmother and in the mythic-symbolical figure of the Fool in the first draft, who represents and is a voice of nature. The force of fate is most powerful in the first draft, Winkler writes, but it continues to predominate in the later drafts as well, as might be expected from an author who, in connection with his study of the French Revolution, "felt annihilated" by his discovery of the "dreadful fatalism of history" (II.425–26) and whose revolutionary hero Danton likewise discovers that his actions have been determined by forces outside his control (Winkler 135–38).

As a pervasive part of nature, sexual drive is indeed a determining immanent or inborn force in man, as Kupsch maintains. It reveals itself to be irresistible in Büchner's figures, Winkler writes, in the love between Woyzeck and Marie as well as in the strong sensual attraction between Marie and the Drum Major. The same force effects both love and hate in the figures in *Woyzeck*: "The sensual union of Marie and the Drum Major and Woyzeck's murder of Marie are the compelling consequence of a single law of nature. The attempt by Woyzeck and Marie to resist this force is futile" (139). Büchner's treatment of the erotic force becomes clearer and more general in the final version. While Marie is only slightly developed in the first draft and appears to be little more than a whore, in the final version she truly loves Woyzeck and becomes a tragic figure in her own right as she attempts to resist her irresistible passion and feels guilty in her betrayal of Woyzeck and her son (139–40, 157). Winkler concludes that sexual drive as a determining force is both transcendent and immanent. One cannot distinguish between the two because it is impossible to determine to what extent Büchner's figures project their own beings into nature and to what extent the figures are themselves expressions of nature (140).

The conclusions Winkler reaches through his careful study of the manuscripts and the changes made in the different stages of development are supported by his analysis of content and of the "idea" or Weltanschauung which determine the play's style and form. Except for Lipmann, who considers *Woyzeck* to be a Dionysian myth, he is the first critic to attribute the tragic fate of Woyzeck and Marie primarily to the effects of transcendent and immanent forces rather than to social forces resulting from their poverty and inferior social class. The importance of their social standing and oppression, which Kupsch identifies as the play's main force, plays no role at all, Winkler notes, until the introduction of the Captain and the Doctor in the second draft, and none of the drafts begins with this motif. The social motif centering around these figures is further developed in the final draft but is still subordinate to the two forces Winkler identifies as primary. The episodes involving the Captain and the Doctor are subplots, according to Winkler, which play on a different level from the main plot (142–43).

Winkler thus argues against the prevailing interpretation of the play as primarily a social drama and proletarian tragedy with emphasis on environment and class. In his view, it is a tragedy of the soul and a myth of the people and of nature (162, 168). The source of Woyzeck's tragedy is not the Captain or the Doctor but the Drum Major and

Marie, members of his own class; it originates in the figures themselves, not in the environment. Woyzeck's desire to exact retribution and achieve atonement becomes an obsession but is not madness (163–67). As in the case of Danton, Lenz, and Leonce, Woyzeck's suffering derives from dualism, from the disharmony between being and will. His tragedy is not a Dionysian mystery, as Lipmann claims, because Woyzeck does not experience a unity between man and nature. His necessary yielding to the force of fate is almost religious; it is a Christian passion and desire for atonement (170–73). This inexplicable fate gives rise to feelings of dread and despair and to fear of the meaninglessness of existence. These feelings and fears, Winkler maintains, are the main themes of the play and dominate Büchner's view of life and all his works. For Büchner there are two paths out of absolute pessimism and disintegration: salvation from chaos through love and suffering, which is the path taken by Leonce and Lena, Woyzeck, and perhaps Marie, and destruction of existence through madness and death, through the birth of nothingness longed for by Danton and Lenz (180). Woyzeck's salvation proves to be temporary, however: through Marie's betrayal his life and the world lose their meaning. (Winkler speculates on the basis of some suggestions in Büchner's manuscripts that Woyzeck would have found salvation through suffering, had Büchner lived to complete the play.) Woyzeck's tragedy becomes the tragedy of man in general, whose tragic fate it is to suffer in what for him is a meaningless world, a world which can be made meaningful by love, but only temporarily (184).

In the concluding section of his study Winkler analyzes Büchner's unique style. Only Rudolf Majut and Heinz Lipmann before him had given any attention to style, and their studies are one-sided and limited, Lipmann's to a comparison of Büchner's stylistic means to those of Romanticism and Majut's to Büchner's use of color and light. Because Winkler believes that style or form mediates between the body and soul of a literary work, and because it is the foundation for the transmission and effect of the material and the idea, he concludes that it must be taken into consideration in any attempt to analyze and interpret such a work. Winkler distinguishes further between an inner or internal style, which he calls the "style of conception" (*Stil der Auffassung*), and an external style or "style of representation" (*Stil der Darstellung*). The inner style depends on the author's Weltanschauung, which in turn is a product of the individual spirit (*Geist*) of the author and the collective spirit of the times. It includes the manner in which the author experiences space and time, his choice of material, the manner and intensity of his sensual perceptions, his feelings for nature, and so on. This style must be deduced from the work. The style of representation is manifest in the use of language and the structure of the work (188–89).

In his experience of time and space Büchner stands between Romanticism and naturalism, Winkler continues. Whereas the Romantics longed to escape from the confines of definite time and place into an ideal eternal time and an ideal infinite space, eternity and infinity for Büchner have entered into the complete and fulfilled moment and state; the present moment and state are complete and valid in their own right, not symbolic, as for the Romantics, nor segments of a causal chain or of a milieu, as for the naturalists. According to Winkler, "*Woyzeck* consists of a divided series of moments, of segments of time; the spiritual state of the participants changes in the moments." Each scene plays in a definite place, not a naturalistic space filled with things but in a space filled with atmosphere which is created by the figures themselves (190–91).

Winkler concludes his discussion of the author's style of conception with a lengthy and enlightening analysis of Büchner's extraordinary sensitivity to sensual impressions and sensations. In keeping with the fact that almost all the scenes in *Woyzeck* take place in the evening or night and are infused with an uncanny and disturbing twilight and darkness occasionally penetrated by glaring light, the contrast between dark and light overshadows the use of colors (197–99). Büchner also uses music to create atmosphere. Consistent with his love of contrasts, Winkler observes, is his preference for both melancholy and gay songs. The songs are complemented by other forms of music that tend to be stimulating and rhythmical and to have a demonic, grating, and disharmonious effect on Woyzeck: military music, dance music, and organ grinder music. Odors, too, contribute to the play's atmosphere, especially in connection with the manifestation of sexuality and as a defining component of certain settings such as the inn and the barracks (197–205).

Büchner is also sensitive to gesture, mime, and physical bearing. The continuous motion of the characters in *Woyzeck* prompted Kupsch to compare the play with the commedia dell'arte, a connection Winkler rejects. In his view, the motion and gesture in *Woyzeck* is a second, expressionistic language; it is usually implied by the words themselves: in order to convey their full meaning, the sentence fragments, exclamations, and questions suggest and demand gestures, motions, pauses, and changes in tempo and tone of voice. Only seldom are stage instructions required to indicate movement or gesture (206–7).

From his analysis of the inner style of *Woyzeck*, Winkler concludes that the play contains some elements of the Sturm und Drang movement but that it is above all a predecessor and powerful embodiment of impressionism and expressionism. In disagreement with Lipmann and others who attempt to connect Büchner with Romanticism, Winkler finds that he completely frees himself from Romanticism and accomplishes what the drama of impressionism and expressionism longed for but were unable to achieve (210–11).

In his discussion of the external style, the style of representation, Winkler anticipates many of the findings of subsequent analyses of the play's open or episodic form. The development of plot is not constant as it is in the classical drama; it consists not of "Handlungslinien" (plot lines) but rather of "Handlungspunkten," that is, points or stages of plot development that form around individual moments which are especially fateful and emotionally charged. Each scene is a self-contained station, complete in itself, a microcosm that contains the whole. The individual scenes are variations and developments of the same theme, of the idea. In some scenes a tension or conflict arises, in others a preexisting tension is revealed, one that arises from a moment preceding the actual scene (311–13).

The structure of the individual scenes is extremely simple: usually the scene is entirely monologue or dialogue; sometimes it consists of part monologue and part dialogue, and it may have a "chorus" in the background, that is, a group of people who take sides or provide a neutral foil. The characters are not developed during the course of the drama; they are fully drawn in the first scene in which they appear (213–16).

As the scenes are a microcosm within the macrocosm of the whole tragedy, so the individual sentence is a microcosm within the scene. According to Winkler, each sentence, indeed each fragment of a sentence arises from an extreme tension. The tension of the individual scene and of the whole play lives in each sentence, sentence fragment, and word. What Winkler describes is a paratactic structure which occurs on all levels. He counts 348 simple sentences in the final manuscript as opposed to only sixty nine compound sentences, seventeen of which are connected by "and." Most of the compound sentences are spoken by the Captain and the Doctor and serve to contrast them with the simple people whose language is not logical and analytical but expressive and based on association (223–28).

Winkler's analysis of the play's style and structure was soon followed by Erwin Scheuer's study of the open form of drama in Büchner's plays (*Akt und Szene in der offenen Form des Dramas dargestellt an den Dramen Georg Büchners*, 1929). Disagreeing with Hoyer's claim that a four-act structure is characteristic of Büchner's plays, Scheuer considers the division into acts in *Dantons Tod* and *Leonce und Lena* to be arbitrary and irrelevant, since in these plays, as in *Woyzeck*, the scenes are the basic units of construction. The closed or classical drama consists of specific and limited subject matter which is clearly divided into discrete parts organized according to the principle of antithesis or contrast. It presents "*formed or constructed* world (*gestaltete* Welt)" and is architectonic in structure. The open form of drama, on the other hand, presents "formed or constructed *world* (gestaltete *Welt*)." It is realistic and contains as much breadth and variety as is compatible with its content, which includes repeated reference to material not directly related to the immediate plot. Its form is musical rather than tectonic (6–14).

In the open form of drama, Scheuer continues, we get the impression that we are observing the growth and becoming of a living being. If such a play contains acts, they usually represent different stages of maturity and intensity. The diversity of their content is unified by a pervading atmosphere or mood. Whereas the act is a part of a whole, the scene is a primary whole in its own right, a moment which seems to contain the essence of the world. There is a "hierarchy" of scenes in the closed form of drama: some scenes are subordinate to others in a complex hypotactic structure. Changes of scenes usually occur with the coming and going of figures. In the open form of drama, on the other hand, the scenes constitute a sequence of equally important moments. The change is often determined by change of setting, and the setting with its particular atmosphere often contributes to the scene's inner symbolism and formal finish. It was Büchner among all the great German dramatists who developed this form of drama most fully, Scheuer writes, and he did so in *Woyzeck* (14–16).

Although Scheuer recognizes the importance for Büchner of the "social moment" and the sympathy with the poor that was a key element in his revolutionary political program, he also shares the critical tendency of the 1920s to downplay the social revolutionary intent of Büchner's works. In his view, the Captain and the Doctor, who were only added in the second draft, are simply foils for Woyzeck; the action involving them provides contrast to the true tragedy, which takes place between Woyzeck and Marie. Büchner did not think that political change could be effected through literature, Scheuer asserts, and his plays are not meant to be weapons in the political struggle, which is not to say that Büchner had given up his desire for revolutionary change. "Büchner has his tragedy take place in the world of the poor and 'uneducated,'" Scheuer writes, "because there alone true tragedy is still possible." In his belief that the authenticity of the people lies in their proximity to nature, Büchner wanted to get as close to nature as possible in the portrayal of his characters. The love between Woyzeck and Marie, which is the subject of the play, is an elementary but also a sa-

cred natural process. Nature c[...]
recognizes and tries to underst[...]
and all being. Scheuer agrees [...]
between nature and man as the[...]

In her inability to resist th[...]
Drum Major, Scheuer writes, [...]
ture, but at the same time she[...]
that demands her loyalty to th[...]
her inner drive, she experier[...]
mented by feelings of guil[...]
Woyzeck's life loses its focus [...]
its meaning for him if such[...]
unatoned. He feels compelle[...]
becomes guilty himself and m[...]
are tragic in the way they are [...]
price they have to pay. As the end or almost every scene [...],
to escape one's fate are futile. Because he experiences what others
merely talk about, the abyss and the threat of the abyss, Woyzeck's fate
is symbolic and universal, according to Scheuer, who agrees with Lipmann and Winkler in considering this elemental story to be truly
mythical (60–61, 66–67).

Scheuer goes beyond earlier critics in the importance he ascribes to
Marie. In his view, she is the first center of attention, and her story represents a separate plot line that runs parallel to Woyzeck's and only
merges with his in the beginning and at the end. Scheuer considers her
relationship to the Drum Major to be an independent, closed development in which Woyzeck does not participate, just as she does not participate in what takes place in Woyzeck following his discovery of her
betrayal (63–64). While the emphasis Scheuer places on Marie as a
tragic figure in her own right is surely justified, his claim that she is the
first center of attention is not convincing, since it is Woyzeck and not
she who appears in the first scene. However, the plot involving her
does begin before, and is a prerequisite for, the primary plot development, which consists of Woyzeck's discovery of her infidelity and the
impact this has on him.

Scheuer agrees with Landau, Winkler, and others that *Woyzeck* can
be compared to folk songs dealing with the murder of unfaithful lovers
or to the Norse folk ballads in which uncanny figures cast spells on and
destroy their victims. Indeed, the play's open form corresponds to the
form of the ballad, which, for the sake of brevity, must concentrate on
the elemental parts of a narrative and deal only briefly or by implication
with what lies between. *Woyzeck* goes beyond the ballad, however, in its

addition of scenes — Scheuer calls them "Milieuszenen" — that provide breadth and constitute retarding moments in the tragic development (61–62).

Continuing a trend of the time and at least in part out of political expediency, critics in the 1930s tended to downplay or deny the political and social dimensions of Büchner's works. In a 1975 study of Büchner's reception, Dietmar Goltschnigg identifies Friedrich Gundolf as the first to make a step in this direction (67), but, as seen above, Scheuer, who is not mentioned by Goltschnigg, preceded Gundolf in downplaying the social-political content of *Woyzeck*. For his part, Gundolf, with his nebulous style and impressionist approach, has little to add to our understanding of the works. Gundolf's essay is included in a volume on Romantic writers and begins with the claim that Büchner's thoughts are not his own, since they derive from German Romanticism and various other sources, but that his form of expression is entirely his own. In Gundolf's view, authenticity of atmosphere (*Stimmung*) is Büchner's unique contribution; indeed, his works are based on atmosphere rather than on plot or character. By the end of his essay, Gundolf appears to have convinced himself that Büchner is more original than he at first thought, at least in *Woyzeck*:

> no other German poet has created something of more original "genius" than *Woyzeck*, no matter what one thinks about the work's purely human value. Only someone enchanted could conjure up this dark face. It cannot be penetrated by reason, and its idea can scarcely be identified. What in the bourgeois tragedy was social criticism, cry of distress, portrayal of sympathy, psychology, that glows down in Woyzeck into the prehuman realm of power (*Mächtereich*). No German who wanted to depict poverty, gloom, evil has reached so close to his foundation as Büchner. (1930, 395)

The tendency of the twenties and thirties to consider Büchner's view of man to be decidedly pessimistic and nihilistic is also represented by Karl Viëtor, one of the most influential of Büchner scholars. Like others of his generation, Viëtor writes, Büchner suffered from the breakdown of faith in the Enlightenment and German idealism, but unlike his contemporaries, he did not find solace in compromise or the distracting participation in the activities and events of the day. Instead, he had the determination to penetrate to the "law of the whole," which brought him eye to eye with the mystery of the conditions of the world.

> A disappointed lover of life and a despairing seeker of faith, who was compelled by his nature to act and create, Büchner constructed in his works anti-idealistic images as an indictment of God and life. They do not arise out of certainty and faith but out of disintegration and despair.

Hence what they contain of criticism of the world and interpretation of life is of limited validity. A decisive nihilism is expressed here long before Nietzsche by someone who was not allowed to climb out of the abyss and to seek a new meaning of life and a new path. (1936, 205)

A major reason for Büchner's despair and nihilism, Viëtor continues, is the realization that man lacks free will and the possibility of determining his own fate, a view which prevails in all his works. In strong contrast to the cold-blooded, heartless Doctor, who sees in Woyzeck an interesting case of "aberratio mentalis," the poet recognizes a defenseless man who is inexorably controlled by the "nameless demons" who have taken possession of his soul (202). As described in Büchner's *Lenz*, the poet should love and attempt to understand his fellow man. To be sure, Büchner finds it easier to love and have sympathy for the poor people, who are close to nature in their elemental simplicity, than for the representatives of old and outmoded ideals and morality such as the Doctor and the Captain. Viëtor cites a letter of Büchner's to his parents in which he claims to "despise no one, least of all because of his intellect or education, since it is in no one's power not to become a blockhead or a criminal — because through the same conditions we would all probably become the same, and because the conditions lie outside of us." He does not laugh in scorn at individuals for what they are, but he does find the human condition to be risible, and he defends the kind of scorn that is based on hatred: "Hate is just as permissible as love, and I harbor it in the fullest degree toward those *who despise*. There are a great many of them who, in possession of a ridiculous externality called education, of a dead commodity called learning, sacrifice the great masses of their brothers to their egoism" (II,422. Büchner's emphasis). Viё ... he Doctor to be Büc ... uthority
and learning," ... he considers to be pr ... f feeling
they will not re ...

Büchner's ... ple for
whom he risk ... , which
Viëtor calls the ... Büchner
creates the firs ... nsiders
Büchner's mo ... to his
rejection of the ... oyzeck
and Marie em ... t since
Gretchen in G ... German
drama to creat ... ndeed,
Marie is an atte ... uthen-

ticity, as may be seen by comparing the scenes in which they admire the earrings that have been given them by their lovers. In contrast to Gretchen's six lines of rhyming iambic verse, Marie's comment is extremely terse: "It must be gold. How good it will look on me when dancing." (It is even terser than Viëtor assumes, since Büchner crossed out the second sentence in his manuscript.) But with Marie there is also a "polemical turn against the morality of the bourgeois world," Viëtor adds, as she compares herself with the "grandest ladies with their full-length mirrors and their handsome gentlemen, who kiss their hands. I'm just a poor woman" (I.170; Viëtor 197).

Büchner represents all the characters from the folk with the highest seriousness. Their actions, speech, and singing have the force and truth that are indicative of genuine nature (185–86). (Viëtor identifies a few departures in Woyzeck's language and thinking from the genuine folk tone, but the examples he cites are all from earlier drafts and do not appear in H4 [186].) The contrast of these natural and authentic beings with the educated and supposedly superior representatives of the middle class is polemical. The domination and rule of the latter is evil, according to Viëtor, for they are evil:

> their power is tyranny, for they degrade man in those who are inferior, their culture is in truth barbarism, for their actions are sordid. Between them and the folk there is no human relationship, because they have fallen out of nature, out of the power and the truth of real life. Woyzeck couldn't reach them with his thinking; and their thinking is so foreign to him that it goes past him, and from such meetings nothing remains but the helpless humility of his "But I am a poor guy." (187)

Viëtor considers it a weakness in the play that Woyzeck is made for nothing but suffering. Büchner tries to offset Woyzeck's suffering passivity by the insertion of scenes of a polemical and tendentious nature, Viëtor claims, scenes that are everything but organic from the perspective of dramatic form. In these scenes Büchner engages in the battle that is denied Woyzeck, the fight against society and his tormentors. "In these scenes the epic play *Woyzeck* is actually a drama of social combat; the figures from the bourgeois world are drawn in a different style from those from the people. Indeed, there are two styles in this piece, a tendentious 'activist' style and an epic realistic one" (185). Through his caricatures, Büchner judges, condemns, and scorns the representatives of the middle class. Despite this polemic, Viëtor does not consider the play to be primarily a social "Tendenzstück," (thesis play) since its social-critical content is secondary to the statement it makes about the nature of the world. The social conditions can be changed, but the human condition cannot be. Viëtor agrees with Winkler and Scheuer that the main source of Woyzeck's suffering is in the behavior of Marie and the Drum Major, which, like his own reaction to it, is an unalterable part of human nature. Woyzeck's tragedy is based on fundamental givens, not on transitory social conditions.

Dietmar Goltschnigg's collection of writings on Büchner from the period of Hitler's Third Reich (*Büchner im "Dritten Reich". Mystifikation, Gleichschaltung, Exil. Eine Dokumentation* [Georg Büchner in the "Third Reich": Mystification — Leveling — Exile. A Documentation, 1990]), begins with a "Vorspiel in Literaturgeschichten und geistesgeschichtlichen Literaturbetrachtungen" (Prelude in Literary Histories and Literary Observations Relating to Intellectual History) which includes excerpts from Adolf Bartels's *Geschichte der deutschen Literatur* (History of German Literature, 1902) and Josef Nadler's *Literaturgeschichte der deutschen Stämme und Landschaften* (Literary History of the German Tribes and Regions, 1928), the title of which clearly reveals its *völkisch* orientation, and Paul Fechter's *Dichtung der Deutschen* (German Literature, 1932). Also included in this section are short pieces by Arthur Moeller van den Bruck (1904), Herbert Cysarz (1928), the Swiss Germanist Emil Ermatinger, and the essay by Gundolf discussed above.

What these works have in common with the criticism in the Third Reich is the tendency to depoliticize Büchner, to claim that he gave up his political involvement and his desire to change the social conditions of the common people. Like his Danton, Büchner supposedly abandoned all hope of changing the political and social conditions of his homeland; he became pessimistic, even nihilistic in his belief that our actions are determined by forces outside ourselves and that life is therefore meaningless. *Woyzeck* is considered to be Büchner's attempt to get closer to the Volk, to the common, albeit poor, people, who are preferable to the intellectual and cruel representatives of the bourgeois ruling class, who have become distant from life and humanity. Considering Gundolf to be representative of this tendency, Goltschnigg characterizes his criticism as the mystification of the author's work as poetry for its own sake, without political and social associations; the complete departure from historical thinking in favor of a mythicized experience of reality; the depotentiation of reason and the renunciation of rationalistic attempts at interpretation; and the "abnegation of verifiable concrete analysis of detail in favor of speculative, abstract syntheses" (14). According to Goltschnigg, Büchner scholarship in the Third Reich was largely determined by Karl Viëtor's 1934 essay "Die Tragödie des heldischen Pessimismus. Über Büchner's Drama 'Dantons Tod'" (The Tragedy of Heroic Pessimism: Concerning Büchner's play *Dantons*

*Death*). Viëtor celebrated Hitler's seizure of power and the victory of
the National Socialist movement, Goltschnigg claims, in the context of
which he advocated considering the literature of the German past as a
manifestation of national will and a celebration of power, heroism, and
the ethics of the German ancestors. In V̶i̶ëtor's i̶nterpretation, the "heroic pessimism" ~~~~~~ ; an heroic attitude
in ~~~~~ skepticism towards
ide ~~~~~ he void (17–19).

*[handwritten: pg, 24 — Woyzeck is poor and belongs to the lowest class.]*

Vië ~~~~~ g considers to be
"les ~~~~~ ange in his 1949
boo ~~~~~

1 ~~~~~ rmany during the
Thir ~~~~~ me in his emphasis o ~~~~~ *Voyzeck*. Only in a
limit ~~~~~ rian tragedy, he
claim ~~~~~ ss, but he is not
explo ~~~~~ s, both of whom
are fa ~~~~~ importance, but
to ful ~~~~~ rstand the existential ~~~~~ n and the Doctor, w ~~~~~ and who live in
an unr ~~~~~ through which they
attemp ~~~~~ and control nature, Woyzeck is the archetype of man
in his elemental state, which, as Schmid sees it, is a state of suffering.
Whereas the Captain, the Doctor, and the Barker at the fair represent a
world that is intellectual, loveless, and hostile to nature, Woyzeck,
Marie, and the Drum Major are more natural and human in their
yielding to natural drives. Unlike Marie and the Drum Major, however,
Woyzeck transcends the natural world inwardly through his loyalty and
his selfless caring for Marie and their child (1940, 106–110).

It is part of the human condition, Schmid argues, to be tormented
by fear and feelings of guilt, as Woyzeck is in his visions and as Marie is
following her betrayal of Woyzeck and their child. Through his discovery of Marie's infidelity, Woyzeck again becomes subject to his chaotic
drives. The same forces that cause Marie to submit to the Drum Major
now command Woyzeck to kill her and cleanse her of her sin, an act
which greatly increases his suffering and which calls for his own death
in retribution. As defined by Schmid, tragedy, or the tragic, does not
depend on moral law but is "guiltlessly guilty suffering from existence"
(das schuldlos-schuldige Leiden am Sein). Only "cosmic suffering that
stems from existence and takes hold of man in his totality is tragic," according to Schmid, and Woyzeck experiences such suffering in its most

elemental form. Indeed, "elementary suffering [*Urleiden*] rarely reveals itself so directly in its numinous character as it does in *Woyzeck*" (115–16, 118).

In a development indicative of the political conservatism and nationalism of many German literary scholars in the first half of the century, the author who was celebrated as a political radical and revolutionary by socialists in the late nineteenth and early twentieth centuries came to be represented by some Germanists as a misguided but well intentioned young man who discovered through his own experience and his study of the French Revolution that society and political structures cannot be changed by revolutionary means. Following his rejection of the Enlightenment, German idealism, and what these critics consider to be his pessimistically, even nihilistically motivated renunciation of political activity, Büchner's orientation supposedly became mythical and "demonic" as he turned to nature and to the Volk to find positive values. Even this trend of criticism was eventually silenced by the "leveling" of the Third Reich.

By this time, however, Büchner scholarship had been given a solid foundation by studies establishing the cultural and historical context of Büchner's works and their relationship to the author's biography. Furthermore, once Büchner's stature as a writer had been recognized and his manuscripts acquired by Insel, the editing of *Woyzeck* was greatly improved, reaching a high point in Fritz Bergemann's edition of 1922 that remained unexcelled for more than four decades. Likewise unsurpassed for some time was Hans Winkler's thorough investigation of the play's language, form, and content, a study that anticipated the close textual analysis of post-war criticism.

## Works Cited

Bergemann, Fritz. "Der Fall Woyzeck in Wahrheit und Dichtung." *Inselschiff* 1 (1920): 242–49.

Bergemann, Fritz. *Georg Büchners Sämtliche Werke und Briefe*. Leipzig: Insel, 1922.

Bieber, Hugo. "Wozzeck und Woyzeck." *Das Literarische Echo* 17 (1914): 1188–91.

Büttner, Ludwig. *Georg Büchner. Revolutionär und Pessimist: Ein Beitrag zur Geistesgeschichte des 19. Jahrhunderts*. Nuremberg: Verlag Hans Carl, 1948.

Franzos, Karl Emil, ed. *Georg Büchner's Sämmtliche Werke und handschriftlicher Nachlaß. Erste kritische Gesammt-Ausgabe*. Frankfurt: J. D. Sauerländer, 1879.

Goltschnigg. Dietmar, ed. *Büchner im "Dritten Reich": Mystifikation, Gleichschaltung, Exil; eine Dokumentation.* Bielefeld: Aisthesis-Verlag, 1990.

Gundolf, Friedrich. "Georg Büchner." Chap. in *Romantiker*, 375–95. Berlin-Wilmersdorf: H. Keller, 1930. Also in Martens, ed., 1965, 82–97.

Hausenstein, Wilhelm. *Georg Büchner: Gesammelte Werke, nebst einer Auswahl seiner Briefe.* Leipzig: Insel, 1916.

Hoyer, Walter. "Stoff und Gestalt bei Georg Büchner." Ph.D. diss., Leipzig, 1922.

Johann, Ernst. *Georg Büchner in Selbstzeugnissen und Bilddokumenten.* Hamburg: Rowohlt, 1958.

Kupsch, Walter. "'Wozzeck.' Ein Beitrag zum Schaffen Georg Büchners (1813–1837)." *Germanische Studien* 4. Berlin: Emil Ebering, 1920.

Landau, Paul. *Georg Büchners Gesammelte Schriften.* 2 vols. Berlin: Paul Cassirer, 1909.

Lipmann, Heinz. *Georg Büchner und die Romantik.* Munich: Hueber Verlag, 1923.

Majut, Rudolf. "Farbe und Licht im Kunstgefühl Büchners." Ph.D. diss., Greifswald, 1912.

Martens, Wolfgang, ed. *Georg Büchner.* Darmstadt: Wissenschaftliche Buchgesellschaft, 1965.

Mayer, Hans. *Georg Büchner und seine Zeit.* Wiesbaden: Limes Verlag, 1946.

Renker, Armin. *Georg Büchner und das Lustspiel der Romantik: Eine Studie über "Leonce und Lena."* Berlin: Emil Ebering, 1924.

Scheuer, Erwin. *Akt und Szene in der offenen Form des Dramas, dargestellt an den Dramen Georg Büchners.* Berlin: Emil Ebering, 1929.

Schmid, Peter. 1940. *Büchner: Versuch über die tragische Existenz.* Bern: Verlag Paul Haupt, 1940.

Viëtor, Karl. "Die Tragödie des heldischen Pessimismus. Über Büchners Drama 'Dantons Tod.'" *Deutsche Vierteljahrsschrift* 12 (1934): 173–209. Also in Martens, ed., 1965, 98–137.

Viëtor, Karl. "Woyzeck." *Das innere Reich* 3 (1936): 182–205. Also in Martens, ed., 1965, 151–77.

Winkler, Hans. *Büchners 'Woyzeck.'* Greifswald: Ratsbuchhandlung L. Bamberg, 1925.

Witkowski, Georg. "Büchners 'Woyzeck.'" *Inselschiff* 1 (1919–20): 20–30.

Zobel von Zabeltitz, Max. *Georg Büchner, sein Leben und sein Schaffen.* Berlin: G. Grote, 1915.

# 2: Post-War Criticism: 1946–1962

IN A SURVEY OF SCHOLARSHIP ON BÜCHNER that was added to the 1959 reprint of *Georg Büchner und seine Zeit* (Georg Büchner and his Times), Hans Mayer claims that his book, which was published in 1946, was the first larger literary-historical study to appear in West Germany following the war. Eugen Diem's *Georg Büchners Leben und Werk* (Georg Büchner's Life and Works) was published the same year, but it is not a critical or literary-historical study. Instead, in anticipation of the fact that Germans will now be seen as pariahs among people who love freedom, Diem wants to point out that, despite Germany's long tradition of obedience to absolute authority, some revolutionary Germans, including especially Georg Büchner, placed freedom and the individual above the state and subordination to authority. In the aftermath of the collapse of the Nazi terror, Diem wants to introduce to his countrymen as a positive model and guide the writer who made a deep impression on him when he first discovered him in an army hospital in 1916 (1946, 7, 63).

Hans Mayer, a Marxist critic, began his investigation in the belief that Büchner had portrayed two kinds of revolution: the liberation of the bourgeoisie (*Dantons Tod*) and social revolution (*Woyzeck*). Mayer soon discovered that the relationship between Büchner and his historical period was not as simple and clear as he had assumed. He thus became committed to a lengthy and detailed study, written — as were most of Büchner's works — while in exile in France and Switzerland. Though completed before the outbreak of the war, Mayer's book had to wait until after the war to be published: since Büchner was not yet well known internationally, a publisher in Zurich abandoned the project when the possibility of reaching German readers was lost.

Unlike other Marxist critics, Mayer finds that he must agree with Viëtor and admit that Büchner's view with regard to revolutionary change was pessimistic and without hope. He also agrees with Viëtor in recognizing the central importance of determinism in Büchner's Weltanschauung. It never occurred to Büchner, Mayer claims, that changing the social determinants would lead to a change in the determined conditions. This being the case, Büchner's only recourse is to sympathize with the suffering of the poor and oppressed people and to hate those who cause the suffering (1959, 104). Mayer also agrees with Viëtor in recognizing a positive element and a ray of hope in Büchner's return to the natural life as exemplified by the common people, the Volk (255–56).

Mayer considers both these motifs, determinism and sympathy, to be of central importance in *Woyzeck*. Woyzeck is driven into madness by his poverty and the conditions of his material existence, which result in his self-destructive crime. Büchner's purpose in this play is to reveal the causes of Woyzeck's thinking and the conditions of his existence. The consequences of determinism, which were presented in a broad historical context in *Dantons Tod*, are seen here on the level of the individual deed. Woyzeck is compelled by forces he does not understand to kill the person he loves and upon whom his own existence depends. He cannot comprehend the sermons on morality and reason to which he is repeatedly exposed, because his life is controlled by forces that have nothing to do with reason and morality. The words of his social superiors have little effect on him — they talk past him rather than to him — but finally he is affected in the sphere in which he felt safe from their attacks, in his existence with wife and child. With no visible or conceivable salvation for Woyzeck in this situation, his suffering can evoke feelings of sympathy and love, but again, Büchner can offer no real comfort or possible solution, no indication of how determinism can be overcome (331–37).

Mayer's book was soon followed by Karl Viëtor's comprehensive study of Büchner's political, literary, and scientific activities and accomplishments (*Georg Büchner: Politik, Dichtung, Wissenschaft* [Georg Büchner: Politics, Poetry, Science], 1949). Like Mayer, though in less detail, Viëtor also considers Büchner's political views and activities in the context of his time and reaches similar conclusions with regard to his position and goals. From his more conservative perspective, however, he is critical of Büchner's lack of sufficient judgment and knowledge to evaluate properly the possibilities for revolutionary change in Germany at a time when conditions were not ripe. In Viëtor's view, radicalism has never created better conditions but instead has always had a destructive effect. That a young poet of Büchner's gifts succumbed to the demons of radicalism is symptomatic of the deep crisis which had overcome the bourgeois spirit in Germany at the time (91). The claim that Büchner realized the futility of revolutionary activity and forsook his own earlier commitment to revolutionary change continued to aggravate Marxist-oriented critics and tended to divide critics for some time into those who sided with Mayer and those who favored Viëtor.

In a book written a year before Viëtor's, in 1948, Ludwig Büttner takes the position that Büchner was not a radical socialist and that his "dangerous pessimism" and doubt destroyed his hope for change and his will to act. His poetic works reveal his historical pessimism and his belief that man is an "arbitrary instrument of soulless, terrible demons" (1948, 11, 13–14). (The importance given to "demons" continues a trend of criticism from the Third Reich which Büttner helped to formulate.) Tragedy does not come from evil deeds or from transgressing divine laws but rather from life itself. By the time he wrote *Woyzeck*, Büchner was able to accept and affirm the world, in which he now recognized a certain consistency and necessity. Insofar as it is destructive and incomprehensible, the world evokes horror and anxiety, but insofar as it is constant and orderly, it gives rise to tragic resignation (22–23).

Betrayal by his lover destroys Woyzeck's last possibility for existence, his only hold on life. The natural drive, Büttner continues, the sexual passion that overcomes Marie, makes visible the abyss of life, the world of naked instincts, of uninhibited egoistic nature. To the extent, however, that Woyzeck feels himself to be an instrument of a necessary law and atones for Marie's disloyalty by murder — and his deed must also be atoned for through his death — a law of sinister consequence reveals itself. Woyzeck submits to his fate; the outcome is inevitable and therefore tragic. His tragedy is not caused by his poverty and social misery, which are of secondary importance, but by the instinctual behavior of Marie and the Drum Major and by his own instinctual response which take place out of necessity according to laws of nature. Necessity replaces the chance and meaninglessness that prevailed in Büchner's earlier works. In *Woyzeck*, Büchner's tragic pessimism moves beyond pure negation and despair along the path toward tragic affirmation (95, 141–42).

In a later study Büttner continues to argue against a deterministic, nihilistic, and socialistic interpretation of *Woyzeck*. Woyzeck is not a victim of his poverty and social status, he argues, but of the biological and emotional urges to which Marie succumbs in submitting to the Drum Major. Woyzeck is not paranoid or schizophrenic in his response to this betrayal, and he is no atheist or nihilist (1967, 58). On the contrary, his judgment and critical abilities are sound; his thinking is clear and acute. His visions are not a result of schizophrenia; they are consistent with his religious background and with the magical, superstitious beliefs of the common people. His primary difference from the Captain and the Doctor is in his lack of education, and he differs from the Drum Major in his diminished vitality (54). He is not forced to work for the Captain or to submit to the Doctor's experiments but does so voluntarily to support his woman and child. Not allowing himself to be disdained, insulted, or scorned, he defends himself against the criticism of the Captain and the Doctor, and he fights with the Drum Major (57).

When betrayed by his beloved, he wants to defend and revenge himself, even at the cost of his own life. His revenge, according to Büttner, is a "Müssen und ein Wollen," a must and a desire. It is a moral imperative. He can't live without Marie and he can no longer live with her, though he still loves her. He must kill her to keep her. His resistance to committing the murder and his reaction afterward indicate that he feels guilty and deserving of punishment. Büttner thus differs from the majority of critics by finding Büchner in agreement with Clarus's affirmation of Woyzeck's accountability for his deed. The moral law prevails and he too must pay for his transgression. By not including many of the historical Woyzeck's negative attributes and deeds, however, Büchner makes his hero into a positive figure whose fate transcends the individual and becomes a universal and tragic example (59–61).

The first "proper account of Büchner" in English, as the author calls it, was published in 1951 by A. H. J. Knight. Written from a "cautious, pragmatic, English standpoint," Knight's book is aimed at serious students and specialists and presupposes "reasonable knowledge of the general political, cultural, social, and economic background of Germany in the 1830's" (4). In his chapter on *Woyzeck*, Knight follows the by-then standard procedure of reviewing the information on the historical figure and events, noting where Büchner is faithful to and where he deviates from his sources, and discussing the editions and problems of editing the work. Distinguishing between "authentic" scenes, "partly authentic" scenes, and "sketches," Knight provides a sequence of scenes derived primarily from Witkowski and Bergemann, but also incorporating Kupsch's suggested placement of the scene "At the Doctor's" (H4,8) in second position following the scene in which Woyzeck shaves the Captain (H4, 5). His text consists of twenty-four scenes and ends with Woyzeck at the pond (H1,20). He omits three scenes which in his view may have been intended for the final version but are incompatible with the extant sequences of scenes, namely, the children playing on the street (H1,18), Woyzeck supposedly returning from the pond after the murder (H3,2), and the fragmentary assessment of the murder by a policeman (H1,21).

Knight considers Büchner's historical sources to be little more than the initial impulse for the play. In his view *Woyzeck* is not a *pièce à thèse* meant to criticize Clarus and the legal system. Rather, it is an essay on the psychology of murder loosely based on the historical case. The impact of poverty on character and actions is but one of the play's essential elements. Its excellence as a work of art, the fact that it is also an "essentially 'pure' tragedy — that is, tragedy not intended to illustrate any idea or view of life, but constructed simply for its essentially *aesthetic* effect," is accidental, for at this time Büchner was "so good an unconscious artist that even something undertaken in this spirit turns out, in his treatment of it, to be a piece of work of great aesthetic merit." Whatever political, social, or economic moral one draws from the play is done at one's own risk, Knight states, since "the dramatist has not told us to do so" (130–32).

What makes the play so aesthetically satisfying, according to Knight, is its extraordinary concision and simplicity, which he considers most un-German, and the author's honesty and lack of sentimentality in presenting his extremely tragic view of life. The play makes excellent use of the episodic, scene-by-scene style and is better adapted to the stage than is *Dantons Tod*. While the sequence of scenes appears to be more episodic and less logically connected than is the case in the earlier play, "the events are actually linked together with an almost perfect logic, the theme develops with an economy and inevitability seldom found in the work of any dramatist." Rather than speaking to each other, the characters talk at or past one another more than in any drama before the mature works of Strindberg. Yet they are "complete, real, and convincing to a degree almost unparalleled in German literature." This seeming inconsistency intensifies the effect of genuine realism by eliminating conventional dramatic action and concentrating on the essentials of the action. The results, Knight observes, are close to those obtained by the Greek dramatists (133–34).

An even greater factor in the play's excellence and effectiveness, according to Knight, is the depiction of character. Whatever Büchner's thoughts on fate and determinism may have been, Woyzeck and Marie are presented as if they were free. The emphasis in the play on moral questions, on the nature of good and evil and of responsibility and irresponsibility, suggests a possible change in the author's attitude. Büchner's departure from the sources in his depiction of Woyzeck and Marie indicate that he is not reopening the case as presented by Clarus: the problem for Büchner is not, as it was for Clarus, whether or not Woyzeck is insane and therefore not accountable for his deed. Büchner's Woyzeck is not insane. He knows "perfectly well what he is doing, and his ideas on good and evil, or right and wrong, are acute, and on the whole sensible." He is a poor man who earns some money by letting himself be used by others, "but there is no indication that he absolutely must allow himself to be so used." One of his defining characteristics is his "muddleheadedness": "his ideas are not clear or consistent; he is partly rational, partly pious, partly superstitious, and he possesses far too lively an imagination for his own comfort or for the good of those with whom he has to do, especially Marie and Andres" (136–37).

Woyzeck and Marie represent Büchner's concept of "ordinary people" in their closeness to nature, in the warm-hearted affection they feel for each other and for their child, and in the strength of their religious feelings. The latter are dangerous and unsettling, however, for the powerful conscience with which they are endowed seems to work in a disruptive, disintegrating fashion. In Woyzeck there is apparently a close connection between religious belief, "religious reminiscence, one might say, and incipient, *but only incipient*, insanity" (137, author's emphasis). Woyzeck is fundamentally a just man. His suspicion is not easily aroused, but once he is persuaded of Marie's infidelity, he reacts violently and with "clumsy premeditation," clumsy because it is out of character for Woyzeck (137).

If there is a moral to the story, Knight concludes, it is contained in Woyzeck's inconspicuous line: "Eins nach dem andern." For some men in some circumstances life is just "one [evil] thing after another," and nothing can be done about it (137–39). Marie, for her part, is basically a good and moral person, but she is also sensual, passionate, and naive. Because she is human and animal, she falls for a more virile, normal, and cheerful man than Woyzeck, but her powerful conscience then makes her distrust herself and undermines her vitality with feelings of remorse. If that were not the case, Knight assumes, she would never have allowed Woyzeck to kill her. As representatives of their class and kind, Woyzeck and Marie are also "'timeless' figures representing humanity at large in many of its most important aspects" (139–41). They are not poor proletarians who are destroyed by the social consequences of their poverty but rather frail human beings who succumb to passion, jealousy, and anger and who commit the real sins of infidelity and murder.

Unlike Hans Mayer, Knight considers the play to be entirely new and not closely connected to its time. In his view it is not dependent on any preceding work of literature. In opposition to Viëtor, he sees no similarity between Woyzeck and Faust, Gretchen and Marie, or between their respective themes and situations. Whereas *Faust* is characteristic of the Sturm und Drang in the misalliance based on social difference and the enormous disparity in intelligence of the protagonists, Woyzeck and Marie are from the same social class and have similar views and levels of intelligence (127–28).

A further step in the shift of emphasis away from class difference and toward the human condition of the characters is taken by Wolfgang Martens, who writes that Woyzeck is not a proletarian but a poor man in the more comprehensive and deeper meaning given that word by Christianity. He appears prefigured by the figures in the Bible who are possessed, downtrodden, and leprous. Marie, too, is of "biblical stature in the force and authenticity of her actions and conscience." These figures are not healthy, innocent, uncorrupted manifestations of nature and the folk, as Mayer claims, but rather "creatures who are in need of mercy, healing, and salvation" (1957–58, 19–20).

In this as in his other works, Martens writes, Büchner's primary concern is with the nature, condition, and destiny of man. In *Woyzeck* as in *Dantons Tod* he confronts the human with the animal and finds little difference between them. As demonstrated in the fair scene interpolated into *Woyzeck*, the differences between man and beast are not truly great or significant, especially in the area of sexuality. Like Marion in *Dantons Tod*, with whom Martens compares her, Marie is driven and determined by her sexual drive and passion and suffers a similar, if more tragic fate. In both cases "sensuality has become a factor in the subjection of the ego, in the reduction of the personality, and in dehumanization" (15–17). In his despair, Büchner contradicts the Epicureanism he seems to advocate in *Dantons Tod*: as exemplified by Marion and Marie, following one's nature, that is, being subject to one's drives, can have devastating results. Marion's lover commits suicide after nearly killing her, and Woyzeck kills Marie, for which he pays with his life. Their tragedy is not caused by society, but by the members of society, like the Captain and the Doctor, who are caricatured and criticized for their lack of understanding and love and for "ignoring the dark possibilities of man and his need" (18). In a radical departure from the idealistic concept of a free, harmonious and self-determining individual, Büchner sees man as threatened by internal and external forces, as isolated and suffering and therefore in need of understanding and brotherly love (20).

In another essay Martens focuses on the Captain, whom he considers to be as unforgettable as Woyzeck and Marie. His peculiar attributes go beyond the socially critical and satirical thrust of caricature and the scornful laughter it evokes to intimate the precarious and endangered situation of humankind and to arouse uncanny and oppressive feelings (1958, 64–65). Büchner's Captain deviates from the traditional representation of the military figure in that he is fat, bloated, and, in the words of the Doctor, has an "apoplectic constitution." He loves domesticity, is respectful of clerical authority, and has a penchant for order and moderation. Lacking all the heroic attributes of the traditional soldier, he is represented as a half-hearted, complacent, and arrogant representative of the bourgeoisie. This is the first time in German literature, according to Martens, that the basic values of a rigid "bourgeois-idealistic ideology" are attacked so directly and aggressively (66–67).

Martens discovers elements in the Captain that stand in paradoxical contrast to the satirical caricature previously identified by critics, namely a nervousness, fearfulness, and restlessness which appear to contradict his philistine bearing and his principles of order and propriety. He is emotional and sentimental. His manner of speaking is disconnected, as he switches from one topic to another and from one attitude to another. Like other figures in Büchner's works, he suffers from neurotic unrest, which motivates him to urge Woyzeck and the Doctor to slow down. Like Woyzeck, he suffers from vertigo, attacks of anxiety, and feelings of being threatened from within; and he too is a potential subject for the Doctor's experiments. Like Danton and Leonce, he worries about the meaning of life and experiences boredom, which Martens considers to be a symptom of the loss of transcendence that is related to melancholy and anxiety about life (68–69).

Given these characteristics, the Captain can no longer be seen as merely a satirical caricature, as a comically distorted counterpart to major figures in Büchner's works. According to Martens, he expresses the fundamentally tragic condition of human existence independent of social class: "In the representative of an unworthy bourgeoisie appear characteristics that point to the disharmony of existence itself: a hidden terror of the trans-social wretchedness of the world is integrated with social criticism." In reflecting the frightening, unchangeable, negative components of existence without a thesis and in a comic manner, the caricature takes on the characteristics of the grotesque (68–70).

From his investigation of another secondary figure, the Barber, Martens makes a convincing argument against constructions of the play that leave Woyzeck alive at the end. The scene "Gerichtsdiener. Barbier. Arzt. Richter" (Court Clerk. Barber. Doctor. Judge), with which the first version ends, has led some critics to assume that Woyzeck, whom they identify with the Barber, is apprehended after the murder and would, like the historical Woyzeck, have been brought to trial, had Büchner lived to complete the play. This is the only scene — and it is fragmentary in the extreme — that can legitimately be seen as indicating that Woyzeck does not drown, that he lives beyond the scene in which he goes into the pond. And such an interpretation is possible only if one identifies the Barber with Woyzeck, as do Bergemann and his followers in their editions, which reverse and supposedly correct Franzos's added stage instruction indicating that Woyzeck drowns. Following the lead of Hans Winkler, Martens presents irrefutable arguments against identifying Woyzeck with the Barber.

To begin with, it makes no sense that Büchner's hero, who is called Louis in the first version, would be identified in the play's final scene as "Barber" rather than by name, and it would also go against Büchner's practice not to list his hero's name first in the list of figures who appear in the scene. It also makes no sense to characterize this figure at the end of the play as "Dogmatischer Atheist. Lang, hager, feig, gutmütig [?], Wissenschaftl [?]" (Dogmatic Atheist. Tall, thin, cowardly, good-natured, scientific [question marks indicate uncertain readings]), attributes which for the most part do not apply to Woyzeck. They do apply, however, to a Barber who appears in an earlier scene in the first draft (H1,10). Through a detailed analysis, Martens demonstrates that the Barber in these scenes belongs to a completely different conception. "He is obviously conceived as a risible figure — a farcical caricature with grotesque elements, hence a contrasting figure to the simple, loyal, suffering human being Woyzeck." Büchner thinks in motifs, according to Martens; his secondary figures function as carriers of certain motive elements and formulations that are not bound to a certain character. Several of the motifs associated with the Barber in H1,10 were later assigned to other characters, and the Barber was eliminated as a figure (1960, 364–68).

Why does the Barber appear in H1,21 along with a Court Clerk, Doctor, and Judge? As Martens points out, barbers treated wounds and performed other medical functions into the nineteenth century. They also took part in investigating wounded or murdered victims for juridical purposes. Thus the Barber is part of an official delegation sent to investigate Marie's corpse and the crime committed against her (371–72). After considering other examples of barbers from German and world literature, Martens concludes that Büchner's Barber has much in common with his predecessors, both in physical attributes and in his function, and that he is therefore based on literary models and not on someone Büchner actually knew, as Winkler assumed (371–81).

Since there is no evidence in Büchner's manuscripts for any plot development that goes beyond Woyzeck's entry into the pond and the Court Clerk's observation about the murder of Marie, one can safely conclude, according to Martens, that Woyzeck does die in the pond — whether intentionally or not is irrelevant. Furthermore, the play is not a torso, as many critics have claimed, but an essentially complete work. The inclusion of the "Court Clerk" scene, as fragmentary as it is, is an appropriate conclusion: as official representatives provide banal commentary on a human tragedy, the play ends in a way that precludes any form of sentimentality (381–82).

An early example of a *werkimmanent* or New Critical analysis of Büchner's language and style is included in Walter Höllerer's investigation of the occurrence of laughter and crying in the literature of the transitional period between classical and modern German literature. According to Höllerer, the rhythm of Büchner's language binds the separate parts — words, sentences, and parts of scenes — together with the greatest possible tension. Rhythmical construction rather than explanation and reflection about connections is the binding principle of Büchner's prose. Compactness and integration are achieved through the repetition and variation of rhythmical units, a practice that reaches its high point in *Woyzeck*, where the individual units are briefer and more separated from each other and the crescendos closer together. The use of stressed and almost entirely unstressed rhythmical elements results in "pantingly breathless, rhythmically varied sequences of sentences" (1958, 111–15). Connected with the rhythm and also contributing to the impression of unity and compactness, according to Höllerer, is the "Klangleib," the fabric of sounds consisting primarily of full and accented vowels (115–16).

Appearing in a series edited by Höllerer, Helmut Krapp's *Der Dialog bei Georg Büchner* (Dialog in the Works of Georg Büchner, 1958), greatly expands the investigation of the style and poetic qualities of Büchner's works. Krapp applies what Höllerer calls a "dichtungswissenschaftliche Betrachtungsweise," an approach similar to the close textual analysis of New Criticism, to contrast Büchner's plays with those of Schiller and the classical tradition and to refute the claim by some critics that Büchner's works are nihilistic in form and content. Idealism and nihilism are similar in their formal structure, Krapp writes, but they differ in the fact that the dramatist can represent the idea but cannot represent nothingness. "Just as the classical hero could not withstand the encounter with God without being blinded, so Büchner's hero cannot endure the confrontation with nothingness. Insight into nothingness is momentary." For Büchner, nothingness appears in order to be overcome (25–26). In Krapp's view, the argument for Büchner's nihilism is compellingly refuted by the fact that his figures are so fully and completely present in their every word and in every scene, even as they confront the abyss and chaos of the world, as Danton does consciously and Woyzeck unconsciously (70).

Whereas Danton and his colleagues identify and analyze their political and existential situation and problems, Woyzeck's psychic condition is *directly expressed* in his confusion and stammering use of language, his interjections of pain, despair, or ecstasy. Pauses and silence predominate over words. Thoughts are not developed in continuous speech: individual words and word motifs are isolated by repetition and by their liberation from the order imposed by syntax, and they serve as signals connecting one scene with another. For example, the "immer zu" (go on) with which Marie encourages the Drum Major in the inn scene (H4,11) is overheard by Woyzeck and becomes a sign of her infidelity. In the following scene it echoes in his mind and gains power over him like a magic spell; it also becomes connected in his mind with the command to stab Marie: "Hör ich's immer, immer zu, stich todt, todt" (Do I always hear it? Go on! Stab dead! Dead!). The reduction of language to individual words and phrases with strong accents creates a powerful rhythm, which is constantly obstructed and therefore prevented from developing into a broad arch as in classical drama. In Krapp's view, rhythm predominates as an ordering principle; words are used like building blocks (79–84).

Isolated and repeated words, phrases, scenes, and parts of scenes gain their expressiveness, their rhythm, and their meaning from a complex web of interconnections that Krapp characterizes as being organized in the depths (*in die Tiefe organisiert*). In place of the causal and chronological connections that form a continuum in the classical drama, Büchner's plays resemble a collage or montage in the juxtaposition — almost with a suggestion of simultaneity — of the particles of speech and segments of scenes. Like the epic drama later developed by Bertolt Brecht, Büchner's plays are composed of situations, which Krapp calls "statuary moments" (*statuarische Momente*), that reveal the momentary behavior of the figures toward typical constellations of forces that control them or that they oppose. Büchner differs from Brecht, however, in his use of contrast as a structuring principle and as a source of tension; the modus of contrast, according to Krapp, is lyrical rather than dramatic (85–87, 103–106, 137).

Krapp uses the term "statuary moments" in specific reference to scenes in which the figures derive their expressive force from borrowed quotations. For example, Marie's anxiety and sense of guilt are expressed through her exclamatory responses to passages she reads in the Bible. In the same scene, the Fool quotes disconnected passages from fairy tales while counting on his fingers. His words do not form sentences that move from subject to predicate to object; rather, they are like things, the building blocks mentioned above, which can be rearranged without significantly altering the meaning. They are "organized in the depths" in that they formulate with unconscious simplicity fragments from fairy tales and, through the broken, fragmentary manner of their construction, also indicate the Fool's confusion. The words he speaks are not his own, just as Marie's are not her own: the juxtaposition allows her words to attain greater expressive power in contrast to his, but it also allows his to take on the darker meaning of an oracular or prophetic utterance. The Fool's words may be seen as an anticipation of and parallel to the scene in which he again entertains Woyzeck's child by counting on his fingers (H3,2), this time repeating the words: "Der is ins Wasser gefallen" (He fell in the water), which can be interpreted as a premonition of Woyzeck's fate (85–91).

Another example of the collage-like juxtaposition of dramatic moments that could be occurring simultaneously is the inn scene in which Woyzeck discovers Marie dancing with the Drum Major (H4,11). The scene begins with comic banter between inebriated journeymen interspersed with fragments from a song and a brief quotation relating to drink. It ends with an absurdly comic and parodistic sermon by one of the journeymen. Between those segments, and in strong contrast to them, is Woyzeck's shattering discovery of Marie's infidelity. Other scenes are broken up into separate dialogue particles which jump from one motif to another in a series of statuary moments. The murder scene (H1,15) may be cited as an example: none of the particles consists of more than two or three short statements by each of the speakers, and some consist of a single monologic utterance (103–107).

Krapp concludes that the fragmentary ending of *Woyzeck*, as of *Lenz*, is consistent with the form and structure of Büchner's works. Like the sequence of images Lenz describes as his aesthetic program (I,88), the statuary moments or situations continue in an uninterrupted chain. Likewise, the scheme of contrasts Büchner uses has no beginning or end: contrasts, too, can follow each other in an unending chain. Büchner's intention is not to present the resolution of a conflict but to allow us to see Woyzeck's hopeless situation following the murder: he is misunderstood and abandoned by his friend Andres, rejected by his son, and recognized as a murderer by the people at the inn. Like the child in the Grandmother's tale, he is totally and tragically alone (92–93, 138–39, 145).

According to Krapp, the folk songs and other verse included in the play come from a reality in which there is still the possibility of an existence that is not yet fragmented and in conflict with the world. They serve as proof of a fundamental disillusionment that has already taken place and of a longing to escape it. By contrasting with Woyzeck's situation, they reinforce the tragic condition of his existence and lose their original function of creating and representing community (147–49).

In a more comprehensive investigation of Büchner's use of folk songs and verse, Gonthier-Louis Fink concludes that they are an expression or representation of authentic and unadorned life and of a

truth that appears inescapable and inevitable (1961, 560). They function like the chorus of Greek tragedy to provide commentary on the
play, and their message is pessimistic, even nihilistic. Without them,
Woyzeck's drama would be nothing but a banal story of murder.
Rather than elevating the spectators, however, Büchner's chorus pulls
them down from their ideals into the poorest reality. It gives the play
an uncanny dimension by pointing to the unavoidability of fate. The
songs expand the play and give it universal validity through their focus
on love and suffering, transitoriness and death. They destroy without
mercy the illusions that keep people in bondage in this world. What
remains is man's bestiality and inescapable suffering (588, 590–91).

Krapp's New Critical investigation of the structure, style, and language of Büchner's works was followed by three remarkably similar,
detailed studies of repeated and varied motifs that were published at
about the same time by authors apparently unfamiliar with each other's
work: Volker Klotz's *Geschlossene und offene Form im Drama* (Closed
and Open Form of Drama, 1960), Franz Heinrich Mautner's "Wortgewebe, Sinngefüge und 'Idee' in Büchners 'Woyzeck'" (Tapestry of
Words, Structure of Meaning and "Idea" in Büchner's *Woyzeck*, 1961),
and a chapter on Büchner in *Enttäuschter Pantheismus: Zur Weltgestaltung der Dichtung in der Restaurationszeit* (Disappointed Pantheism:
Concerning the Concept of the World in the Literature of the Period
of Restoration, 1962) by Walter Weiss. By analyzing the unifying, char-
acterizing, and expressive function of recurring motifs and complexes of
motifs and images, these authors build on the foundation laid by
Scheuer's and Krapp's investigations of the open form of drama.

In an article published in 1961 that is an updated revision of a lecture delivered at the annual meeting of the Modern Language Association in 1950, Franz Mautner finds Krapp's study to be excellent in its
analysis of the mimic and monologic nature of Büchner's language but
almost blind to the individual, usually repeated word as an expression
of the characters' mental and spiritual essence and as the element that
creates the atmosphere in many scenes. In Mautner's view, the individual word is the characteristic attribute of the play: it dominates the
scenes and creates the characters. This occurs in two forms: (1) the
same words or cluster of words deriving from a particular realm of
meaning or mood recur in the speeches of the same person; (2) individual scenes take their meaning or atmosphere from words or word
groups, which in some cases contain contrasting elements that indicate
conflict (511–12).

Mautner finds the repetition of words to be especially effective in
revealing Woyzeck's psychopathic hallucinations and compulsive be-

havior, but it applies to the other figures as well. The erotic content of Marie's unconscious and her sensual nature are repeatedly expressed in her words and in the songs she sings. When she and her neighbor first see the Drum Major, for example, Margret says of him: "What a man! Like a tree," to which Marie adds: "He stands on his feet like a lion," a response that transforms Margret's "statically lifeless" image into one of animal vitality. Even in the completely unerotic fourth scene, in which Marie holds her child on her lap and admires her new earrings, she sings a song about abduction that reveals where her thoughts are. And when admiring her beauty in the same scene, she compares herself with the wealthy women, to whom she is inferior only because of her poverty. According to Mautner, all but one of the scenes in which Marie appears or in which she is spoken about have erotic content or erotic implications, and that indicates, "considering the paucity of words in the play, an erotically colored vocabulary." The Drum Major is Marie's counterpart in his erotic or sexual orientation, but he lacks her heart and her conscience (525–26).

Turning to Woyzeck, Mautner sees his neurotic character as clearly manifest in his manner of expression, which alternates between stuttering hesitation and explosive outbursts. Mautner finds his vocabulary concentrated on three emotional areas and three or four rational themes. The emotional areas are eroticism, fear, and murder. At least one of these motifs occurs in all but two of the scenes in which Woyzeck appears, and the impending murder is the suppressed content of one of those, namely, the scene in which Woyzeck comes for Marie (H1,14). The only scene in which none of the motifs appears is the so-called testament scene (H4,17). The subjects of Woyzeck's rational thinking are nature, the world, man, and poverty, the last of which is, like the word "must," perceived as an expression of fateful compulsion. Once Woyzeck's jealousy is aroused, a small number of words take on very specific personal meaning and recur in his speech. These are (1) "warm," "hot," "cold," "freeze"; (2) "go on" (*immer zu*) and "still" (*immer noch*); and (3) "stab," which is connected to "knife" (527–28).

When Woyzeck refers the word pairs "warm, cold; hot, freeze" to himself, they indicate his fear and his feeling of being driven. "Hot" indicates his fear of the murder and of its discovery, "cold" the terror after the deed, the horror of knowing, of suffering. When applied to Marie the same pairs indicate either the opposition between life and death or that between vitality or sensuality and its eradication. Just before he kills Marie, Woyzeck's observations, feelings, wishes, and deliberation are expressed in his groping with the contrast of cold and warm:

> Are you freezing Marie? And yet you're warm.
> How hot your lips are! Hot — hot whore's breath.
> But still I'd give heaven to kiss them once more.
>> When you're cold, you don't freeze any more.
> You won't freeze in the morning dew. (H1,15)

Life and sin become one for Woyzeck in the word "hot." In the inn scene following the murder, he describes himself as hot. When dancing with Kate, who becomes associated in his mind with Marie, he tells her that she is hot but that she too will grow cold. In a similar development, the phrase "immer zu" also becomes symbolic following its appearance in a unique, concrete situation. Woyzeck's jealousy turns to rage when he hears Marie encourage the Drum Major with these words. He then hears them coming from everywhere, demanding that he kill her in revenge, but also in punishment for her transgression of a moral law (528–30).

As Mautner demonstrates in a scene-by-scene analysis, the repetition of words is also used to create thematic and atmospheric unity. The tone of a scene is often set in the first sentence. The Captain's first words to Woyzeck in the opening scene of the Bergemann edition (=H4,5), for example, point to a key element in the contrast of their characters and worlds. "Slow down, Woyzeck, slow down," he admonishes him, afraid that he will run out of activity before his time is up. The Captain's fixed idea centering around boredom and fear of empty time contrasts with Woyzeck's urgency in his attempt to supplement his meager wages. The Captain uses the word "langsam," (slow or slowly) four times in the scene and refers twice to Woyzeck as being driven (*verhetzt*). This is but one of several sets of opposites that define their contrasting personalities and views on "morality" and "virtue," which are also recurring words (532–33). Similar contrasts in vocabulary and the repetition of words also occur in Woyzeck's scenes with the Doctor and the Drum Major as well as in the meeting on the street of the Captain and the Doctor. It is this recurrence in the various scenes of words and phrases associated with specific characters and clusters of motifs that creates thematic and atmospheric unity (532–42). These word motifs thus have three different functions and tasks, Mautner observes: they are used to characterize the figures psychologically, to identify the play's themes and problems, and as building blocks that bind the scenes together (552).

The one scene that does not contain any recurring motifs is the final scene in H4, which, Mautner assumes, is the last scene Büchner wrote before his death. In anticipation of his death, Woyzeck gives away the few things he possesses. As he speaks about his mother and sister and the religious objects they gave him, Woyzeck appears for a moment not as a doomed psychopath but as a creature created by God and bound through blood to his mother and sister. In the second half of the scene he reads his military papers, which place him impersonally in the context of the military machine. The two parts are connected by the verses he finds in his mother's Bible: "As your body, Lord, was red and sore, // Let my heart be for ever more." In Mautner's view, these lines extend the play's horizon beyond its merely psychological or social or nihilistic content: "The poor devil Woyzeck becomes a representative of suffering in the world, especially that of the poor and despised people, and he takes that suffering upon himself." Woyzeck thus stands before us in a "transfiguring light" that transcends his individuality and places him in a Christian context. In his suffering, Woyzeck becomes an imitator of Christ. This scene is the counterpart to the preceding scene, which could be taking place at the same time, in which Marie confronts her guilt by reading passages in the Bible (542–45).

These scenes achieve their full impact as a thematic unity, like two wings of an altar or diptych. In his scene, the only one free of motifs expressing fear, jealousy, or killing, Woyzeck appears to be completely composed, transformed, and no longer damned. He has undergone a profound transformation, according to Mautner, one which has been all but ignored in previous interpretations, probably because the scenes that follow take no notice of this transformation. But these scenes are supplied from the first draft (H1) and begin with the Grandmother's tale, which has been cited as the primary justification for a nihilistic interpretation. Mautner does not want to claim by his emphasis on these scenes that *Woyzeck* is a Christian play, but he does note the similarity between Woyzeck's acceptance of suffering and Büchner's reported deathbed affirmation of suffering, spoken not long after the scene was written: "We don't have too much pain; we have too little, for through pain we go to God. We are death, dust, ashes; how can we complain?" (542–47). Büchner's task in *Woyzeck*, as Mautner sees it, is to represent human existence, which is experienced primarily as suffering. This includes the individual's relations to nature and society and the impact of fate and guilt. Through the successive stages of composition, Mautner concludes, Büchner increases the emphasis on Woyzeck's and Marie's morality, softens the determinism, reduces the antireligious forms of expression, and presents a more positive view of the world (552–54).

In a chapter of a book published in 1962, Walter Weiss sees a correlation between the lack of connection between the scenes in Büchner's plays and the isolation or lack of connection between the figures, who do not engage in real conversation. Weiss disagrees with those who consider the isolation of speech particles and the emphasis on the moment to be characteristic of realism. Such interpretations overlook what he calls the "convergence" that serves as a unifying force in the composition of the language, the figures, and the scenes. The repeated words and motifs, which Weiss refers to as "Kernwörter, Grundbilder, und Grundgebärden" (core words, basic images, and fundamental gestures) form a sequence, a juxtaposition, and what Weiss calls *Tiefenspannung und Tiefengliederung* (a tension and articulation in the depths) of which the speaker is unaware (1962, 276–80).

One such complex involves the word *hetzen* (to rush, be frantically in haste), which the Captain connects to death. He says to the Doctor: "Rudern Sie mit ihrem Stock nicht so in der Luft. Sie hetzen sich ja hinter dem Tod drein" (Don't paddle like that with your cane in the air. You're chasing after death) (H4,9). And in the first draft of the same scene he also says to Woyzeck: "He Woyzeck, was hetzt er sich so an uns vorbey? (Hey, Woyzeck, why are you hurrying by us like that?) (H2,7). The phlegmatic, lethargic Captain, considers death to be the end result of haste. In slowing down the Doctor, he claims to have saved his life. He connects Woyzeck's haste with an open razor that cuts its way through life. This basic gesture is connected with a particular place, namely, the street. In a previous scene the Captain urges the departing Woyzeck to walk slowly down the street (H4,5). Furthermore, the scene in which Woyzeck fetches Marie with the intent of killing her begins on the street, and the children are on the street when they learn about Marie's death. The street thus takes on symbolic meaning as the path to death (281).

The motifs of the knife or razor and of stabbing also occur in the opening scene in Bergemann's construction (H4,5), in which Woyzeck has a razor in his hand and is shaving the Captain, and the second scene (H4,1), in which Woyzeck is cutting sticks in a thicket. Following the confrontation between Woyzeck and Marie over the earrings she claims to have found, Marie says: "I really am a whore. I could stab myself" (H4,4). In scenes from the drafts included in Bergemann's text, Marie defies Woyzeck with the words: "Dare to touch me, Franz! I would rather have a knife in my body than your hand on mine" (H2,8), and the Captain reacts to Woyzeck's piercing stare with the words: "You stab me with your eyes" (H2,7). In general, Woyzeck's staring is connected with the motif of stabbing and with his disturbed state of mind. Finally, following Woyzeck's discovery of the dancing pair, the motifs of the knife and stabbing recur with compelling frequency until the murder itself (282–83).

As noted by previous interpreters, Marie and Woyzeck are associated with and characterized by contrasting colors and temperatures: she with red and hot, he with white and cold. Marie's red mouth is a metaphor for her beauty. The color red functions as a reference to her beauty, her hot passion, her sinful transgression, and, as the color of blood, to punishment and retribution. Both Woyzeck and the Drum Major see Marie as hot in her sensuality and passion. Just before killing her, Woyzeck says: "How hot your lips are! Hot — hot whore's breath" (H1,15). In contrast to Marie, according to Weiss, Woyzeck is cold and white, but the passages he cites occur in the drafts and not in the final manuscript: in Woyzeck's meeting with the Captain on the street (H2,7), which is omitted in Büchner's final draft (H4,9), Woyzeck responds to the Captain's reference to Marie's infidelity as follows: "Captain, Sir, the earth is hot as hell — I'm ice cold, ice cold. Hell is cold, do you want to bet"; and Woyzeck is "*very cold*" when he tells Andres he has dreamed of a knife (H1,8) (285). In the inn scene following the murder, it may be added, Woyzeck says he is hot. After removing his jacket, he tells Kate that she is hot, but that she too will grow cold. In his mind heat is associated with life and sin, cold with death and punishment. In addition to being the color of life, sensuality, sin, and blood, red is also associated with suffering in the religious verse Woyzeck quotes in the testament scene (H4,17), a meaning also contained in the reference to the "red cross" near Marie's corpse and, according to Weiss, to the red of the socks in the verse sung before Woyzeck fetches her (H1,14) (285–87).

The word *Mensch* (person, human being, mankind) is another recurring motif. The Captain repeats the phrase "ein guter Mensch" (a good person) especially in reference to Woyzeck: like the word "morality," this phrase is nothing but a formula for him that is empty of any real meaning. Woyzeck also uses the word frequently and at key moments: everything he experiences is related to his image of man, but, unlike the Captain, he struggles to understand the word's meaning. Woyzeck repeatedly uses the word *Mensch* as an exclamation, or, as Weiss sees it, in a position somewhere between exclamation and address. Weiss again takes his example from H2,7: following the Captain's revelation of Marie's infidelity, Woyzeck exclaims: "Impossible! Man! Man! [*Mensch! Mensch!*] impossible!" Later, when his doubt becomes certainty, he says: "Much is possible. Man! [*Mensch!*] Much is possible." The words *Mann* and *Weib,* (man and woman) on the other hand, are used to refer to the human animal, man and woman as sexual beings. These are the terms used by Marie and the Drum Major in referring to each other, and when Woyzeck sees the two dancing, he too uses these terms, followed by a linkage of human being (*Mensch*) and animal: "Man [*Mann*] and woman, man [*Mensch*] and beast" (H4,11). The tension between an untrue, illusory, and abstract concept of man, like the Captain's, and man as an animal, as represented by the Drum Major and, when she comes under his spell, Marie, runs through the entire play, according to Weiss (287).

In two scenes, the fair scene and the first inn scene — both of which are settings that have traditionally served as mirrors and models of the world, according to Weiss — the nature of man becomes the object of examination and interpretation. The Journeyman in the inn scene (H4,14) parodies a sermon about divine wisdom that has created everything for the best, and he provides an ironic answer to the question "Why is man [*der Mensch*]?" He then falls out of his assumed role and undermines his apparent optimism by concluding that "everything earthly is vain — even money falls into decay." His message is also contradicted by Woyzeck's discovery of Marie's infidelity and his vision of chaos, which immediately precede the sermon. The fair scene makes clear that there is no real difference between man and beast and that man should be ashamed for trying to be more than he is. The Doctor's view of man is an example of the kind of idealization the fair scene ridicules. He supposedly believes that man is free, that "individuality is exalted in man to freedom," yet he treats Woyzeck as an experimental animal and values his life even less than an animal's: "God forbid that I should get upset about a man. A man! Now if it were a proteus that easily dies on you!" (H4,8) (287–89).

Nearly all the settings have the deep or meaningful interconnection Weiss refers to. The open field, for example, is the setting for Woyzeck's visions. The inn scenes serve as a model of the world and are characterized by images of chaos and circularity. The latter is a basic motif in the play. It is represented by the mill wheel referred to by the Captain (H4,5) and the dancing in the inn, which is associated with the recurring phrase "immer zu" (Go on). In the following examples Weiss sees circularity in what could be considered linear. When Woyzeck wonders where Marie's seducer stood, she answers: "Because the day is long and the world old, lots of people can stand in one place — one after the other" (H4,7). And after Woyzeck is thrashed by the Drum Major, he says: "One thing after the other" (H4,15). According to Weiss, Woyzeck is driven by the inescapable circularity of his existence to madness and murder. Eventually he breaks out, or, in keeping with the knife metaphor, cuts out of the circular motion of life, when he kills Marie (281–82).

Opposed to the pessimism and nihilism expressed in the play is the positive value of Woyzeck's suffering and of the love he feels for Marie and their child. Weiss refers to the verses Woyzeck reads from his mother's Bible: "Let suffering be my reward // Through suffering I praise the Lord," which are similar in content to verses from a hymn quoted in *Lenz*: "Suffering shall be my gain, // Suffering my liturgy." Like Mautner, Weiss considers these lines to be in agreement with and an authentication of Büchner's deathbed affirmation of pain. Suffering is also the message of the Grandmother's tale, in which the child's pain creates a counterweight to the play's negative images, according to Weiss, because it is deeply human and awakens human feelings that can counteract the alienation and destruction represented in the tale. It thus becomes a model for the entire play; the child in the tale becomes the mirror image for Woyzeck (298).

In an important study of drama based on the contrasting concepts of closed or tectonic and open or atectonic form — which were introduced by the art historian Heinrich Wölfflin to compare and define classical and baroque art — Volker Klotz bases his analysis of the open form of drama on *Dantons Tod* and *Woyzeck* along with plays by Lenz, Wedekind, and Brecht. As Klotz acknowledges, Oskar Walzel was the first to apply Wölfflin's opposites to literature, especially to drama, and, as seen above, Erwin Scheuer and Helmut Krapp preceded him in applying the concepts to Büchner's plays. Klotz's study surpasses its predecessors, however, in its clear and comprehensive investigation of plot, time, place, dramatis personae, composition, and language.

According to Klotz, the means used in the open form of drama to construct, coordinate, and unify the plot and subplots may consist either of complementary strands of plot in which individual and collective lines of action are integrated, or, as is the case in *Woyzeck*, of a central figure, "das zentrale Ich," who holds together the fullness of the diverse scenes and the conditions of the world represented in them that stand in an oppositional subject-object relation to the central figure. Rather than being in conflict with similar antagonists, as in classical drama, the protagonists in these plays are in confrontation with fate and the world. The development of plot is not linear, as in the closed form of drama, but circular, as Weiss, too, concludes from his analysis of motifs. Scenes coming later in the play, such as Woyzeck's meeting with the Doctor, are no closer to the conclusion, Klotz claims, than earlier ones; such episodic scenes broaden the depiction of the world confronted by the central figure (1960, 99–101, 106–108).

Especially effective for creating unity in *Woyzeck* is what Klotz calls "metaphorische Verklammerung," that is, a complex of repeated and varied word-motifs and chains of images that interconnect the scenes in which they occur. Chains of images Klotz identifies include "red," "blood," "stab" and "knife," "moon," "hot" and "cold," and the rhythmic motifs "stab dead" and "immer zu" (go on), which are transformed into "Dead! Dead!" and "immer noch" (still), many of which sound together as a chord in the words preceding the murder: Marie: "How red the moon is rising." Woyzeck: "Like a bloody knife" (H1,15). Because of Woyzeck's compulsion to repeat these words, they become, as Krapp has pointed out, not only an element of form but, in reflecting Woyzeck's state of mind, also of content. Words take on the quality of things that act upon the person through whom they speak. "Texture undertakes the functions of structure," as Klotz puts it (1960, 104–106).

The scene is the primary unit of construction in the open form of drama, Klotz writes, and the sequence of scenes is discontinuous rather than linear as in the closed form. Each scene is complete in and of itself, though it may begin and end *in medias res*. There is no need for exposition or for messengers or observers to supply background information not presented on the stage. This form of drama does not explain, and it does not tactfully exclude unpleasant, ugly, or violent events. The scenes represent stations, and their arrangement is determined by contrast or variation. The focus is on the specific and unique aspects of a definite person, situation, or place, not on what is characteristic and typical. Often an episodic scene is included, such as the Grandmother's tale in *Woyzeck*, which serves as a "point of integration," a place where diverse elements are brought together and placed in a greater context: in this case, Woyzeck's individual fate is localized in a world without salvation and intercommunication (109–112).

As opposed to the unity of time and place that is characteristic of the closed form of drama, Klotz continues, the open form requires an extended period of time and various settings in order to represent the fullness and variety of the realistic world. In keeping with the relative autonomy of the scenes, time and space are discontinuous: rather than being connected through a linear progression, the scenes are separated by intervals of time and changes in setting. The uniform, constructed, aristocratic world of the closed form opens up to include all social classes and all potential settings. The sense of belonging in a definite context in a hierarchically structured society gives way to feelings of isolation and loneliness. Space or setting becomes a means of characterization. In closed spaces such as Marie's room and the barracks, Woyzeck and Marie appear to be confined, imprisoned, cut off from others. They feel uncomfortable, anxious, and threatened. Walls may be used to separate and exclude, as when Woyzeck stands outside the inn and looks through a window to discover Marie and the Drum Major dancing. Here and in other scenes the window serves as a means of communication between inside and outside, between outer and inner worlds, between the individual and the external world. Some scenes in *Woyzeck* are set outdoors, and reveal Woyzeck's relationship to nature, which is a "powerful, active partner and antagonist" and participant in the drama (113–134).

As already noted, Klotz considers the social class of the figures in the open form of drama to be unimportant. They lack the completeness and polish of figures in the closed form: often they are not fully aware of themselves, or they are aberrant in one way or another: Woyzeck, for example, is psychopathic, and Marie cannot control her sexual urges. Physical and biological elements play no part in the closed form of drama, according to Klotz, but a significant one in the open form. Woyzeck is defeated in a fight with the Drum Major, for example, and Marie feels oppressed in her room following Woyzeck's disturbing account of the visions he has seen. The immediate response to physical perceptions goes along with the general spontaneity of these figures, who are more individual, comprehensive, and closer to life than the figures of the closed form. They lack the distancing self-awareness of those figures that enables them to compare, judge, and plan their actions, and their thoughts and actions are not prescribed by the conventions of a preexisting meaning system or by what has preceded and what will follow in time. Instead, they strike back almost automatically and without contemplation at the attacks of their opponent, the world. They see only what is closest to them, not the whole, and their actions and reactions are determined more by unconscious forces than by consciousness and reflection (137–45).

The language in the open form of drama is not uniform and in verse, as in the closed form, but pluralistic and individualized to reflect the differences in status and character of the speakers. The simplicity and lack of education of the primary figures in *Woyzeck* is reflected in the paratactic simplicity of their language. Their groping attempts to express themselves are frequently characterized by the occurrence of ellipsis and anacoluthon, which Wolfgang Kayser has identified as syntactic figures that occur particularly in spontaneous speech. The greater education and refinement of the Captain and the Doctor, on the other hand, are evident in their use of more complex sentence structures and, in the case of the Doctor, technical terms. Pseudoscientific language occurs in the tirades of the proprietor of the fair booth, and the Journeyman speaks out of character in his parody of a sermon (157–58, 160, 165–68).

According to Klotz, the open form of drama lacks a uniform perspective, a point of view that determines the place of the individual components. The subject changes constantly, and the complexity of reality confronts the individual polyperspectivally as a fullness of confusing details. The dramatic hero not only confronts a variety of opponents representing aspects of the world, he is also acted upon by impersonal forces that are ineffable and unnamable, forces represented by the impersonal "es," as in the following examples: "Es geht hinter mir . . ."; "'S is so kurios still"; "Wie's heraufzieht!" (H4,1); "Es ist hinter mir hergegangen . . ."; "Es wird so dunkel. . . . Ich halt's nicht aus. Es schauert mich!" (H4, 2); "wenn ich die Aug zumach, dreht sich's immer . . . und dann spricht's aus der Wand"; "Es redt immer: stich, stich!" (H4, 13). (Something's moving behind me . . ."; "It is so curiously still . . ."; "It's coming closer." "It followed me . . ."; "It's getting so dark. . . . I can't stand it. It gives me the creeps"; "when I close my eyes, it keeps spinning . . . and then it speaks from the wall!"; "It keeps saying: stab, stab!") This force, against which the individual is completely defenseless, may appear as a force of nature or as a supernatural being (169–75).

As opposed to the clear contrast between dialogue and monologue in the closed form of drama, dialogue in the open form tends to be monologic. What it conveys, Klotz maintains, is primarily the self-expression of the figures and the reflection of their situation, the inner condition of the figures, and what they feel as they speak. It contains little conflict between opponents, because the hero's conflict is with the world rather than with individuals. The figures have little in common with each other and little to communicate to each other. Rather than speaking to each other, they speak past each other (182–84). Klotz does not cite examples from *Woyzeck* for this argument, but the lack of communication between Woyzeck and Andres in the first scene and Marie's response to Woyzeck's attempt to describe his experience from the first scene could serve as examples. Neither listener comprehends Woyzeck; they are frightened (Andres) and disturbed (Marie) by his peculiar behavior and words.

Finally, as the speakers in the closed form of drama use metaphors and allusions to mythology, history, and literature, those in the open form have recourse to the Bible, folk songs, proverbs, and fairy tales. These are sources with which they are familiar; the material is retrieved unconsciously and used to elucidate and comment on the speakers' own situations. For example, Marie confronts and attempts to come to terms with her guilt through Biblical passages, which she selects arbitrarily but as if guided by an external force, and Woyzeck's visions are experienced and described in language from the Old Testament and the

Apocalypse. Folk songs occur throughout the play. They may be analogous to situations in the play, as when Marie sings about an illegitimate child (H4,2) or, while admiring herself with the earrings given her by the Drum Major, about the gypsy lad who will come and take her away (H4,4). Similarly, Woyzeck sings about the maid who sits in her garden watching the soldiers (H1,17). In the "Lied vom Jäger aus Kurpfalz" (A Hunter from the Rhine) sung by journeymen just before Woyzeck discovers Marie dancing with the Drum Major (H4,11), Klotz sees the "transindividual" demonism that evokes Woyzeck's inner compulsion and despair at seeing the dancing couple. Likewise, the seemingly light and clear song about Candlemas (H1,14) takes on a threatening meaning in connection with the murder that immediately follows, the circumstances of which the song can be seen to anticipate (188–93).

In the seventeen years covered in this chapter, we have seen how, following the hiatus imposed by the intolerant cultural barbarism of the Third Reich, Büchner scholarship resumed in the second half of the forties with monographs on Büchner's life and works and on their historical and cultural context. Of particular interest because of their lasting influence and their opposing positions are the studies by Hans Mayer in 1946 and Karl Viëtor in 1949. Published in 1951 by Blackwell in Oxford, A. H. J. Knight's book was the first major study in English or any foreign language and can be seen to represent the beginning of Büchner's recognition as a world-class author. Then, beginning at the end of the fifties, the development of a new methodology, the *werkimmanent* or New Critical approach, gave rise to a series of close investigations of the language, form, structure, and content of Büchner's works. Though based on an editorially contaminated text, as will be seen in the following chapter, studies of dialog by Helmut Krapp (1958), of the open form of drama by Volker Klotz (1960), and of various motifs by Franz Heinrich Mautner (1961) represent major contributions to the understanding of the works and of Büchner's stature as a writer.

# Works Cited

Büttner, Ludwig. *Georg Büchner: Revolutionär und Pessimist. Ein Beitrag zur Geistesgeschichte des 19. Jahrhunderts*. Nuremberg: Verlag Hans Carl, 1948.

———. *Büchners Bild vom Menschen*. Nuremberg: Verlag Hans Carl, 1967.

Diem, Eugen. *Georg Büchners Leben und Werk*. Heidelberg: Meister, 1946.

Fink, Gonthier-Louis. "Volkslied und Verseinlage in den Dramen Georg Büchners." *Deutsche Vierteljahrsschrift* 35 (1961) 558–93. Also in Martens, ed., 1965, 433–87.

Höllerer, Walter. "Georg Büchner." Chap. in *Zwischen Klassik und Moderne: Lachen und Weinen in der Dichtung einer Übergangszeit.* Stuttgart: Ernst Klett Verlag, 1958. 100–142.

Klotz, Volker. *Geschlossene und offene Form im Drama.* Literatur als Kunst. Munich: Hanser, 1960.

Knight, Arthur H. J. *Georg Büchner.* Oxford: Blackwell, 1951.

Krapp, Helmut. *Der Dialog bei Georg Büchner.* Literatur als Kunst. Darmstadt: Gentner, 1958. (Since 1959: Munich: Hanser.)

Martens, Wolfgang. "Zum Menschenbild Georg Büchners. 'Woyzeck' und die Marionszene in 'Dantons Tod.'" *Wirkendes Wort* 8 (1957–58): 13–20. Also in Martens, ed., 1965, 373–85.

———. "Zur Karikatur in der Dichtung Büchners. (Woyzecks Hauptmann)." *Germanisch-Romanische Monatsschrift* 39, new series 8 (1958) 64–71.

———, ed. *Georg Büchner.* Darmstadt: Wissenschaftliche Buchgesellschaft, 1965.

Mautner, Franz Heinrich. "Wortgewebe, Sinngefüge und 'Idee" in Büchners 'Woyzeck.'" *Deutsche Vierteljahrsschrift* 35 (1961): 521–557. Also in Martens, ed., 1965, 507–54.

Mayer, Hans. *Georg Büchner und seine Zeit.* Wiesbaden: Limes Verlag, 1946. 2nd ed., 1959.

Viëtor, Karl. *Georg Büchner: Politik, Dichtung, Wissenschaft.* Bern: Francke, 1949.

Weiss, Walter. "Georg Büchner." In *Enttäuschter Pantheismus: Zur Weltgestaltung der Dichtung in der Restaurationszeit.* Dornbirn: Voralberger Verlagsanstalt, 1962. 247–301.

# 3: Construction of a Reading and Acting Text

A NEW PHASE OF BÜCHNER SCHOLARSHIP began in 1967 with Werner R. Lehmann's publication of a new historical-critical edition. In a "Prolegomena" to that edition published in 1963, Lehmann reminds his readers that the interpretation of a text is largely dependent on the quality or accuracy of the text, and he questions the assumptions of modern interpreters with regard to the reliability of the texts they are using: To what extent do they represent the will of the author rather than the intervention of editors? Those who want to deal seriously and critically with Büchner's texts find themselves in a hopeless situation, he claims: they must work with at least two editions, Bergemann's historical-critical edition of 1922, which has become difficult to obtain, and his subsequent incomplete "reading editions" (190–91).

Lehmann's study of Büchner's manuscripts in the Goethe and Schiller Archive in Weimar led him to the conclusion that Bergemann's editorial decisions reflect the aesthetic consciousness of the twenties and that his edition contains many misreadings that change and distort meaning (190–92). With regard to *Woyzeck*, Lehmann promises a large number of new readings and claims to have established a new sequence of scenes for the final manuscript on the basis of unambiguous evidence that Bergemann and Witkowski overlooked, a sequence "of which can be said with a probability bordering on certainty that it is authentic" (215).

A year following Lehmann's announcement of a new edition and three years before it appeared, Ursula Paulus published a detailed and convincing critical analysis of Bergemann's edition.[1] Like Lehmann, she considers it unfortunate that Bergemann departed from his original edition in order to present subsequent editions in a "more popular form" and with greater appeal to the "aesthetic pleasure" of the reader. She also points out that Bergemann changed his view of the state of the final manuscript: in the first edition he considered it to be a "fragment that is lacking above all the conclusion," but that nevertheless represents Büchner's latest intention and is therefore to be considered an authentic sequence of scenes which should not be contaminated by the addition of material from earlier versions. In his second edition (1926) Bergemann considers the same manuscript to be a "fragment that is lacking not only the conclusion but also the final dramatic arrangement." In the belief that different arrangements are possible, he now constructs *his* version of the play and leaves it to his readers to construct theirs from material he claims to describe exactly in an appendix. But in fact, as Paulus notes, it is no longer possible for the reader to establish the poet's final and most complete version. Bergemann states in the appendix that the final manuscript is the foundation for his text, and he indicates where he has made "basic departures" from that manuscript, but he does not reveal the many changes he has made in individual scenes, changes involving the contaminating inclusion of material from the earlier drafts (1964, 227–28).

Users of Bergemann's editions from 1926 on are therefore able to reconstruct the drafts (H1–3) but not the final version (H4). Hence criticism not based on the 1922 edition, including the studies of form by Krapp and Klotz, relies on a text that departs from Büchner's final manuscript in the sequence of scenes and in the content of individual scenes. And of course Bergemann's interventions have consequences for interpretation. To intensify the play's social criticism, for example, Bergemann makes changes that place greater emphasis on Woyzeck's poverty and inferior class status and on the abuse he suffers at the hands of his social superiors. Other alterations are motivated by Bergemann's lack of appreciation for the episodic form of drama and his attempt to make Büchner's play accord with the conventions of classical drama. He strengthens chronological and causal connections, for example, in order to create greater unity of plot, but in so doing he reverses the re-duction of such connections made by the author during the process of composition (231–32).

In the second scene, for example, which takes place in Marie's room, Bergemann adds material from the second draft that establishes connections to the preceding and following scenes. To Marie's greeting of Woyzeck Bergemann adds the question: "Did you cut sticks for the Captain?" which connects to Woyzeck's activity in the first scene. As Woyzeck leaves, he says in H4: "I must go," to which Bergemann adds from H2: "This evening let's go to the fair. I have saved some money again," which connects to the following scene. As Paulus points out, Woyzeck is so distracted by what he has experienced that he does not even look at his child; it is scarcely possible, she concludes, that he would think of the fair at this moment (233). One might add that Woyzeck's ability to save money and spend it at the fair might detract from the impact of his poverty.

In another contamination, Bergemann adds the following lines from H1 to the beginning of the scene in which Marie is admiring her new earrings (H4,4): "The other commanded him, and he had to go," which specifically establishes a link to the Drum Major and suggests that a meeting has taken place between them. According to Paulus, "this brutal beginning counteracts the effect of Marie's symbolic self-reflection" (233–34), and it also introduces the probability that Woyzeck already has reason to be jealous. The interpolated line not only has an impact on the interpretation of Woyzeck's behavior in this scene, it also undermines the purpose of Bergemann's contaminations of H4,8 — which are undertaken in an attempt to provide a "visible" provocation for Woyzeck's discovery of Marie's infidelity and to drive the action forward — contaminations that in their turn demand the transposition of a number of scenes, including the placement of H4,5 (The Captain. Woyzeck) at the beginning of the play, where it supposedly will be "least disturbing," but where it creates a different exposition and shifts the meaning of the play from Woyzeck's existential condition to his social situation. Paulus identifies such contaminating changes in eleven of the sixteen scenes of H4 (230–31).

From her investigation of the manuscripts, Paulus concludes that all the scenes of the first two versions, H1 and H2, are used "in a narrower or broader sense" in H4, which is therefore to be considered the last and most complete version. Any attempt to supplement the scenes in H4 by the addition of superseded material from the earlier versions and any alteration in the sequence of scenes of H4 constitutes an unauthorized intervention. There are three clearly defined and delimited problems faced by editors who attempt to complete the fragment for performance, and each of these involves unfilled space in the final version (H4): the first consists of one and one-half blank pages under the heading "Fair Booths. Lights. People"; the second consists of two-thirds of a page following scene H4,8, the meeting of the Captain and the Doctor on the street; and the third involves the construction of a conclusion.

From the heading and large space left blank in the manuscript, it is apparent that Büchner intended to include a substantial fair scene. There are no fewer than five scenes in H1 and H2 dealing with this material, and Bergemann had recourse to all of them for his construction. What is more, he also changed the text and, as Paulus writes, "composed" scenes of his own. Paulus argues against the inclusion of the earlier material in the fair scene, because it was later incorporated in other scenes. She relies entirely on scenes from the second draft. Her solution, admittedly "an expedient solution" (*Notlösung*), consists of H2,3 (Public Place. Booth. Lights) through the line ending ". . . the lowest level of the human race," to which she adds the final exchange between the Sergeant and the Drum Major and the words of Marie and Woyzeck from H2,5 (235–37). Because it involves minimal contamination, it is a valid proposal, certainly an improvement over Bergemann's construction.

Paulus's solution to the problem of H4,8, which she considers one of the most problematic in H4, is less satisfying. As she indicates twice in the same paragraph, the action between the Captain and the Doctor is "abgeschlossen," that is, self-contained and concluded. In the first working of this scene in H2,9, however, Woyzeck appears before the Captain and the Doctor take leave of each other. The Captain taunts him about Marie's infidelity, and the Doctor delights in observing the physical signs of his distress. They treat him as an object, as they do each other in H4,8. Since H4,8 cannot be replaced by H2,9, Paulus's solution is to incorporate some of the material from the earlier scene into the later version, a solution that is undermined by her own arguments. She notes, for example, that H2,9 is the first appearance of the Captain and that some of what he says to Woyzeck is later incorporated in H4,5. Furthermore, since Woyzeck has been treated by the Doctor as an object for investigation in the scene immediately preceding, the similar material from H2,7 is redundant. Furthermore, awakening Woyzeck's suspicion and jealousy no longer fits into the causal nexus of H4 (237–40). A solution consistent with Paulus's minimal contamination of H4,3 would be to leave H4,8 as it stands; it is indeed "abgeschlossen."

Since Büchner's final manuscript ends with scene 17, the testament-scene, it is necessary to complete the play by the addition of the only scenes that continue the action, namely H1,14–20. Further possible additions are the two scenes of H3, "The Professor's Courtyard" and "The Idiot. The Child. Woyzeck," and the fragmentary H1,21, "Court Clerk. Barber. Doctor. Judge," which Paulus considers to be the first scene of H2. Since the scenes from H3 cannot be added to H4 or to the concluding sequence of scenes from H1 without disrupting an authorized sequence of scenes, their inclusion would require special justification. Paulus eliminates H3,1 (The Professor's Courtyard) because the action involving the Doctor is completed in H4,8. Her arguments for the inclusion of H3,2 are based on her interpretation. As opposed to Bergemann's emphasis on the socially critical content of the play, she emphasizes Woyzeck's existential situation, his isolation and exposure to forces beyond his control. This interpretation is reinforced by what she considers to be the identification of the child in the Grandmother's tale with both Woyzeck and his child. From this identification she concludes that the end of the tale can be related to the end of the play as a whole. In keeping with this interpretation, she argues against the possibility that Woyzeck drowns (240–41).

In Paulus's view, the sequence of discoveries by the people who come onto the scene (H1,16), the people at the inn (H1,17), and the people Woyzeck hears coming at the end of H1,19 must lead to the discovery of the scene of the crime and the murderer and must result in society's demand for retribution (241–42). Consequently, the "Court Clerk" scene (H1,21) must be included, she argues, because it is probably followed by Woyzeck's arrest. This scene appears by chance at the beginning of the second draft, Paulus maintains, and really belongs to the first version, for which it provides an appropriate conclusion. A drawback to the inclusion of this scene is the emphasis it puts on social criticism, which is reduced, according to Paulus, in the final version. Moreover, for reasons she does not explain, she assumes that the Barber must be eliminated from the scene and replaced by the Captain or the Doctor. Despite Martens's evidence to the contrary, she appears to identify the Barber with Woyzeck (242–43).

Paulus argues for the inclusion of "The Idiot. The Child. Woyzeck" as the final scene. Parallel to H4,16, the Bible scene, in which the inner events relating to Marie are concluded, the Idiot-Child scene constitutes a similar conclusion for Woyzeck and the Child, who is also present with the Idiot in H4,16. It also connects to the Grandmother's tale, in which a child's relationship to both parents is described. "The observations that the scene is 'parallel' to Marie's plot line and points to something beyond it predestines it for the conclusion of Woyzeck's plot line and for the conclusion of the play in general: in both scenes [H4,16 and H3,2] the Child is shown in the care of the Idiot," which demonstrates its terrible desperation. His gesture of love and goodness having been rejected by his son, the suffering Woyzeck is left standing all alone before an incomprehensible God, and the Child is all alone with the Idiot. Both are isolated and exposed in an absurd existence (243–44).

Paulus's arguments are supported by J. Elema in an article published the year after hers but evidently written before hers was in print. From his study of the manuscripts, Elema, too, concludes that H4 was indeed a final version in which all the scenes are in their proper chronological and causal sequence. It integrates scenes from the first two drafts, which are themselves in proper sequence. Elema argues that the first draft is a "balladesque sequence of scenes" that already contains everything essential except for Woyzeck's arrest, sentencing, and perhaps his execution. Büchner's need to deal with this part of Woyzeck's story may have sent him back to Clarus's report, Elema speculates, the findings of which are much more apparent in H2 than in H1. The second sequence of scenes (H2) does not represent a new beginning so much as a consistent and well-thought-out continuation and expansion of the first. Except for the revision of, and renewed attempt to write, a fair scene, all the scenes in this manuscript are completely new. They add to the development of the main plot and broaden the action to include Woyzeck's humiliation by the Captain and the Doctor (1965, 134–38, 142).

Elema agrees with Paulus that the reworking of the fair scene supersedes the first version. The scene inside the booth should therefore not be included in a final version. By not including it in the reworking of the scene, Büchner cut it, Elema concludes, perhaps for the technical reason that it would be difficult to have animals perform on the stage (139, 144). Like Paulus, Elema also argues against the inclusion of H3,1 (The Professor's Courtyard), which he considers to be a first version of the meeting between the Doctor and Woyzeck. The scene was rewritten and improved in H2. A doubling of this scene is redundant and not in keeping with the concision of Büchner's art (140–41).

Without referring to Walter Müller-Seidel's 1964 edition of *Woyzeck*, which was cited by Paulus, Elema agrees with both critics that the scene "The Captain. Woyzeck" should not stand at the beginning of the play, where Bergemann placed it in his second and subsequent editions. Bergemann's desire to strengthen the socially critical content of the play is an attempt to improve upon what needs no improvement, Elema maintains, and it changes the author's intention (144). Likewise, the contamination of H4,9 by the addition of material from H2,7 is not permissible (141, 145).

Since Elema considers the composition of H4 to be complete and consistent, he concludes that, with the exception of a few details, it is to be treated as a final version. Editors should present it in this version, and the "beautiful and meaningful scenes" from H1 and H2 should be included in an apparatus of variant readings. Elema does not make it clear whether his concept of a final version includes the few missing details, but his final listing of scenes does include H2,3 and H2,5 in the gap left for the fair scene. His recommendation does not preclude the addition of the concluding scenes from H1, in which he is again in agreement with Paulus. Like Paulus, he too is then left with the problem of the disposition of H3,2, which he thinks cannot be used if Woyzeck drowns. He sees some merit in the argument that the Idiot's words can be seen as an anticipation of Woyzeck's drowning, just as in another scene (H1,5) he had anticipated the murder, but Elema is not willing to accept this possibility, since it is not represented in the text (146–49).

Elema's solution is to place H3,2 at the end of the sequence of scenes from H1 but before the "Court Clerk" scene, which both ends the play and anticipates its further development. Though he, unlike Paulus, considers the "Court Clerk" scene to be the final scene of H1, he sees it as the beginning of a new dramatic section leading to

Woyzeck's arrest and trial. In his view, the plot line involving the Doctor and the Captain continues in this scene, in which they are supposedly present. (The scene heading lists the Doctor but not the Captain.) The Policeman presumably addresses them and reveals an attitude similar to theirs in his description of the "beautiful, authentic" murder, that is, by his dehumanization and objectification of the tragic situation. It is a terrible paradox of this upside-down world, Elema writes, that the inhuman, cruel murderers of men's souls are in a position to judge the desperate and mentally disturbed murderer of his beloved (147–50, 153).

In a second "Prolegomena," which was published along with the first volume of the Hamburg edition of Büchner's works in 1967, Werner R. Lehmann continues his criticism of Bergemann's text, which he claims is based on the editor's normative aesthetic assumptions with regard to drama and on his subjective aesthetic judgment: Lehmann demonstrates how Bergemann contaminated scenes in H4 by adding material from the earlier manuscripts and how his modernization of punctuation and orthography effects meaning and interpretation.

The goal of Lehmann's edition is to allow the reader access to the extant material unchanged by editorial intervention, which always presupposes the editors' interpretation. To that end he presents in the presumed order of composition all of the material contained in the manuscripts. Since he is concerned with achieving clarity and consistency rather than pedantic accuracy, he completes Büchner's abbreviations, standardizes his spelling and rather idiosyncratic use of the apostrophe, and corrects "obvious" slips of the pen. To meet the need of the more serious reader for more detailed knowledge of what is actually contained in the manuscripts, such as what spelling Büchner used, where and how he abbreviated, what he crossed out, and what he added as an afterthought or revision, Lehmann includes a more exact reproduction or representation of the text in a section entitled "Synopse." (His promise to provide notes and variant readings in a separate volume has not yet been fulfilled. Only two of four announced volumes have been published.) By presenting the corresponding scenes of the various manuscripts side by side, the "Synopse" also facilitates comparison of the various stages in the development of individual scenes as well. Finally, Lehmann also constructs a "non-authentic" version for reading and performance (42–45).

In the introduction to another new edition of *Woyzeck*, Egon Krause repeats and adds to the by-then-familiar criticism of Bergemann's editions. He also rejects Müller-Seidel's edition and all others based on Bergemann's 1922 text rather than on a renewed study of the manuscripts. Instead of finding support for his own endeavor in Paulus's article, he dismisses it as unconvincing because it is intended to support Müller-Seidel's edition, a claim that is only partially justified (1969, 13–23). Krause criticizes Lehmann's edition for not presenting the manuscripts in the sequence of their composition and for presenting a reading and acting text, which is based on editorial decisions and which supposedly blocks the readers' true access to Büchner's fragments. Krause's book reveals its beginnings as a dissertation (1966) that was not thoroughly revised before being rushed into print: though published after the appearance of Lehmann's text, Krause's criticism is based on the text announced in the 1963 "Prolegomena" followed by the acknowledgment that Lehmann's actual edition includes a third and unannounced version that does present the manuscripts in the order of their composition (22–25). Since the goal of Krause's edition is to do just that, and since the sequence of manuscripts and scenes he establishes is the same as Lehmann's, Krause's text could be considered superfluous, were it not for the more than fifty pages of variant readings and explanations he includes in an attempt to reproduce the manuscripts as exactly as possible, short of a facsimile edition.

Krause does disagree with Lehmann's view of the relationship of the manuscripts to each other and with his interpretation of Büchner's changing concept of the whole. Krause does not consider H2 to be an addition to, or expansion of, H1, as Lehmann does, but the beginning of a completely different conception and thus closely connected to H4. He assumes that the new version was not to include the murder, which is represented only in the first version. The use of quotations from and references to the Bible are an important indicator of the changed concept: in H1 they refer or relate to the murder; in H2 they increase in number and significance and relate to Woyzeck's apocalyptic feelings of being threatened, which result from his existential anxiety and the shock of Marie's infidelity. Notwithstanding the retention in H4 of the Biblical references to murder which also occurred in H1, Krause concludes from Büchner's inclusion in H4 of additional references to Marie's repentance and desire for forgiveness that Woyzeck no longer feels compelled to kill her. In H4,17, the testament scene, he supposedly assumes an attitude opposed to the "must," an attitude equivalent to the desire for forgiveness expressed by Marie in H4,16, and he appears to overcome the compulsion to kill her. From this evidence Krause concludes that Büchner did not intend for Woyzeck to murder Marie in H4 (26–27). Unfortunately, he does not indicate what it is in this scene that justifies his puzzling and unconvincing interpretation. He claims that Lehmann's interpretation relies too much on the historical figure of Woyzeck and not enough on the case of Daniel Schmolling, but Schmolling, too, killed his beloved, as did a third murderer cited by Krause, a former soldier named Diess. (Both men felt remorse after their deeds and surrendered voluntarily to the authorities. Schmolling had planned to and tried to kill himself after murdering his lover, and Diess wept repeatedly during his trial.)

One might think that the corroboration by Lehmann and Krause of the sequence of manuscripts and scenes established by Bergemann in 1922 might lay this issue to rest, but that is not the case. Based not so much on the evidence of the extant manuscripts as on his assumptions concerning changes in Büchner's conception of Woyzeck, Wilfried Buch argues for a different sequence of scenes in the first manuscript, which he considers to be two versions instead of one, and for a slight rearrangement of scenes in H4. In his view, the first or "murder version" begins with scene H1,11, an inn scene, and runs through H1,20, a division that results from the reversal of the order of the first two folded sheets. Buch finds justification for such a reversal in the fact that the first sheet, as identified by the earlier editors, ends and the third sheet begins with scenes including a barber. For some unstated reason, Buch thinks these scenes should go together. Since H1,11 cannot have been intended as the play's first scene and is similar to one or another inn scene appearing later in H4, Buch assumes that a beginning sheet may have been lost or destroyed by Büchner. It is also conceivable, he argues, that Büchner simply began writing *medias in res* with this scene, a supposition that he feels gains some support from the uncertainty in its execution, including three attempts at a beginning. Buch also believes that H1,13 was written before the similar H1,7, both scenes involving Woyzeck and Andres. Finally, the "murder version" is based more on the case of Schmolling, Buch claims, while the subsequent versions are based almost exclusively on the more complicated figure of the historical Woyzeck (1970, 11–13).

Buch calls what he considers to be the second stage in composition, H1,1 to H1,10, the "jealousy version" to reflect the shift in focus from the murder to Woyzeck's reaction to the developing discovery of Marie's infidelity. Unlike Krause, however, he still considers the murder to be the "central point of reference" for all the versions. In disagreement with Lehmann's view that H2 is an addition or supplement to H1, Buch argues that it is a new version. His only evidence for this questionable assumption is the belief that H2,3 (Public Place. Booth. Lights) appears to be a reworking of H1,1 (Booths. People) (7). Because of the "grotesque" behavior of the Captain and the Doctor toward Woyzeck and each other, Buch calls this the "grotesque version" and assumes that Büchner broke off work on it because of another change in his view of Woyzeck (43).

Büchner's concept of Woyzeck supposedly changes again in the final revision, which Buch calls the "suffering version." Again based on his interpretation rather than on the evidence of the manuscripts, Buch places scene H4,9 (The Captain. The Doctor) after H4,6 (Marie. Drum Major), his purpose being to develop the chronology of Woyzeck's discovery of Marie's infidelity. Buch assumes that Woyzeck was meant to appear in H4,9, as he did in the preliminary scene H2,7, and to have Marie's infidelity revealed to him by the Captain. This only makes sense if H4,9 precedes H4,7, in which Woyzeck looks at Marie's face for a physical sign of her deadly sin (50–52).

Buch assumes that the two scenes of H3 were written after H4. H3,1 (The Professor's Courtyard) was probably written to replace H4,8 (Woyzeck. The Doctor), the latter part of which supposedly does not fit Büchner's new conception. Woyzeck's suffering in the new scene is "almost unbearable and almost ineffable" (54, 64). Buch places H3,2 (The Idiot. The Child. Woyzeck) just before H4,17, the testament scene, which he considers to be the last scene of the play. According to Buch's interpretation, Woyzeck encounters his child on the way back to the barracks and is rejected by him. He is now completely alone, as is the child in the old woman's tale. Back in the barracks he puts into order "what he still has and what he still is," as far as that is possible. Rather than having gone mad, as Krause interprets, Woyzeck has recovered himself and is ready to face the consequences of his deed (62, 65).

In a chapter on *Woyzeck* contained in his extensive study *Das Bild in der Dichtung* (The Image in Literature, 1969), Hermann Pongs sides with those editors and critics who willingly accept editorial contaminations that support their interpretations. He agrees with Lehmann's retention of Woyzeck's appearance in H4,9, for example, which is especially important for his thesis. Because of the metaphor of the knife and the image of the stake driven into heaven, Pongs considers this scene to be a central pillar of the play. The Captain's comparison of Woyzeck to a razor and his reference to his cutting eyes anticipate the subsequent appearance and importance of the knife and indicates the "cutting hardness" that is part of Woyzeck's character. Furthermore, the severity of Woyzeck's disturbance caused by the Captain's allusion to Marie's infidelity is revealed not only by the Doctor's examination of his physical condition but also by his response to the Captain, whom he addresses as an equal. Taking this as an outrageous insubordination, the Captain threatens him: "Rascal, do you want to be shot? Do you want a couple bullets in your head? ["Will Er ein paar Kugeln vor den Kopf haben?" This could be a reference to Woyzeck's bulging eyes, to which the Captain next refers, rather than to bullets.] You stab me with your eyes, and I mean well with you . . ." (637–39).

The pressure of this encounter again evokes or compels the manifestation of Woyzeck's visionary power: "We have beautiful weather, Captain, Sir. Do you see the beautiful, solid, coarse heaven? One could get the desire to hammer a stake into it and hang oneself on it, just because of the dash between yes, and yes again — and no, Captain sir, yes and no. Is the no guilty of the yes or the yes of the no? I'll think about it" (H2, 7). Pongs sees in this response a balladesque movement toward the *Urdrama*, to the decision between yes and no. Büchner here impels Woyzeck forward into consciousness and the responsibility for deciding between yes and no. According to Pongs, this scene, in which we "feel the symbolic cosmos which is given to poets," is the turning point in Woyzeck's fate (639–40).

By placing scene H4,7 (Marie. Woyzeck) after H4,8, Pongs restores the sequence of scenes of H2. In agreement with Paul Landau, "who had the courage to contaminate both versions" in his 1909 edition, and with Bergemann's incorporation of Landau's contaminations in his post-1922 editions, he also contaminates H4,7 by the addition of material from the earlier version (H2,8). Pongs notes that Büchner left some space in the manuscript following H4,7 where he undoubtedly intended to include the final moments from H2,8, in which Woyzeck advances threateningly on Marie, referring to her as "Mensch!" which in this context is equivalent to calling her a slut. But Marie regains or reasserts her superiority in her defiant reply: "Dare to touch me, Franz! I would rather have a knife in me than your hand on mine. When I was ten years old my father didn't dare touch me when I looked at him." Marie's words connect to an earlier self-rebuke: "I could stab myself," and they also convey the extremity of the alienation between her and Woyzeck, Pongs claims, an alienation, one might add, that is not in accord with the later version, where she confronts her guilt and inability to resist temptation and expresses discomfort at the fact that Woyzeck has not visited her for two days (H4,16). Pongs writes of this scene that it gives Marie the halo (*Gloriole*) she deserves and raises her above the fate of a slut (*Dirnenschicksal*). Woyzeck's response to Marie's defiance conveys the "dread that has seized him": "Woman! — No, there must be a mark on you! Every person is an abyss; one gets dizzy when looking down. So be it! She goes like innocence. Now, innocence, you have a mark on you. Do I know it? Do I know it? Who knows it?" (641–42) Woyzeck's image of the human abyss is much cited by critics, but it does not occur in the final version, perhaps because it is stated in a language Woyzeck no longer uses in that version.

In other comments relating to the text, Pongs assumes that the first part of the carnival scene should be constructed from both earlier versions, and he agrees with Elema that the second part, which takes place inside the booth (H1,2), should not be included. Marie's brief comment that constitutes the entirety of H1,3 ("The other commanded him and he had to go. Ha! One man above another") is interpreted by Pongs as referring to the Drum Major and the Officer rather than to the Drum Major and Woyzeck. Thus, following the fair scene, the Drum Major commands the officer to go so he can be alone with Marie. It is here that he supposedly gives her the earrings she admires in H4,4 (630–33).

As for the problematic scenes of H3, Pongs agrees with Landau, Bergemann, and Lehmann that H3,1 (The Professors Courtyard) should be included. He disagrees with them, however, in placing it after H4,13, which he contaminates with additions from H1,7 and H1,8, in which Woyzeck relates his dream of a knife and utters the moving words many critics want to retain: "Aber Andres, sie war doch ein einzig Mädel" (But Andres, she surely was a unique girl). The scene in the Professor's Courtyard does not add much to the depiction of Woyzeck, Pongs admits, but it is effective as a contrast to the sequence of jealousy scenes leading up to Woyzeck's decision to kill Marie, and it takes Woyzeck's degradation to a new extreme (643–44).

Pongs places the second scene of H3 (The Idiot. The Child. Woyzeck) after the final inn scene (H1,17). When he leaves the inn, Woyzeck comes upon his child and the Idiot. His child pulls back from him in fear, and the Idiot stares at him as if he sees the murderer in him. Both then run away from him, increasing his isolation. The Idiot's repeated reference to falling into the water has impressed itself on Woyzeck's mind, and the water seems to attract him. Pongs shares the opinion that Woyzeck drowns, but, in agreement with a conclusion of the play suggested by Landau, he assumes that Marie's and Woyzeck's corpses were to end in a dissecting lab, as did the corpse of the murderer Diess in the Giessen lab at the time Büchner was a student there. He bases this assumption on the fragmentary scene H1,21 (Court Clerk . . .), which could be taking place in a dissecting room. According to this reading, the play was to end not with a court trial and execution, but with the representation of divine judgment (655–57).

Werner Lehmann's construction of a reading and acting text of *Woyzeck* was criticized by David G. Richards and defended by Lehmann in articles published 1971 in *Euphorion*. While Richards considers

Lehmann's edition of the Büchner texts to be exemplary, he identifies several places in Lehmann's proposed reading and acting text in which the editor deviates from his own stated principles of editing and introduces contaminations of the kind he rejects in Bergemann's text. Like Lehmann, Richards assumes from the fact that scenes in H1 and H2 were crossed out as they were reworked for H4 that H4 represents the author's final intention in the preparation of a manuscript that, as he wrote to his fiancée shortly before his death, would be ready for publication in eight days at most. Any alteration in this sequence of scenes or alterations within scenes, such as those undertaken by Bergemann, are not justified. According to an editorial principle formulated by Hans Werner Seiffert and cited by Lehmann in his *Textkritische Noten*: "It is not permissible to construct a text that never existed (which the author himself did not know). For that reason, contaminations must definitely be avoided." In the case of *Woyzeck*, however, in which the author himself was not clear about its continuation, "the question is not whether to contaminate or not," Lehmann maintains, "but how and where" (1967, 59). Just as Lehmann considers most of Bergemann's contaminations to be unnecessary, Richards questions the necessity of Lehmann's.

The first of four problems involves the page and one-half left blank under the title "Booths. Lights. People." The first two scenes of the first manuscript deal with this material, which was obviously of central importance for Büchner: they were the only scenes in H1 to be reworked in H2. Although Lehmann recognizes "that H2,3 not only goes beyond H1,1–2 but also makes use of parts of H1,1–2 and tries to render it in a tighter, denser form stylistically and compositionally," he nevertheless maintains that the latter version does not supersede the earlier one. He assumes that Büchner would have used material from both scenes in a final revision (*Textkritische Noten*, 62). Richards considers it justifiable to include the intact presentation of the action inside the booth (H1,2) following the introductory material contained in H2,3, since that is the only and therefore the latest rendition of this material, but he argues against Lehmann's supplementation of H2,3 through the addition of parts of H1,1 (1971, 51–52).

Lehmann appears to have introduced a third contamination in order to establish a causal connection between the two halves of the scene. Having heard the Barker's pitch outside the booth, Woyzeck asks Marie whether she wants to go in, to which she responds: "All right. That must be a fine show. Look at the man's tassels! And the woman wears pants!" (I.411). Referring to Lehmann's rejection of Bergemann's similar attempts to establish causal connections where Büchner had eliminated them, Richards argues against the inclusion of this material (51–53). In his reply to Richards's criticism, Lehmann states that neither H1 nor H2 can be considered authorized material: to be authorized, a scene for H4 would have to be constructed from H1, H2, or both H1 and H2, or a scene in H2 would have to be based on H1 in such a way that it supersedes the earlier version, neither of which Lehmann considers to be the case here (1971, 71–72).

Concerning the first two contaminations identified by Richards, Lehmann admits that they include repetitions (*Textdoubletten*) in the Barker's address to the public, but he considers them of sufficient importance to justify their inclusion. He also refers to the "principle of connected or interdependent contamination" (*Prinzip der zusammenhängenden Kontamination*) which demands that the "transplanted" material be transferred along with its immediate context in order to preserve the authenticity of the transplanted material. He now explains that what he does not wish to lose is the question and answer that connect the two halves of this double scene, an exchange he considers of major importance, because "Marie and Woyzeck, not each separately, but both together, are now definitely and finally drawn as actors into a play in which they had been spectators until now." Lehmann takes Marie's word of agreement or submission ("Meinetwege" [All right]) to be an indication of the "intersection and unification of action and commentary," since she later uses the same word in yielding sexually to the Drum Major. It is a question of preserving the correspondence between Marie's acquiescence in two separate scenes (Lehmann 1971, 75).

The use of corresponding themes and motifs is indeed an important formal and structural principle in Büchner's works, as the studies by Mautner, Klotz, and Krapp cited by Lehmann demonstrate. However, since there is scarcely a scene or scenic fragment in all of Büchner's manuscripts to which Lehmann's argument could not be applied, Richards countered in 1975, it can scarcely be used to justify such a questionable complex of contaminations. Furthermore, Richards adds, if Lehmann's interpretation of the lines he does not wish to sacrifice were correct, that would further justify their omission, since this play, like all of Büchner's works, is not about togetherness, but about loneliness and isolation. From the preceding scene it is clear that there is little understanding between Woyzeck and Marie. And not only do they not act together, they scarcely act at all, but are acted upon by people and forces that use them as instruments. (Marie's "All right" is an expression of passive acquiescence.) When she does act in the fair scene, it is to *leave* Woyzeck and to be better seen by, perhaps even make contact with, the man who becomes responsible for their permanent separation (1975, 21–22).

Richards sides with Lehmann and Müller-Seidel on the inclusion of scene H2,5, the exchange between the Drum Major and the Sergeant, as a transition between the two halves of this scene. Paulus opposes its inclusion because some of the words used here recur elsewhere, but her proposal to include a part of it is unacceptable, Richards argues, for methodological and aesthetic reasons. Making cuts in a completed scene violates principles of editing, and attempting to avoid the repetition of words and motifs runs counter to Büchner's use of corresponding words and motifs as a means of interconnecting separate units (1971, 52–53).

The second problem faced by editors of a reading text involves the three-quarters of a page left blank following scene H4,9 (The Captain. The Doctor), an encounter between the Captain and the Doctor in which each relates to and treats the other in a characteristic way, that is, according to his particular fixed idea. The presentation in pure form of these caricatures may be meant to provide comic relief in the manner of Shakespeare. Richards agrees with Paulus that the intention of the revised scene is completely different from the earlier draft, in that it is "entirely oriented toward the juxtaposition of the Captain and the Doctor" (Paulus 237). Arguing against the inclusion by Lehmann and other editors of the material from H2,7 in which Woyzeck appears and is callously taunted about Marie's infidelity, Richards demonstrates that the Captain's reference to her betrayal can no longer have the impact on Woyzeck at this point in H4 that it did in H2,7, since his suspicion has already been confirmed by more direct and convincing evidence. A further argument against contamination of H4,9 is the incongruity between Woyzeck's language in H2,7 and his idiom in H4. In H2 Woyzeck frequently employs an obscure, complicated, metaphorical means of expression (1971, 54). Viëtor writes of this and similar passages: "The illusion of authenticity and undiminished truth is broken in only a few passages, passages in which the poet himself speaks through his figures." It is the style of *Leonce und Lena* (1949, 193). Viëtor did not question their place in the play, but we now have good reason to do so.

Lehmann claims in response to Richards's arguments that the blank space in H4,9 is also authorized and that the fact that H2,7 was not crossed out indicates that Büchner had not yet completed this scene, which can therefore not be considered fully authorized, and that he would have used the material from H2,7 to do so. With respect to Woyzeck's jealousy, Lehmann claims that Woyzeck's suspicion based on appearances does not become jealousy until corroborated by the

Captain: "Suspicion is followed in H2,7 by debasement through the infamy of the word, since the Captain, seconded by the Doctor, confirms and makes obscene comments about the suspicion: this must destroy Woyzeck" (1971, 76–77). At this point in the play Woyzeck could indeed be humiliated by such a debasing comment, but, as Richards counters, given the knowledge he already has, he could not be destroyed, and the vehemence of his reaction is no longer appropriate or convincing (1975, 24).

Lehmann's defense of this contamination and of his inclusion of H3,1 (The Professor Courtyard) indicates that they are based less on editorial principles than on his desire to emphasize the play's social criticism: "It would result in a questionable reduction of the play's social criticism if H3,1 and H2,7 were to be suppressed, for Büchner left keys (if not passe-partout) in them, as it were, that we must try" (1971, 77). Like Bergemann, Lehmann also imposes his own aesthetic preconceptions and interpretation on the text. According to Richards, such argumentation leads to the heart of the problem both of constructing a text and of interpreting it, for each of these procedures depends upon the other. In an attempt to avoid being entrapped in that vicious circle, it is necessary to limit contaminations to those, such as the conclusion, that are required for the construction of a playable text and, more problematically, to those that, like the carnival scene, are clearly in keeping with the author's intention and that do not alter the meaning of authorized material (1971, 25).

From the evidence provided by the relationship of H4 to H1 and from the fact that all the scenes of H2 find their way with varying degrees of revision into the final manuscript, as do almost all the scenes from H1 up to H1,14, the beginning of the murder sequence, Richards concludes, in disagreement with Krause and others, that Büchner did not change the basic concept of his play during the different stages of composition and that he would have continued to follow the sequence of scenes in H1 to complete the play. Büchner began work on the play with the historically given material; in the second draft he filled in the background, developed his characters more fully, and placed the main action in a broader context, thereby transforming a basically melodramatic story into a powerful tragedy. Once Woyzeck discovers Marie dancing with the Drum Major, he is possessed by the irresistible urge to kill her, as an act of punishment and retribution. Büchner would undoubtedly have made changes and revisions in the scenes of H1 depicting the murder and its aftermath, but in view of the fact that he considered the play to be almost ready for publication, he apparently did not foresee the need for major rewriting (1971, 54–55; 1975, 25–27).

The two scenes of H3, "The Professor's Courtyard" and "The Idiot. The Child. Woyzeck," present editorial problems of a different kind. Since nothing in Büchner's manuscripts indicates whether or not he intended to use them, the incorporation of either scene constitutes a contamination which can be justified only if its interpolation does not in any way alter the meaning of the authorized text. Lehmann includes "The Professor's Courtyard" between H4 and the beginning of the murder sequence from H1, a position that does not disturb either authorized sequence of scenes. Richards argues against the scene's inclusion because it belongs to the exposition, which is concluded with Woyzeck's discovery of the dancing couple in H4,11. It cannot legitimately be interpolated into the authorized sequence of scenes of H4, nor is there any reason it should be, since further humiliation of Woyzeck by the Doctor is superfluous, and therefore at odds with the play's concision (1971, 57).

As noted above, Lehmann's inclusion of H3,1 is based on the desire to emphasize the play's social criticism. He regards Woyzeck's diet of peas as the cause for his mental aberrations and therefore as a key without which the "Doctor-Woyzeck scene . . . and perhaps the whole problem of social criticism would be incomprehensible to us," and H3,1 contains additional information about Woyzeck's diet and the effects it has on him (1971,78). Richards sees this explanation as another example of circular argumentation, whereby the inclusion of a scene is justified on the basis of an interpretation based on the inclusion of that scene. By comparing H4,8 (At the Doctor's) with the earlier version (H2,6), Richards refutes Lehmann's claim that the diet of peas is "more strongly and exclusively" emphasized in H4 than in H2. In both scenes, moreover, as Richards points out, the Doctor's main interest is not in the diet's effect on Woyzeck but in the chemical content of Woyzeck's urine. The Doctor's experiment is but one contribution to the cumulative effect of all the odd jobs Woyzeck undertakes in an attempt to support his family and that strain and exhaust him and help to undermine the stability of his psyche (1975, 28–29).

Richards agrees with Winkler's assumption that H3,1 preceded H2,6 in composition and was superseded by it. The Doctor, identified as a professor in the beginning of H3,1, was originally conceived as a caricature of a professor with whom Büchner had studied in Giessen and of the famous chemist Justus von Liebig, also a professor, who was engaged in experiments with soldiers in Giessen involving the influence of diet on the chemical content of urine. From this caricature combining traits of two specific professors, Büchner's Doctor develops into a representative of the general type of modern scientist for whom ideas and theories are more important than the suffering and humiliation of his fellow man. The transition from professor to doctor occurs to some extent within H3,1, Richards observes; in H2,6 and H4,8 he is no longer presented in his capacity as a teacher, but only as a medical doctor engaged in research. In neither of these later scenes is Woyzeck's malady presented as physiological in nature, nor does the Doctor make a connection between Woyzeck's symptoms and his diet (1971, 29–31).

An argument may be made for the inclusion of H3,2 (The Idiot. The Child. Woyzeck), Richards maintains, but its placement by Müller-Seidel, Paulus, and Lehmann at the end of the play is unacceptable because it imposes an ending and an interpretation on the play that Büchner may not have intended. Since Woyzeck appears in this scene, the possibility of his drowning is precluded. In her defense of this contamination, Paulus cites the parallel between Woyzeck and the child in the Grandmother's tale: like the child, Woyzeck is now completely alone (241). It is a persuasive argument for the inclusion of the scene, but not for its placement at the end. Richards suggests placing the scene after the murder and just before the final inn scene (H1,17), where it can reinforce the important theme of loneliness and isolation without adding a conclusion that goes beyond what the author wrote and may very well disagree with what he intended, and it can also function as a foreshadowing of Woyzeck's going into the water. To be sure, this contamination disrupts an authorized sequence of scenes, but it does not force an ending on the play or change its interpretation. On his way from the murder scene to the inn, Woyzeck meets and is rejected by his child, who may sense that Woyzeck has murdered his mother. This does indeed leave Woyzeck completely alone (1971, 55–56). Pongs's placement of the scene following the inn scene is a possibility, but in this position it interrupts and detracts from Woyzeck's agitation following the discovery of blood on him at the inn and his haste to eliminate the evidence of his crime.

The play's conclusion as presented in H1 remains open: after throwing the murder weapon into the pond, Woyzeck goes into the water to retrieve it and throw it further out where it won't be discovered. In the final scene of H4 Woyzeck anticipates and prepares for his death, but nothing in any of the manuscripts indicates what might follow his entry into the pond. Because of a stage instruction added by Franzos, the assumption of interpreters for some time was that Woyzeck drowns. Then, following the discovery of the historical source material for the play in 1914, some interpreters began to assume that Woyzeck was to be arrested, brought to trial, and executed. The only evidence in the manuscripts for this interpretation, however, is the appearance of a barber in the fragmentary scene H1,21 in which only the Court Clerk speaks: "A good murder, an authentic murder, a beautiful murder, as beautiful as one can expect. We haven't had one like that for a long time" (I,431). Even though the barber is identified in a stage instruction that, as seen above, can scarcely be seen as a description of Woyzeck and that makes no sense, coming as it does at the end of the play, as a description of the play's main character, interpreters have nevertheless identified this figure with Woyzeck, who has supposedly been arrested, is being confronted with his murder, and will be put on trial, an interpretation that was convincingly refuted by Wolfgang Martens in the 1960 article discussed above. Richards argues against the inclusion of this scene because it is fragmentary in the extreme and because in his view it detracts from Woyzeck's tragedy (1971, 56).

Lehmann responds that he does not agree with those who consider Woyzeck to be present in this scene, which is nothing more than a forensic autopsy. The loving and appreciative way the professionals respond to what is a catastrophic and tragic event for the participants provides an additional confirmation and demonstration of the isolation and suffering referred to in the Grandmother's tale. What is tragedy for the one is nothing but sensationalism for the others, who have lost their humanity and their sense of human connectedness. Those who would condemn Woyzeck are themselves condemned. Lehmann claims that the incorporation of such a fragmentary scene is justified in the construction of a text from fragmentary drafts. Furthermore, he objects to what he claims to be Richards's "decimation" of the socially critical content of this scene (1971, 82). Whereas the inclusion of this scene for its socially critical content does not agree with sound principles of editing, a valid argument can be made for its retention as part of an authorized sequence of scenes, an argument Richards now accepts.

Finally, Richards objects to Lehmann's placement of H1,18, in which children comment on the discovery of Marie's corpse, following H1,20 (Woyzeck by a Pond). Such a transposition contradicts Lehmann's own principles of editing and, in Richards's view, weakens the play's conclusion (1971, 57). Lehmann admits in his reply that he made this change reluctantly as a "concession to the pragmatic nexus" and to chronology, since he can't imagine that the children would be awake at a time which he calculates to be around midnight. Furthermore, he is not certain about the chronology of the scenes H1,18–20. The space between lines in scenes 19 and 20 is different from that in 17 and 18, and these scenes are squeezed in at the bottom of a page. It is possible, Lehmann concludes, that they were added later and that their placement was determined by external circumstances. Nevertheless, he concedes, their transposition is problematic (1971, 83).

An indication that Büchner had fully emerged from the underground to become a classic of German literature is the publication by Philipp Reclam in 1972 of an inexpensive *Kritische Lese- und Arbeitsausgabe* (Critical Reading and Working Text) of *Woyzeck* and an accompanying volume in the series *Erläuterungen und Dokumente* (Commentary and Documents), both edited by Lothar Bornscheuer. Bornscheuer accepts and attempts to add further support to Buch's hypothesis concerning the sequence of manuscripts, which, as seen above, involves primarily the separation of the first twenty scenes into two groups of ten each and a reversal of their order. In addition to the argument based on the supposed sequence of three sets of parallel scenes put forth by Buch, Bornscheuer claims that the lesser uniformity of script and the greater number of corrections in H1,11–20 indicate that it is an earlier and less certain stage of composition than H1,1–10. But this assumption is undermined by Bornscheuer's observation that the seven scenes of the "murder-complex" (H1,14–20) constitute the only whole group of scenes which does not undergo a revision or a deletion (*Lese- und Arbeitsausgabe*, 78–79). In maintaining that these were the most mature of the scenes that were not crossed out (81), Bornscheuer contradicts his earlier claim that H1,11–20 is a "groping rough draft" (78).

In his critique of Bornscheuer's edition, Richards argues that since the handwriting already begins to become less certain in H1,10, it is this scene rather than H1,11 that must be seen as the first of the series of sloppily written scenes. Furthermore, since H1,21 clearly follows the murder, it belongs at the end of the sequence ending with H1,20 and not after H1,10 where Buch and Bornscheuer place it. And finally, the fact that H4 uses material from the first group of ten scenes indicates that these come chronologically before the last ten, which must provide the play's conclusion and which would no doubt have been crossed out once Büchner had incorporated them (Richards 1977, 255).[2]

For his edition of the play Bornscheuer reduces the number of editorial decisions to the minimum required for constructing a playable text: the only addition he makes to H4 is the complex of murder scenes H1,14–20. With this minimal text he wants simply to provide a "basic framework" and the parts from which the reader, exercising his "right to interpret," can make his own construction or adaptation (*Lese- und Arbeitsausgabe*, 3). Bornscheuer makes further suggestions for building on the framework he provides, but since they are incorporated in a complicated discussion of manuscripts and scenes, they will be of little use to the general reader.

To solve the major problem, the space left for the carnival scene, Bornscheuer advocates the simplest possible solution, which is to include only H2,3, or part of H2,3, since the latter part of the scene is obviously fragmentary and should be excluded. Bornscheuer favors this scene "because its core, the Barker's text, represents a visible concentration and maturation of the main role, which is divided in Hb [=H1,1–10] between two scenes" (83). "While the role of the Barker (*Ausrufer*) is indeed somewhat expanded in H2,3," Richards comments in 1977, "it seems doubtful that it was intended to subsume the role of the showman (*Marktschreier*) presented in H1,2." The fact that Büchner rewrote the beginning part of this scenic complex and did not include it in H4 does indeed indicate that he was not yet satisfied with it. But the same cannot be claimed for the part of the scenic complex that takes place inside the booth (H1,2). Richards concludes from the lack of corrections, the regular script, and the seemingly finished nature of this scene that Büchner may have been satisfied with it as it stands. Bornscheuer's solution is editorially defensible, but in Richards's view it is less desirable and effective than a construction that also includes H1,2 (1977, 258).

As for H4,9 (The Captain. The Doctor), Bornscheuer presents a convincing argument for its completeness as it stands. He argues that Büchner left blank spaces in the manuscript with the intention of returning to them and filling them with revised versions of the material contained in the preliminary drafts. The elimination of Woyzeck's appearance in the revision of H2,7 resulted in a much shorter scene than he had anticipated (86).

With regard to the two scenes of H3, Bornscheuer agrees with Lehmann's placement of H3,1 (The Professor's Courtyard) in the seam between H4 and the complex of murder scenes from H1, where it provides "thematic intensification" without disrupting authorized sequences of scenes (86). He disagrees with Lehmann's placement of H3,2 (The Idiot. The Child. Woyzeck), however, because it limits the possible interpretations of the play's open ending. He is inclined to place it after the final inn scene, as does Jürgen Meinerts in his 1963 edition (*Georg Büchner: Sämtliche Werke nebst Briefen und anderen Dokumenten* [Georg Büchner: Complete Works with Letters and Other Documents]) and Hermann Pongs, among others, but he hesitates to include it at all because it disturbs the inherent rhythm of the murder scenes. According to Bornscheuer, this rhythm consists of an alternation between Woyzeck's frantic movement away from the scene of the murder and orientation toward the corpse as represented in the comments by the people (H1,16) and the children (H1,18) as well as Woyzeck's own return to the scene of the crime (86–88). Richards points out in response to Bornscheuer's argument that the placement of H3,2 *before* the inn scene does not disrupt the rhythm Bornscheuer identifies (1977, 260).

In a report on the state of editing *Woyzeck*, Klaus Kanzog mentions the reciprocal relationship of interpreting and editing a text, describes the extant manuscripts, and assumes the role of referee in the controversy concerning the sequence of manuscript pages and the construction of a reading and acting text. Kanzog agrees with the reversal of the sequence of the two halves of H1 proposed by Buch and adopted by Bornscheuer, except that he considers it likely that H1,19 and 20 were written after H1,21. From the fact that the lines in these two scenes are very close together, Lehmann concludes and Kanzog agrees that they were squeezed onto the final third of the page. They appear to have been written as an afterthought where room was available and not necessarily in the position intended for them. The existence of these scenes argues against Buch's assumption that Büchner had distanced himself from the murder scenes and intended a different conclusion. Kanzog argues that Büchner set the murder scenes aside to work on something else, but that the later inclusion of H1,19 and 20 clearly indicates that his basic concept had not changed (1973, 428–29).

Kanzog disagrees with Buch's division of the manuscripts into different "versions" and therefore also with Krause's argument against the inclusion of the murder sequence. He agrees with Paulus that the whole dramatic development presupposes the murder and that the addition of the murder scenes is necessary and justifiable. (Kanzog cautions in this connection that one should not be guided by theories of the open form of drama in constructing the play, since Büchner was both oriented to the classical norm and at the same time intent on departing from it.) In question is whether the scenes H1,14–21 should be taken over intact. Like Lehmann, Kanzog is disturbed by the placement of H1,18, which presupposes that the children are up past their bedtime. This in itself does not justify altering the sequence of scenes, Kanzog suggests, because it would be based on interpretation alone. But since H1,19 and 20 may have been added out of sequence, in which case H1,18 would immediately precede H1,21, and since the final words of H1,18 ("Let's go so we can still see something. Otherwise they'll take it [Marie's corpse] in") may be seen to connect to H1,21, the reversal in the order of these scenes can be defended, Kanzog maintains, according to editorial principles (429–30).

The other editorial problems Kanzog deals with are the placement of the two scenes of H3. Whether H3,2 (The Idiot. The Child. Woyzeck) is placed after H1,21, as in Lehmann's edition, or before it, as in Müller-Seidel's, is no longer an editorial problem, according to Kanzog, but a question of interpretation or, as he calls it, the consideration of a director. Influenced by a performance he saw in Munich, he opts for ending with H1,21. His assertion that H3,2 must follow H1,20 (Woyzeck at the Pond) reverts to the assumption that the Idiot's words from a finger-counting game refer directly to Woyzeck, who has just come from the pond and is still wet (438–40).

Considering it the "most controversial scene of the play," Kanzog agrees with Winkler, Richards, and Krause that H3,1 (The Professor's Courtyard) is the first scene Büchner wrote with the Professor/Doctor, in which case it would have been written before H2,6. Kanzog does not accept Lehmann's solution of placing this scene in the break between H4 and the murder complex. According to Kanzog, it is up to the director to decide whether to include this scene Lehmann considers of central importance for the "entire socially critical problematic" of the play, since this is a directorial and not an editorial decision. Kanzog refers to a performance by the Berliner Ensemble that begins with this scene, thus creating "through the teaching situation doctor-students a framework that is closed in the final scene (H1,21, with the setting considered to be a dissecting room). He takes this as evidence that scenes like H3,1 belong in the exposition (438–40).

Kanzog concludes that it is not possible to construct a playable text without contaminating and therefore violating sound principles of editing. His solution, which he calls an "Orientierungstext," is virtually identical to Lehmann's except for the elimination of H3,1 and the placement of H3,2 following rather than preceding H1,21. His suggestion with respect to the carnival scene is to print the material from the earlier drafts side-by-side, and with respect to 4,9, to print the earlier version parallel to it (440–41).

In a translation of *Woyzeck* published in 1969, Henry J. Schmidt relies on Lehmann's text for what he calls his "reconstruction." Schmidt believes, however, that the "scenes can be moved around with no particular damage to the play's structure," and that the reader must be allowed to piece the fragments together himself; an editor should not perform this task for him and deprive him of the opportunity of examining the variants" (81). This is an invitation to the kind of arbitrary and inaccurate statements Richard Schechner includes in his "Notes Toward an Imaginary Production," which introduces Schmidt's text. The play is a "masterpiece of indeterminacy," he writes, whose scenes don't go anywhere and can be arranged as one pleases. "Indeterminacy. The murder could come first, absolutely first. Each event has happened; everything is in the past. Time is a thing, and Woyzeck has a geography rather than a temporality." Or: "Büchner is as hard on Woyzeck as the doctor is" (11–12). The struggle is not between classes, he writes, but between species (16). "To Marie, appearances are essences; and Woyzeck sees things. Marie screws with the drum major, while Woyzeck is unfaithful with the grass. She knows that her infidelity is justified" (20). These and other *aperçus* are presented without discussion or justification. Schechner's position may have some relevance for directors wanting to use *Woyzeck* as a vehicle for their own creativity, but they contribute little or nothing to our understanding of Büchner's text. Presumably, Schmidt's suggestions for contaminating several scenes by adding material from others is meant for such directors.

In his 1977 edition of Büchner's complete works, Schmidt takes a more critical approach to the problem of constructing a text. He accepts Richards's suggestion that scene H2,3 is a reworking of H1,1 and he also follows Richards in the elimination of the fragmentary passages that frame the Barker's speech. Furthermore, in an argument echoing Richards's, he now finds it

> inappropriate to supplement Scene H4,9 with the Woyzeck-Captain-Doctor dialogue of Scene H2,7 because there is a stylistic discrepancy between Woyzeck's philosophical speculations in the earlier version and his blunt manner of speaking in the Fourth Draft. More important, the Captain's taunts have lost their motivation: in the Fourth Draft Woyzeck becomes aware of Marie's infidelity in the previous scene. (359–60)

Recognizing that "it does not introduce significantly new material," Schmidt also eliminates H3,1 in his new version, but regretfully, since he considers it "dramatically more effective than the other Woyzeck-Doctor scenes." He strongly encourages directors to do what the scholar cannot, namely, to include it in their stage productions (357). Schmidt recognizes that the inclusion of H3,2 at the end eliminates the possibility that Woyzeck drowns, as unlikely as that conclusion may be. He acknowledges that H3,2 could be placed before the final inn scene as Richards suggests, but he prefers to omit it and again leave the decision to the theater director. Schmidt's new version therefore ends with H1,21. Finally, Schmidt restores H1,18 to its original position in the manuscript. The "chronological enigmas" of children being up so late would seem to lose significance, Schmidt writes, "upon consideration of the expressionistic quality of these final scenes. Their frenzied pace, their nightmarish abruptness — in short, their form symbolizes and in-

tensifies Woyzeck's desperation, his inner derangement. In consequence, it seems singularly inappropriate to pause and ask the time of
day" (355).

According to Maurice B. Benn the only sound procedure for
studying the manuscripts of *Woyzeck* is a genetic method, which accepts
the fragmentary drafts as they are given in the extant manuscripts and
attempts to study them in chronological order and to ascertain at least
the direction in which the composition was moving. With respect to
the sequence of manuscripts, Benn agrees with Winkler, whose arguments he recapitulates, that H3 precedes H2, in which case scene H3,1
(The Professor's Courtyard) was written before and replaced by H2,6.
This is sufficient reason not to include H3,1 in a text construction. If it
were to be included in a final version, Benn adds, it would have to be
after the point where H4 breaks off, which is where Lehmann places it,
but this is impossible because H3,1 "does not, as Lehmann supposes,
follow and 'radicalize' H2,6; but, on the contrary, H2,6 follows and
radicalizes H3,1." Benn argues that this is an expository scene that
would have to come early in the play, preferably, he suggests, following
the first scene with the Captain (H4,5). "Its late position in Lehmann's
stage version produces an anticlimax and a most undramatic interrup-
tion and retardation of the action at a point where it is moving swiftly
toward the catastrophe" (1976, 218, 223–25).

In the first draft or "fragment," as Benn refers to it, Büchner out-
lines the action of the play, from Marie's first meeting with the junior
officer who seduces her, to the official examination of her dead body. It
is a framework in which only the murder sequence is worked out fully
and only a few scenes are magnificently realized (226–27, 236). At this
point Büchner had both Schmolling and Woyzeck in mind; the hero of
the first fragment, Louis, has more in common with the "peaceable and
industrious" Schmolling than with Woyzeck, "who had some very
brutal characteristics." According to Benn, Büchner's wavering may be
seen in alternative possibilities of developing the action: in H1,7 Louis
apparently buys a weapon, as did the historical Woyzeck; in H1,11 he
seems to find it, as did Schmolling. At this early stage of composition,
Benn writes, Büchner is less concerned with the portrayal of character
than with the "imaginative realization of certain experiences of
Schmolling and Woyzeck" and with the suffering of his hero and its
metaphysical implications" (227–30, 234).

As can be seen from the inclusion of numerous details from
Woyzeck's life in H2 and H3, Büchner appears to have reread Clarus's
report before continuing work on his play. Moreover, H3,1 is the first
scene in which the name Woyzeck is regularly used and also the first in

which Büchner attempts to expand the representation of his hero's social situation. Benn considers H1 and H2 to be substantially different conceptions rather than two groups of scenes belonging to the same version, as seen by Lehmann. In H2 Büchner begins to round out Woyzeck's character and to stress his poverty. The hero of H2 "presents a picture of material distress, of physical and psychical sickness, of degradation and humiliation at the hands of a society which systematically refuses to recognize him as a human being." Marie is the only thing he possesses in a "world of merciless exploitation and inveterate hostility." She represents his longing for escape from the world and his refuge in it (236–38).

Benn considers H2,7, the scene with Woyzeck, the Captain, and the Doctor, to be a "cardinal passage" because it relates to the center of the tragedy, Marie's betrayal, and answers the question "whether *Woyzeck* is a drama of social protest or of universal human passion." From this scene we can see that it is both, he maintains, and that these two aspects are integrally combined. The tragedy for Woyzeck and Marie arises from the contrast between her "natural sensuality" and his "unhealthy spirituality, his persistent sense of mysterious terrors," which frighten and repel her. It is not only a tragedy of character, however, but also of social injustice, of class oppression. It requires that Büchner depict the oppressors, which he does in what Benn calls "perhaps the most powerful piece of satirical portraiture that German literature has produced in the last two centuries" (236–40). One must bear in mind, however, that Benn's interpretation of the Doctor and the Captain and the emphasis he places on social protest are based largely on the material in H2,7, which Benn assumes would have been added in revised form to the space left blank following Büchner's reworking of that scene (H4,9).

Finally, Benn does not consider H3,2 (The Idiot. The Child. Woyzeck) to be an appropriate ending to the play because it is not "properly dramatic" and because "it misplaces the emphasis at the critical moment of the play's conclusion." Büchner is concerned with Woyzeck's relation to society as well as with his personal fate; "and as the story of the historical Woyzeck merges into the story of society's reaction to his crime, so Büchner's play most properly ends, not with the full representation, but with the prospect, the anticipation of that reaction." An expansion of H1,21 would have provided such a conclusion, Benn writes, and even the scene as it stands suggests the beginning of the official proceedings against Woyzeck. Benn finds support for this argument in what he considers to be the play's rhythmical alternation of scenes of social oppression and private agony in an "ascending scale of suffering and injustice culminating in the supreme irony: the condemnation of the lowliest and best human being by those who are socially his superiors but in every other respect immeasurably his inferiors" (257–58).

Benn identifies in H4 a clear tendency to greater concision and force of expression. "Explanation is replaced by action, speech by mimicry"; the style is exclamatory rather than discursive, associative rather than logical in its transitions. Redundancies in the earlier drafts are eliminated in the revised scenes. The play gains in realism and proximity to life (246–47). The new scenes added to H4 bridge the gaps in the action as represented in the earlier drafts and complete the portrayal of the main characters. Marie, in particular, is more fully developed and complex: Büchner deliberately intensifies our impression of her sensuality and depicts fully her contrition, which was barely suggested in the earlier drafts. Because of the conflicts within her, she becomes a truly tragic character. Benn thinks that he "is probably not mistaken" in tracing the source of the mood of apathy and demoralization in which Marie yields to her seducer "to that perpetual poverty and misery which Marie experiences no less painfully than Woyzeck" (247, 249–51). According to Benn, the more frequent recurrence of the words "arm" (poor) and "Geld" (money) in H4 indicates the increasing importance of poverty and "material disabilities" in the final version and confirms his view, he claims, "that Woyzeck is not, as the majority of critics maintain, a tragedy of primitive passion or metaphysical suffering in which social circumstances are more or less irrelevant. It is a tragedy of human feeling in a world of social oppression, and the humanity and the oppression are alike integral to it" (251–52).

Like many of the critics he criticizes, Benn also considers the play to be a powerful expression of metaphysical and political revolt. While some critics may place less emphasis on Woyzeck's poverty than Benn does, very few of them consider the social circumstances to be "more or less irrelevant." Certainly Richards, whose position Benn misrepresents (303, n.53), does not claim that human nature exists independently of social circumstances, though his emphasis does differ from Benn's, who does not give sufficient attention to Woyzeck's mental state: in his only mention of the voices commanding Woyzeck to kill, for example, Benn writes: "He [Woyzeck] does not ask himself what voices are speaking from under the earth, but throws himself to the ground and directly challenges them," which is a questionable interpretation at best. And while he gives considerable emphasis to the material contained in H2,7 which is not included in the revised scene

H4,9, Benn barely mentions and discounts the significance of the carnival scenes and the statement they make about human nature.

With Gerhard Schmid's publication in 1981 of a facsimile edition, it is now possible for scholars everywhere to work with a photographic reproduction of Büchner's manuscripts. Because of the technical care and expertise that went into their preparation, these pages are more legible in some places than the originals. Schmid agrees with Lehmann, Krause, and others on the sequence of the main drafts, H1, H2, and H4, and, with one speculative exception, on the sequence of scenes within the drafts. As for the controversial position of H3, Schmid is certain that it was written after H1 and before H2,6 (34–35, 38–39).

With respect to the construction of a reading and acting text, Schmid argues against Henri Poschmann's assumption that the Professor and the Doctor in H3,1 are two separate figures (see below) and that this scene should therefore be incorporated in a final version. He agrees rather with Richards that H3,1 precedes and is superseded by H2,6, which appears in revised form as H4,8 (35). Schmid considers H3,2 to have been written in close association with H1 rather than with or after H4, as Lehmann argues (37). The disposition of this scene cannot be determined or justified by principles of editing, Schmid writes, and must therefore be considered a question of interpretation or staging (38). In answer to Lehmann's justification for his transposition of scenes at the end of H1 based on the speculation that H1,19 and 20, which are squeezed in at the bottom of a page, may have been later additions, Schmid argues that the retention in these scenes of the name Louis for Woyzeck indicates that they were added before work began on H2.

In his transcription of the texts and in an extensive list of variant readings, Schmid makes a valuable contribution to deciphering Büchner's handwriting and to laying the groundwork for questions that are likely to exercise scholars for years to come, namely, the reading of individual words that are abbreviated by Büchner or that contain obvious inversions and intended or unintended omissions of letters.[3] This task is complicated by the fact that the solutions often depend on whether one assumes that Büchner is using a word in its standard high German form or in some degree of the particular Hessian dialect he employs. As Schmid anticipated, these issues have become the subject of a lively debate among scholars, especially in the pages of the *Georg Büchner Jahrbuch*. Of the new readings that have been proposed and debated, few have any impact on the play's meaning, and fewer still have any consequence for translations into English. It matters little, for example whether the word for a young girls is spelled "Madeln" or "Maderl" or whether it is "duftig" or "düftig," "dämpfen" or "dampfen." In these and other cases involving dialect, the difference may only involve pronunciation. For the most part, these debates yield more heat than light and have little if any significance for most readers and none for those reading the text in English.

In his 1984 and 1992 editions of Büchner's works, Henri Poschmann reproduces the various manuscripts and constructs what he calls a "Kombinierte Werkfassung" (A Combined Working Text) consisting of thirty-one scenes. He considers it justified to use all the scenes of the drafts that were not crossed out and one scene he thinks was mistakenly crossed out. He thus reverts to the introduction of a greater number of contaminations than has been the case in more recent editions. Following the fair scenes, for example, which constitute three separate scenes in his edition, he interpolates the very short scene H1,3: "The other commanded him and he had to go. Ha! One man above another." This is immediately followed by the interpolation of H3,1 (The Professor's Courtyard), which has been the subject of much controversy. In another contamination Poschmann interpolates the barracks scene H1,8 between H4,13, another barracks scene, and H4,14, in which Woyzeck confronts the Drum Major. (H1,8 is the scene in which Woyzeck says of Marie: "But Andres, she was a unique [*einzig*] girl.") Like Lehmann, Poschmann reverses the order of scenes H1,18 (Children) and H1,19 and 20, so the children don't have to be up late. Unlike Lehmann, however, he interpolates H3,2 (The Idiot, The Child. Woyzeck) between H1,18, his scene 29, and H1,21 (Court Clerk . . .). Again in agreement with Lehmann, Poschmann contaminates H4,9 by the addition of the material involving Woyzeck from H2,7.

Poschmann argues that H3 was written after the other manuscripts and represents a final stage of development. In his view, the fact that Büchner adds to the conclusion as contained in H1 authorizes that conclusion and indicates that Büchner considered these scenes more or less complete as they stand. The two scenes of H3 should be considered final additions to the nearly completed play. With respect to H3,1, Poschmann argues that the Doctor and Professor are not two stages in the development of the figure who then appears as the Doctor, but that they are different figures. The reason for what he considers the misinterpretation of these figures lies with Franzos and his tendency to reduce the various names used by Büchner for the same individual to a single name. According to Poschmann, nothing in the manuscript indicates that the Doctor standing with Woyzeck in the courtyard is the same person as the Professor standing above in the window, who thus may be seen as an additional exploiter of Woyzeck's labor (1984, 100–103; 1992, 676, 689–95).

# Notes

[1] In the preface to his 1964 edition of *Woyzeck*, Walter Müller-Seidel refers to the work being prepared for publication by Ursula Paulus, a participant in a doctoral seminar he conducted. I am treating her essay rather than his edition, because her discussion goes beyond his in its detailed criticism of Bergemann's text and in the analysis of editorial problems. Müller-Seidel's edition is not based on Büchner's manuscripts but rather on the text of Bergemann's 1922 edition. With the return of H4,1, Woyzeck and Andres in the field, to its rightful place, Müller-Seidel restores the integrity of H4. What he adds from the earlier manuscripts is distinguished from H4 by the use of a different type face.

[2] In 1975 the Japanese Germanist Mori Mitsuaki proposed a new order of scenes based on a different assumption for the two sheets comprising H1. From his analysis he concludes that one should fit inside the other rather than before or after it. This yields the sequences H1,1–5, 11–20 and H1,6–10, 21. He bases his argument on the correspondence between two groups of two scenes, rather than the three identified by Buch and Bornscheuer, as well as on the close connection of H1,21 to H1,6 in which the barber also appears.

[3] Schmid discusses variant readings along with other problems of editing in a subsequent article. Of particular importance is his reading of "unverdorbene Natur" (uncorrupted or unsophisticated nature) (H1,2 [Inside the Fair Booth]) instead of the "unideale Natur" of the texts edited by Bergemann, Lehmann, and Krause. And in the murder scene (H1,15) where Margreth [=Marie] says, in Bergemann's text, "Ich muß fort das Nachtessen richten" (I must go make dinner), Schmid reads "Ich muß fort der Nachtthau falt [*sic*]" (I must go; the evening dew is falling), which connects to Woyzeck's response: "Friert's dich. . . . Du wirst vom Morgenthau nicht frieren" (Are you freezing. . . . You won't freeze from the morning dew). And where Bergemann, Lehmann, and Krause read "Rind" in Marie's description of the Drum Major: "Uebe die Brust wie ein Rind . . ." "Across the breast like a bullock," Schmid reads "Stier" (bull), which, as the uncastrated equivalent to "Rind," is more fitting (1985, 287–88).

# Works Cited

Benn, Maurice B. *The Drama of Revolt: A Critical Study of Georg Büchner.* London, New York, Melbourne: Cambridge UP, 1976.

Bergemann, Fritz. *Georg Büchners Sämtliche Werke und Briefe.* Leipzig: Insel, 1922.

Bornscheuer, Lothar. *Erläuterungen und Dokumente. Georg Büchner: Woyzeck.* Stuttgart: Reclam, 1972.

———. *Woyzeck: Kritische Lese- und Arbeitsausgabe.* Stuttgart: Reclam, 1972.

Buch, Wilfried. *Woyzeck: Fassungen und Wandlungen.* Dortmund: Crüwell, 1970.

Elema, J. "Der verstümmelte 'Woyzeck.'" *Neophilologus* 49 (1965): 131–56.

Kanzog, Klaus. "Wozzeck, Woyzeck und kein Ende: Zur Standortbestimmung der Editionsphilologie." *Deutsche Vierteljahrsschrift* 47 (1973): 420–42.

Krause, Egon, ed. *Woyzeck: Texte und Dokumente.* Frankfurt: Insel, 1969.

Lehmann, Werner R. *Georg Büchner: Sämtliche Werke und Briefe.* Vol. 1, *Dichtungen und Übersetzungen mit Dokumentation zur Stoffgeschichte.* Hamburg: Christian Wegner Verlag, 1967.

———. "Prolegomena zu einer historisch-kritischen Büchner Ausgabe." In *Gratulatio. Festschrift für Christian Wegner zum 70. Geburtstag,* ed. Maria Honeit and Matthias Wegner. 190–225. Hamburg: Christian Wegner Verlag, 1963.

———. "Repliken: Beiträge zu einem Streitgespräch über den *Woyzeck.*" *Euphorion* 65 (1971): 58–83.

———. *Textkritische Noten: Prolegomena zur Hamburger Büchner-Ausgabe.* Hamburg: Christian Wegner Verlag, 1967.

Meinerts, Jürgen, ed. *Georg Büchner. Sämtliche Werke nebst Briefen und anderen Dokumenten.* Gütersloh: S. Mohn, 1963.

Mori, Mitsuaki. "Der Barbier und die Bogenanordnung der WOYZECK-Handschriften." In *Memoirs of the Faculty of General Education. Kamamoto University. Series of the Humanities* 10 (1975): 157–71.

Müller-Seidel, Walter. "Georg Büchner, Woyzeck." In *Klassische Deutsche Dichtung,* vol. 15: *Bürgerliches Trauerspiel und soziales Drama,* ed. Fritz Martini and Walter Müller-Seidel. Freiburg, Basel, Vienna: Herder, 1964.

Paulus, Ursula. "Georg Büchners 'Woyzeck'. Eine kritische Betrachtung zu der Edition Fritz Bergemanns." *Jahrbuch der deutschen Schiller-Gesellschaft* 8 (1964): 226–46.

Pongs, Hermann. "Büchners 'Woyzeck.'" In *Das Bild in der Dichtung*. Vol. 3, 618–63. Marburg: N. G. Elwert'sche Verlagsbuchhandlung, 1969.

Poschmann, Henri. *Georg Büchner: Woyzeck. Nach den Handschriften neu hergestellt und kommentiert*. Leipzig: Insel, 1984.

———, ed. *Georg Büchner: Sämtliche Werke, Briefe und Dokumente*. Frankfurt: Deutscher Klassiker Verlag, 1992.

Richards, David G. "Zur Textgestaltung von Georg Büchners *Woyzeck*: Anmerkungen zur Hamburger Büchner-Ausgabe, den *Woyzeck* betreffend." *Euphorion* 65 (1971): 49–57.

———. *Georg Büchners Woyzeck: Textgestaltung und Interpretation*. Bonn: H. Bouvier Verlag, 1975.

———. *Georg Büchner and the Birth of the Modern Drama*. Albany: State U. of New York P., 1977.

Schmid, Gerhard, ed. *Georg Büchner: Woyzeck. Faksimileausgabe der Handschriften*. Leipzig: Edition Leipzig; Wiesbaden: Dr. Ludwig Reichert Verlag, 1981.

Schmidt, Henry J., ed. and trans. *Georg Büchner. The Complete Collected Works*. New York: Avon, 1977.

———, trans. *Georg Büchner: Woyzeck*. New York: Avon, 1969.

# 4: International Criticism: 1966–1979

IN THE POLITICALLY ACTIVE LATE SIXTIES AND SEVENTIES, the intensely work-oriented New Critical approach of the late fifties and early sixties was criticized for downplaying or ignoring the importance of the political, social, and biographical context in which the works were written. The focus of critical attention shifted back to content and context. It became more biographical, historical, sociological, and political. Büchner's significance as a political radical and revolutionary contributed to the rapid increase in his international reputation during this period, which saw a dramatic increase in the editions and translations of his works, in their performance, and in the critical literature dealing with them.

As it had been in the politically divided twenties and thirties, a key focus of the debate remained the nature of man: to what extent are his conditions and actions determined by circumstances and forces beyond his control and to what extent can he change the world and himself. For Ludwig Völker, writing in 1966, nature is the play's key idea. Büchner is not so much concerned with Woyzeck's accountability, he maintains, as he is with the essence of man, including especially the extent to which he is free and self-determining or bound and determined by forces beyond his control. Völker concludes that Woyzeck is used as a tool by nature, which gives him the command to kill Marie; he is therefore not accountable. And it is Marie's elementary life force transformed into animality that awakens the voices in Woyzeck that compel him to punish her. Likewise, it is the power of Marie's nature, of her animalistic sexual drive, which causes her to succumb to the Drum Major. She does not act according to a prevailing moral system but according to her nature (1966; 611–19, 629).

Woyzeck's fate is tragic, according to Völker, because he is driven to act by nature, that is, by his inner drives and the effects the drives of others have on him, in a way that strongly contradicts his inherent humanity; he experiences the discrepancy between "nature" and what is human. Büchner equates man and nature in order to demonstrate all the more forcefully that this identification is impossible, that there is something in man that is not entirely congruent with what is "natural." Woyzeck's murder of Marie is an unconscious, instinctive protest against "nature" and therefore against life (625, 627, 630–31).

Considering determinism from a different perspective, Eberhard Henze discusses the contrasting representations of marionettes and automatons by Büchner and Heinrich von Kleist. These motifs were used frequently in early nineteenth-century literature to portray man as determined and manipulated rather than as a self-determining being created in the image of God. According to Henze, Kleist exemplifies the ending of an epoch and Büchner the beginning of a new one. Kleist's heroes are not determined: they act, and in their actions they are deluded and rebellious (1967, 1144–46). Büchner's heroes, on the other hand, are passive rather than active, and they are determined by forces over which they have no control. This is the most terrible form of human existence, since man is reduced to the level of an object. He is alone because he cannot find anyone who understands him or who is able to share his suffering. Unlike Kleist's heroes, Henze writes, Büchner's are not deluded: they clearly see the threads on which they hang. As Büchner's Danton says: "We are puppets, manipulated on our strings by unknown forces. We ourselves are nothing! Nothing! The swords that spirits fight with. One just doesn't see the hands — like in a fairy tale" (I.41). Woyzeck's behavior is compulsive in the extreme when he obeys the voice commanding him to kill Marie. Compared to the impact of this command, the other determining factors such as the Doctor's experiments, Marie's infidelity, and the voices he hears in the beginning are merely the strings on which he hangs. From his comparison of Büchner and Kleist, Henze concludes that Kleist's plays and stories are dramatic, while Büchner's are epic. Kleist observes and records, while Büchner analyzes and diagnoses. Büchner's "autopsy" is the attitude of a scientist applied to the work of art (1146–48, 1154).

In an essay published shortly after Henze's, in 1968, Walter Müller-Seidel also discusses Büchner's scientific attitude and approach. Büchner's mentor Karl Gutzkow already recognized the importance of this approach in his advice to the author, who was thinking of giving up medicine: "Don't be unjust toward this study, for it seems to me that you owe your main 'strength' to it, I mean your unusual candor; I almost want to say your autopsy, that speaks out of everything you write." Like Gutzkow, Müller-Seidel points to Büchner's use of medical vocabulary and concepts from the dissecting room or the morgue, by means of which he makes the poetic process of disillusionment into a scientific process within poetry.

To a large extent, Müller-Seidel adds, Romanticism is the illusion he disillusions. In *Dantons Tod,* history is reduced to natural history, to human drives. In *Woyzeck* it is nature that is disillusioned or disenchanted, that is, stripped of the illusory characteristics that had been projected onto it. Indeed, the reduction of history to the nature of man is a disillusionment that also presupposes the disillusionment of nature (213–17). Disillusioning elements identified by Müller-Seidel include determinism, the confining and oppressive narrowness of space, the feelings of uncanniness and angst caused by this confinement and by other phenomena such as stillness or noise, the conflict and isolation caused by the feeling of being estranged from nature while attempting to cling to it, and, finally, the chaos and collapse of the world (217–21).

Though he does not consider it to be a dominant factor in Büchner's works, Müller-Seidel disagrees with attempts to deny Büchner's nihilism. Beyond all the questioning and challenging of politics or the natural sciences is the goal of searching for meaning, for the meaning of humanity in the midst of a disintegrating world. But nihilism does not have the final word. Although many interpreters refuse to admit it, Müller-Seidel writes, there are also religious motifs in Büchner's works. Whereas the Woyzeck of the earliest draft is conceived of as an atheist, he becomes less so as the work progresses, and he is a believing, Bible-quoting Christian in the final version. The deterministic elements of the play do not preclude the existence of responsibility. Despite his lack of accountability, Woyzeck is guilty from a human, if not a legal, point of view: "A guiltless guilt becomes manifest, which is always a tragic guilt." Woyzeck is compelled as a result of his suffering to commit murder, but he suffers also from the stirring of his conscience and from the awareness that he is guilty before the law. He suffers, that is, from a tragic ambivalence (222–27).

Mario Carlo Abutille adopts a psychological approach for his study *Angst und Zynismus bei Georg Büchner* (Anxiety and Cynicism in the Works of Georg Büchner, 1969). In keeping with his thesis, Abutille focuses on Woyzeck's anxiety and on the cynicism of his persecutors. "Woyzeck consists only of anxiety and suffering," Abutille writes. Büchner's concept of the "terrible fatalism of history" and hence also of the individual is concentrated in Woyzeck. Since he is mentally disturbed and not adapted to the reality of life, he is seized by existential anxiety. A cynical fate controls his life. He is a symbol of man without solace and support, a symbol of human weakness and misery. Because of his hopeless situation, he feels resignation and despair. He is torn by inner restlessness and tension and possessed by anxiety that has no recognizable basis. This anxiety comes from all sides: anonymous demonic forces disturb him internally and are manifest in hallucinatory visions evoked by his surroundings. The agony caused by these forces and by the threat coming from below and above the earth is more terrible than the suffering caused by other people. Once he discovers Marie's infidelity, his hallucinations lose their incomprehensibility and become focused on the command to kill Marie in atonement for her sins and for the suffering she has caused him. Unlike Büchner's other "heroes," Woyzeck does not remain passive. And he too becomes cynical, according to Abutille, in the questions he poses to Marie shortly before the murder: "Do you know how long it's been now, Marie? . . . Do you also know how long it's going to be?"(135–37).

The truly cynical figures, however, are the Captain and the Doctor. The philistine Captain has attributes of Leonce and Lenz, according to Abutille. Like Leonce and like Lenz following his final breakdown, he is hollowed out inside and faces the problem of filling empty time. And like King Peter in Büchner's comedy, his attempts to think and reason are absurd. The Captain covers his own weakness by assuming a self-satisfied posture as he accuses Woyzeck of being immoral, a behavior Abutille considers cynical. Abutille's argument is weakened by the fact that his primary example for the Captain's cynicism is taken from the part of scene H2,7 that Büchner does not include in the revised H4,9, the part in which the Captain maliciously abuses Woyzeck in the area of his greatest vulnerability by calling his attention to Marie's infidelity. According to Abutille, the Captain's malevolent destruction of a fellow human's belief system is the essence of cynicism. But Abutille also finds an element of tragedy in the fact that an "uncertain, tormented, and suffering person feels a kind of relief by causing others to suffer" (121–23).

Unlike the Captain, the Doctor's cynicism, heartlessness, and cruelty are not softened by any human attributes. He is a prime example of the educated man Büchner scorns for the superficiality and emptiness of his learning. The Doctor's goal is to achieve fame; scientific investigation and the use of other humans as guinea pigs are means to that end. The difference in social class between the Doctor and Woyzeck is of no significance, Abutille claims, since he demonstrates his sadism and cynicism with even more brutality and less consideration in his treatment of the Captain. "Here the Doctor outdoes himself in his cynicism. He is diabolical in destroying the hopes of a person seeking help." Through the Doctor, Büchner caricatures the arrogance of scientists as well as the bourgeois world, which is unreceptive to the needs of the lower class. Ironically, Woyzeck disproves through his behavior the existence of free will, which the Doctor is trying to prove. And he does not succumb to the abuse inflicted on him by the Captain and the Doctor. According to Abutille, "He is the only one in the play to preserve human dignity even in his deepest misery" (123–24).

By the end of the fifties Büchner had finally gained recognition as a major figure in German literature. Because of the political and social-critical aspect of his works, his reputation abroad spread rapidly in the politicized sixties and seventies and secured a place for him in the canon of world literature. Almost simultaneous with the beginning of the student protest movement in America was the publication in 1964 of a book on Büchner hailed in the preface by Harry T. Moore as the "first-full-length study of Büchner in English," and introduced by the author, Herbert Lindenberger, as the "first full-length critical study of Büchner's works directed primarily to the English-speaking reader" (v, xi). (A. H. J. Knight's 1951 book does not qualify, Lindenberger claims, because "through its extended quotations in German and its attempt to survey all facets of Büchner's life with equal intensity, [it] is essentially a background guide for the professional student of German literature" [xi].) At about the same time Lehmann, Paulus, and others were questioning Bergemann's edition of the text, Lindenberger, too, would like to see the manuscript problem reopened. Unlike them, however, he does not recognize Büchner's "fair copy" as a final authority; he does not want to proceed according to scholarly principles of editing but in order to "bring future texts of the play in line with what we know of Büchner's dramaturgy" (102), a questionable procedure, as we have seen, given the dependence of such "knowledge" on subjective and historical factors and the tendency to alter the text to fit the interpretation.

Apparently unfamiliar with the discussions by Scheuer and Klotz of the open form of drama, Lindenberger notes the similarity between the complexity Büchner achieves in *Woyzeck* and what has been identified as the "spatial" composition of Shakespeare's major plays. According to this technique, many, if not most, of the scenes are not centrally concerned with furthering the plot line; they provide amplification, ironic commentary, and different perspectives. The play's meanings and effects emerge to a large degree from "side issues" such as the Grandmother's tale and the carnival scenes. One could also speak of a kind of "dispersion" technique, Lindenberger writes, "whereby the central themes are dispersed spatially within the speeches and songs of a large number of characters, many of whom have little or no connection with the temporal sequence" (86, 90–91). The connection, for example, between the carnival scenes and the rest of the play is thematic: the performing animals and the woman in pants are all "de-natured" or "perverted from their natural bent." They serve as analogies to the perverse relationships to nature exemplified by the Captain, the Doctor, and, Lindenberger includes, the Drum Major. In a similar way, Lindenberger agrees with Völker, most of the characters in the play can be defined through their relationship with nature. In her naturalness, spontaneity, and vitality, Marie has a positive relationship to nature, yet her naturalness is also the source of tragedy. Woyzeck's naturalness is less positive, in Lindenberger's view, because it is a reaction to oppression. Through his exploration of his characters' relationship to the natural order, Büchner raises questions about the nature of being (86, 91–94).

According to Lindenberger, Büchner preceded the Symbolists in his discovery that "fragments of statements can have a more powerful effect in an appropriate context than the statements in full." The Fool's citation of fragments of fairy tales in H4,16, for example, provides a kind of ironic counterpoint to Marie's expression of guilt as she reads passages from the Bible. Like the fragments of folk songs that recur throughout the play, the bits of fairy tales the Fool quotes here and in his other appearances serve, according to Lindenberger, "to create effects both of amplification and of ironic commentary on the action," as well as to assert the folk-like character of the play. Furthermore, like Marie's quotations from the Bible, these quotations and references give the characters greater eloquence than they otherwise command and provide a universal framework for what might otherwise have remained a domestic tragedy (87–89).

Just as Büchner approaches a theme such as the nature of man and beast from varying points of view, he also uses words with different meanings in varying contexts. As described by Mautner and others (see chapter two), words such as "red" and "blood" take on different meanings in different contexts, thereby accumulating associations and enriching their expressivity. Especially fundamental to Büchner's central question concerning the nature of man, Lindenberger maintains in agreement with Walter Weiss, is the word *Mensch*, that is, man or human being, and *menschlich*, which can mean both human and humane. These words recur throughout the play with a variety of meanings. Lindenberger considers it "the burden of the play to break down and expose the meanings of the word, which can no longer hold up in the world." The Captain and the Doctor use the word with its most lofty meaning of "man as a free and autonomous being who is intrinsically superior to animals." In proclaiming that the individual's will to freedom is manifest in man, the Doctor speaks in terms used by Kant and the idealist philosophers to present a concept that is made to appear ridiculous by the context in which Büchner places it. The Captain proceeds from the same concept when he prides himself on being a good and virtuous man because he is able to resist sexual temptation. According to Lindenberger, who appears to overlook the Captain's repeated references to Woyzeck as "a good man," the Captain contrasts himself with Woyzeck, who has fathered an illegitimate child and is therefore "excluded from the honor of being a 'human being.'" In the mock sermon delivered by a journeyman in H4,11 (The Inn), it is the Biblical meaning of the word "Mensch" that is subjected to ridicule (94–95).

When Woyzeck sees Marie and the Drum Major dancing together, he recognizes in Marie's faithlessness the basic equivalence between human and animal behavior: "Male and Female! Man and Beast! They'll do it in broad daylight! They'll do it on your hands, like flies!" Woyzeck's conclusion is supported by the carnival scene, in which humanity is seen to exist on several levels: the trained horse is "a beastly man," and the monkey, costumed as a soldier, is on "the lowest level of the human race." The suggestion here and elsewhere in the play is that Woyzeck's status as a human being is close to that of the horse and the monkey: like the horse, he follows his nature and relieves himself in public, and like the monkey, he is dressed as a soldier and made to perform and to subject himself to medical experiments. Ironically, according to Lindenberger, he is finally honored with the designation "Mensch" as he drowns (95–96). (Lindenberger interprets the remarks of the people in H1,16 as referring to the sounds of the drowning Woyzeck, but they more likely come from Marie, who has just been stabbed. And, as noted above, he overlooks the Captain's references to Woyzeck as "a good man," [ein guter *Mensch*]). According to Lindenberger, Büchner does not answer the questions he raises about the nature of man. Although Woyzeck is denied his humanity by others, and although he himself has a low opinion of man, he is endowed with basic human dignity, especially in the testament scene, where he rummages through the remnants of his past with a calmness and clarity not evident elsewhere in the play, reviving family memories and reciting his vital statistics, which serve as an assertion of self-identity (109–110).

Lindenberger identifies two approaches to characterization: "objectively" created characters such as Marie and Woyzeck and the caricatures or marionettes with no autonomy such as the Doctor and the Captain. Lindenberger considers Marie to be the prime example of the objectively drawn figure: she seems to exist independently of the author. "She is simply there; no judgment is passed on her, either directly or implicitly. She reveals herself through the immediacy of her speech and her actions." Although her role in the play is quite minimal, her portrait is fully rounded. Lindenberger considers Woyzeck to be somewhat absurd, even clownlike and comical, but in such a way that we "sympathize with him as with a real human being. . . . He is perhaps the first tragic hero whom we can laugh at and pity at once." In the confrontation between the caricatures and the "realistically" conceived characters, Lindenberger writes, "Büchner was able to achieve a unique blend of comedy and pathos" (102–105, 108–109).

In his 1968 discussion of Büchner's influence on modern literature, Wilhelm Emrich writes: "Georg Büchner's work contains concentrated in form and content all the basic structural elements that constitute modern literature of the twentieth century." Emrich considers the model of this form to be the carrousel or *Weltrad* that reduces people to objects without will, to puppets whose actions are circular and repetitive. The typical plot development of classical drama — exposition, increasing complication and tension, intrigue and counter intrigue, turning point, moment of final tension followed by catastrophe — no longer exists. Instead, the catastrophe exists before the beginning of the drama; the end is already contained in the beginning. Extreme despair and a playfully skeptical cheerfulness exist together in what only appears to be a contradictory conjunction. Tragedy and comedy become identical, which gives rise to the grotesque. The boundaries not only between man and animal but also between man and thing are eliminated: Woyzeck, for example, is compared to an animal, and he is treated like an object in the Doctor's experiments. This degradation of man is accompanied by the ridicule or dissolution of all ideals, Weltanschauungen, and religious norms, which prove to be lies used by those in power to maintain their dominance. A tormented creature such as Woyzeck constitutes a protest against the domination of science, philosophy, and morality, and he represents a new possibility of consciousness that did not fully emerge until the twentieth century and that determines contemporary thought, a consciousness involving the conflict between real existence and false ideology (133–38). As Emrich demonstrates by comparing with Büchner's works similar passages from works by Gerhart Hauptmann, Frank Wedekind, Hans Henny Jahnn, Ernst Toller, Carl Sternheim, Else Lasker-Schüler, Georg Heym, Alfred Döblin, Ödön von Horváth, Bertolt Brecht, Eugéne Ionesco, and Samuel Beckett, Büchner anticipates prophetically this modern conflict.

At the same time Büchner's works were becoming firmly established in the canon of classical German literature and their innovative modernity was being explored, critics sympathetic to the new political and social activism of the sixties and seventies were focusing again, as had readers in the late nineteenth century, on their socially and politically critical content. One of the first and most diligent advocates of this position, the Swedish Germanist Bo Ullman, completed a dissertation on the subject in 1970, which was published in 1972 under the title *Die sozialkritische Thematik im Werk Georg Büchners und ihre Entfaltung im "Woyzeck." Mit einigen Bemerkungen zu der Oper Alban Bergs* (The Social-Critical Themes in the Works of Georg Büchner and their Development in *Woyzeck*. With Some Comments on Alban Berg's Opera). In the same year he also published an article entitled "Der unpolitische Georg Büchner. Zum Büchner-Bild der Forschung, unter besonderer Berücksichtigung der 'Woyzeck'-Interpretationen" (The Unpolitical Georg Büchner. Concerning Scholarship's Image of Büchner with Particular Consideration of Interpretations of *Woyzeck*).

Ullman argues in his book against the New Critical or *werkimmanent* approach, because it excludes extraliterary considerations such as the social implications of Büchner's works and because it rejects interpretations based on intellectual history. In agreement with Theodor Adorno, Ullman considers the intellect or *Geist* to be essentially social, a human capacity that has its origin in society and through whose aesthetic products society manifests and asserts itself. Ullman's rejection of the New Critical approach does not prevent him from recognizing the importance of language and style as analyzed by Klotz, Krapp, Elema, and others, as long as the formal elements are not considered independent of their relationship to society. Though his approach is essentially Marxist, Ullman does not agree with Hans Meyer's definition of realism in Büchner's works. According to Ullman, Büchner's realism is not a copy but rather an *expressive exaggeration* of reality (8–13, 17, 26).

Except in some of its details, Ullman's interpretation of the play is not new. Like others before him, he emphasizes the social origins of Woyzeck's poverty and ignorance. The Doctor and the Captain represent the kind of aristocracy and egoism of class and education Büchner scorned, and they are examples of the worn-out society he hated. Their activities and conversations are meaningless and often cruel attempts to escape the boredom of their inauthentic and useless lives. In observing the niceties of social convention and in their monomaniacal concentration on their fixed ideas, they are grotesque marionettes, yet they have the power and position to persecute, abuse, and demean Woyzeck (38–40, 49–56). In connection with the analogy between man and animal made in the fair scenes, Ullman considers the animalistic elements in the lower-class characters to be a result of social oppression. Likewise, the erotic drive that motivates and compels the actions of Marie and the Drum Major is a part of man's animal nature over which he has no control, and this lack of freedom, according to Ullman, is "not outside of the social problematic of *Woyzeck* and of Büchner's works in general." The hopeless state of the world, which Woyzeck experiences from the first scene on, is related to and punished through Marie. According to Ullman, it is not class but the world itself and the importance society places on property that is to blame. Woyzeck feels so entirely alone when Marie betrays him because he has clung to a possession that is not, or should not be, one. His possessiveness derives from society's rootedness in property, yet his deed is punished by society. The true erotic problem, according to Ullman, is that of erotic possessiveness (59–62, 74–5, 80).

Ullman is familiar with the texts edited by Lehmann and Krause and with Paulus's article, but he is willing to depart from sound principles of editing in order to find support for his thesis. He argues for the placement of H3,2 (The Idiot. The Child. Woyzeck) at the end, for example, because it emphasizes Woyzeck's isolation and anticipates the trial, which would increase his humiliation and abasement by society. Ullman thinks Büchner would have added Woyzeck's appearance in H4,7 (The Doctor. The Captain), but without reference to Marie's betrayal, which is meaningless at this point (33, 35). However, if the reference to Marie's betrayal and Woyzeck's disturbed reaction to this revelation were removed from the scene as contained in H2,9, as Ullman proposes, almost nothing would remain.

In his review of the secondary literature on Büchner to 1967, which is contained in his essay "The Unpolitical Büchner," Ullman provides a brief discussion of selected critical works with emphasis on *Woyzeck*. As suggested by the title of his article, he is intent on identifying the tendency of critics to discount the political content and importance of Büchner's works and on disparaging those studies that do not give this aspect of Büchner the emphasis Ullman considers appropriate, especially those that tend to focus on Büchner's pessimism or nihilism (97–98).

One of the many examples of what Ullman identifies as "the lamentable tradition of depoliticizing Büchner" (119) is the chapter in Benno von Wiese's *Die deutsche Tragödie von Lessing bis Hebbel* (German Tragedy from Lessing to Hebbel, 1948) entitled "Georg Büchner: Die Tragödie des Nihilismus" (Georg Büchner: The Tragedy of Nihilism). Here and in a 1973 article "Der 'arme' Woyzeck. Ein Beitrag zur Umwertung des Heldenideals im 19. Jahrhundert" ("Poor" Woyzeck: A Contribution to the Revaluation of the Ideal of the Hero in the Nineteenth Century) von Wiese gives particular emphasis to the parallel between Woyzeck and the child in the Grandmother's "Anti-Märchen": both figures are sad and totally alone in a world that provides no support, no comfort, and no meaning. In the 1973 article, however, von Wiese has become aware of the tale's political implication "that for poor, abandoned children there is no comforting heaven, no saving God, not even a helping fellow human being" (1973, 310).

Citing Büchner's criticism of Young German liberalism and his analysis of the political conditions of the time, von Wiese writes that "only Karl Marx and in his way Heinrich Heine saw the social conflicts with the precision Büchner partly anticipated already in 1835 and 1836" (310).

Von Wiese concludes nevertheless that the Grandmother's tale is not to be misunderstood as a political manifesto. It should be seen, rather, as a parable that makes a connection between the child's situation and Woyzeck's. For the first time in the history of German tragedy, the central figure of a play is an anti-hero, the very opposite of the traditional heroes of tragedy. "Woyzeck is the hunted, unhappy, degraded, vitally weakened creature, the poor but good-hearted soldier, the simple man who has become simply an object, who in a terrible environment loses the modicum of love that Marie had given him" (314). The question of innocence or guilt, which is of central importance in traditional tragedy, is irrelevant in this play. Woyzeck has no subjective awareness of guilt: he considers the murder of Marie to be just retribution for her sin and lechery, and he is prepared to die himself. Woyzeck is not presented as the hero of a social class struggle, von Wiese maintains. His suffering and fate are not caused, either directly or indirectly, by his poverty or by the representatives of bourgeois society, the Captain and the Doctor, whose ideological positions are subject to ridicule in the play. Rather, he is exposed to the "suffering of existence in general" and suffers at least as much from his inability to communicate as from his economic misery. Büchner's concern is with the essence of man, not with social revolution. He is shaken by the misery and suffering of human existence. In *Dantons Tod* he poses the question "Why do I suffer?" and claims that the existence of suffering is the foundation of atheism and the manifestation of a flaw in creation (I,48). Büchner's Lenz says: "but I, if I were omnipotent. . . I could not bear the suffering; I would save, save" (I,99). This, according to von Wiese, is the core of Büchner's humanism (310, 315, 320–22).

Because Büchner is a humanist and loves his fellow man, von Wiese is no longer prepared to identify him as a nihilist, as he did in his book on the German tragedy. For Büchner the pain of existence is a "Mysterium" that Woyzeck and all humans must endure. Büchner knew that pain is the most human of our attributes and perhaps therefore also the most divine. Von Wiese concludes that one may take the scenes of *Woyzeck* as the confession of a humane, pre-Marxist socialism, but one should not forget that Büchner did not write a dialectical program. As a great tragedian who found life to be an incomprehensible enigma, he is superior to those who believe they have found a final, practical solution for freeing man from suffering with the help of reason (324–25).

In a discussion of the structure of *Woyzeck*, Luc Lamberechts amplifies Klotz's study of the open form of drama and compares what he
considers to be the static form of *Woyzeck* with Brecht's "dialectical
form of drama." Büchner's use of brief moments to create a multiper-
spectival representation of totality approximates Brecht's use of the
*Verfremdungseffect* (alienation or distancing effect). The multiperspec-
tives are focused on the point where the latent meaning of the whole is
represented, that is, on the "point of integration." This form of drama
does not presuppose a generally accepted view of reality; rather, it creates its own reality (1972, 122).

Lamberechts agrees with critics who consider the contrast of the
animal and human realms to be of central importance in *Woyzeck*, but
the two passages he identifies as integration points that supposedly
summarize the content of the play contain no reference to the bestial
side of man. Rather, they contrast positive and negative representations
of the human condition. The Grandmother's tale represents a complete
disillusionment of the universe, according to Lamberechts, in the context of which Woyzeck's fate becomes representative of a general condition in which the "positive, beautiful or friendly effect of the earth,
moon, sun, and stars is only an illusion, and man, suffering eternally in
absolute isolation, cannot hope for improvement" (122,129). The
content of the contrasting testament scene, on the other hand, is positive and Christian. The verse cited by Woyzeck indicates, according to
Lamberechts, that Woyzeck takes the suffering of the world upon himself, thus becoming a kind of Christ figure. This verse contrasts with
the Grandmother's tale to reveal the positive side of Büchner's view of
the world; what is meaningful is contrasted with what is meaningless.
Woyzeck's particular tragic fate becomes the tragedy of mankind. By
taking the suffering of all mankind and indeed, as represented in the
Grandmother's tale, even of the universe, upon himself, Woyzeck
makes a connection between personal and general fate. Fundamentally
tragic in this situation is the fact that both poles exist in a balanced, antithetical equilibrium, so that there is no prospect of a shift in this relationship. Here stasis has the significance of tragedy (129–30).

The two integration points, together with what Lamberechts calls
partial integration points, for example, the carnival scene, quotations
from the Bible, and fragments from folk songs, constitute a form of
commentary on the actual plot that resembles the demonstrations in
the later plays of Brecht. But according to Lamberechts, Büchner's play
differs from Brecht's in that these partial integration points are not
dialectical but static, and they are not directed to the public and obviously presented as a demonstration or model. They have nothing of the

principle of dialectical historicization, which employs contrast to alienate what is shown. There is no prospect of dissolving the conflict in a synthesis, of finding a solution to the problems presented. The imperfect condition of the world and of human nature are the unalterable source of Woyzeck's tragedy. Brecht's dramas, on the other hand, depict a society that presumably can be changed. The emphasis in Brecht's dialectical drama shifts from the individual to the collective, and it goes beyond its beginning point to anticipate or call for change (130–34, 139–41).

A substantial contribution to Büchner criticism in English was made in the mid-seventies with the publication of three full-length studies: *Georg Büchner* by Ronald Hauser, *The Drama of Revolt: A Critical Study of Georg Büchner* by Maurice B. Benn, and *Georg Büchner and the Birth of Modern Drama* by David G. Richards. Ronald Hauser pays particular attention to Woyzeck's psychological state and to his status as a kind of everyman attempting to survive in a chaotic and "grotesquely absurd world." From his analysis of Clarus's reports on Woyzeck's physical and psychological state and his judgment with respect to Woyzeck's accountability and guilt, and from the close proximity of Büchner's representations to Clarus's, Hauser concludes that Büchner does not attack Clarus's theories or put the doctor on trial. Büchner attempts through Woyzeck to answer the question asked in a letter to his fiancée and again in *Dantons Tod*: "What is it in us that lies, whores, steals, and murders?" Büchner does not ask "what is it *in our society* or *in our world* that makes us murder" (1974, 102, author's emphasis), Hauser points out in disagreement with the many interpreters who look for a sociological basis for Woyzeck's tragedy, but "what is it in us." To shape Woyzeck's story as an indictment of the injustices of criminal law enforcement would require presenting him as "indisputably insane in the legal sense of the word," but the very notion of legal insanity is antithetical to Büchner's view that there is no distinction between rational and irrational behavior (94–95).

For Hauser, all that we know about Woyzeck, whether from Clarus's report or Büchner's play, does not explain what it is in this simple, good, ordinary, and perfectly rational man that makes him capable of savagely killing the woman he loves. "Knowing so much and yet not knowing, therein lies the tragedy!" according to Hauser. As much as we know about Woyzeck and his motivation, we cannot understand the deed. Clarus appears to have been equally at a loss: he describes Woyzeck largely in terms of what he is not: he does not have the attributes one might expect of a beast, a sex fiend, a drunk, or a monster capable of killing his lover; and he lists a number of possible reasons for murder — bad circulation, insanity, stupidity, and drunkenness — that do not apply to Woyzeck. Büchner thus assaults the myth of the monster as murderer, but that is not the central theme of the play, according to Hauser:

> The fact that Woyzeck kills because that terrible inner force seizes control over him contains deeply tragic implications for mankind, but it is not the basis of his personal tragedy. Woyzeck . . . loses all the games in life, most of them by default. He cannot even participate, but is, in fact, totally unfit for living. That is his tragedy, and the anatomy of his suffering is the main theme of the play. (106–107)

Woyzeck's tragedy is the "tragedy of every man who opens his eyes and begins to think." According to Hauser, all Büchner's main figures are "victims of an overly uncompromising intellect," and all know that there is nothing to know (95). Büchner's Doctor demonstrates the pointlessness of the "scientific method," which only leads man "into ever greater disharmony with his surroundings, and ever closer to the abyss." The Captain's thinking has gotten him into a state of melancholy lethargy. In the fair scenes Büchner compares man to animals to "establish the idea that man's highly developed brain actually represents a kind of biological defect." The animals presented in these scenes have become denatured by taking on human attributes. The monkey's rise on the "human ladder," for example, makes a mockery of man and his achievements, but the monkey is also the object of mockery, since the human talents it displays lead no further than to being a curiosity at a carnival side show. In a world so devoid of human values, Hauser concludes, it is only the mockers, the fools and charlatans, liars and madmen who can hold a mirror up to society. Hauser sees the "final, and most incisive, definition of the human condition" and the "dramatic climax of the play" in the parodistic sermon of the Journeyman, whose intellect is numbed by alcohol, and whose cynical words point to the lack of purpose in human existence. It is a message similar to the one contained in the Grandmother's tale. Once Woyzeck loses his "romantic conception of love as the inseparable union of two people joined together by the forces of nature," he falls into the abysmal depths of this meaningless world (119–22, 124).

In a chapter on *Woyzeck* in *Georg Büchner and the Birth of the Modern Drama* (1977), which was first published as a monograph in German in 1975, David G. Richards provides an interpretation and analysis of form based on his construction of the text (see chapter three). In his view, the play's socially critical content goes beyond the scornful treatment of Woyzeck's presumed oppressors to question and challenge the legal, social, and religious assumptions upon which our concept of justice and the methods for administering it are based. "The fundamental concern of Büchner's play is not the guilt of one man and the judgment of a few others," he writes,

> but the legal, social, religious, moral, psychological, and even scientific systems, institutions, and presuppositions of society in general. In the spirit of the dawning scientific age, Büchner gives radically new and modern answers to the old questions concerning the nature of man and his position in society, and these answers give rise, in turn, to new questions. Changes in the concept of man demand corresponding revisions of his moral and legal codes and social institutions to the extent that these are based upon presuppositions about man's nature. (1977, 173–74)

Having been unsuccessful in his attempt to change the political and social conditions in his native Hesse, Büchner may have redirected his efforts to preparing for revolutionary change by attempting through his art to change attitudes, consciousness, and awareness.

In connection with Büchner's opposition to idealism and idealistic glorification of man, Richards contrasts Büchner's scientific perspective with a statement by the philosopher Immanuel Kant, a major representative of German Idealism. Kant wrote that man transcends "the mechanical disposition of his animal existence" because nature has given him "reason and freedom of will." As Büchner demonstrates in *Woyzeck* and his other works, man's will is determined by nature and environment, and reason is by no means a strong or reliable attribute. Büchner wrote in a letter: "Reason, moreover, is only a very insignificant side of our mental being, and education only an accidental form of the same" (II.422). And as a schoolboy, Büchner wrote in the margin of a notebook: "Oh, Herr Doctor! What are intellect, sagacity, sound reason? Empty names! — A dung heap of scholarship, the only worthy goal of human striving!" (Bergemann, 1922, 762). If one denies freedom of will and minimizes the role of reason, all that remains of Kant's definition is man's "animal being," and that, according to Richards, is what Büchner demonstrates in his play (180). Woyzeck is not destroyed by the debasement he suffers at the hands of society's villains, Richards claims — that would be the stuff of melodrama and the literature of disaster — but by "members of his own class, who act as instruments of a force far more universal and ineluctable and therefore more terrifying than those represented by the Captain and the Doctor, and that is the force of nature. . . . Fate for Woyzeck as for Büchner's characters in general, is in nature." In betraying Woyzeck, Marie cannot resist her vital, erotic nature, and he cannot resist the compulsion to punish her and exact retribution (177–78).

Consistent with his criticism of the idealistic, teleological, and hier-archical Weltanschauung of German idealism is Büchner's rejection of the classical, Aristotelian dramatic form with its linear, causal plot de-velopment and its complex arrangement of interdependent parts ac-cording to principles of logic and rank. Unlike the idealists, Richards writes, who tend to see the moment as part of a continuum, Büchner considers each moment to be important in its own right; life consists of a series of such individual moments, each of which is complete in itself and its own reason for being. The succession of moments is not deter-mined by a divine will or a Hegelian world spirit, but by the laws of nature, by inherent physical, biological, and psychological patterns and processes, which are their own meaning and purpose. By presenting a sequence of moments that are "especially charged with meaning, ten-sion, and action or those which effectively stretch beyond their own borders to imply what preceded and suggest what will follow," an author attempts to re-present life and history as it actually occurred or might have occurred. This form is particularly suitable for presenting a fragmented world in which clearly defined relationships are lacking and in which the individual is isolated and alone, as is the case in *Woyzeck* (190–91).

Richards does not agree with those critics, however, who claim that one can shift the sequence of scenes almost at will without altering the play. In his view, the sequence of scenes, like the sequence of words in a sentence or sentences in a paragraph, is as much a determinant of meaning and effect as are the parts themselves. In place of the Aristote-lian rules for creating unity in classical drama, Büchner relies on the unity of impression created above all by the repetition and variation of words, phrases, images, themes, and rhythms as discussed by Mautner, Klotz, and others. Through the use of these motifs and motif-complexes, Richards adds, Büchner also achieves "maximal concentra-tion and force of expression" (195–98).

Since Maurice Benn's analysis of *Woyzeck* is closely related to his discussion of the construction of the text, it was included in the pre-ceding chapter. To provide a background for his treatment of the indi-vidual works, Benn includes introductory chapters on Büchner's political, metaphysical, and aesthetic revolt. He considers Büchner's aesthetics to be a revolt against idealism or "idealization," as repre-sented especially by Kant, Hegel, and, more importantly for Büchner, by Schiller. For Kant the "regulative principle in art is 'the ideal of beauty,'" and "the aesthetic ideal also acquires an ethical aspect in so far as beauty is the symbol of what is ethically good." For Hegel "art proceeds out of the absolute idea and its purpose is 'the sensuous representation of the Absolute.'" For both philosophers, then, art is concerned with deeper, more general truth than that of empirical reality. In his classical period, Goethe adhered to the principle of idealization both in the theory and the practice of art, but Schiller, in his classical period, was an eloquent spokesman for idealization in German literature, which is why he was the object of Büchner's attack (1976, 80–81).

Büchner objects to idealization because the idealizing artist attempts to improve on nature, to ennoble, beautify, or transfigure it, to transform it in accordance with some perfect ideal, which, in Büchner's view, cannot "result in something richer or grander or finer than nature but, on the contrary, in something infinitely poorer and weaker and meaner" (84–85). Rather than transcending nature, Benn continues, idealizing art falls short of, and is inadequate to, nature, and such art leaves us completely cold. As indicated by Camille in *Dantons Tod* and by the central figure of *Lenz*, such art produces puppets and automatons instead of living human beings. It is art like Pygmalion's statue Galatea, whom Winckelmann considered to be the representation of the mythical ideal of perfect beauty, but whom Büchner dismisses as sterile. In opposition to classical idealization, Büchner advocates realism, which, unlike classicism, would not be hopelessly inadequate in its representation of nature and history, and which would achieve the true aim of art as Büchner conceived it, namely, the communication of feeling. Büchner advocates a characteristic art, not an art of beauty. As noted by Müller-Seidel, Emrich, and others, he carries into the realm of art something of the cool, clinical attitude of the scientist (86–89).

According to Benn, Büchner believed that literature should not be didactic but should study life objectively, honestly, and without preconceived ideas or ulterior motives. On the other hand, Büchner's aesthetics are not an "Abspiegelungslehre," as Hans Mayer writes, not a theory of the artistic mirroring or reflection of reality. According to Benn, Büchner does not suggest that a "real" rendering of nature can be achieved by any superficial mechanical process of copying. The reality he has in mind is something the artist must discover, just as the scientist must discover it in his domain. Also essential for Büchner's art is his doctrine of sympathy and humility, his own aspiration to human solidarity, which he opposes to the inhumanity and arrogance of idealizing art. For Büchner considers no one too ugly or too lowly to be represented by the artist. "In the aesthetic as in the political sphere he was trying to rescue the submerged classes of society and bring them into the light," Benn writes. Büchner's aesthetic revolt is related to his metaphysical revolt, since the increasing empiricism in literature and art and the attempt to liberate art from inherited dogmas and prejudices was "no doubt in some measure due to the crumbling of religious faith" (94, 96, 98).

In *Georg Büchner: Das dichterische Werk* (Georg Büchner: the Poetic Works) Erwin Kobel concludes that Büchner is less interested in whether man is free or unfree than he is in the nature of human freedom. He believes both in determinism and in free will; the freedom of one person is the lack of freedom of another. The Doctor represents both positions: after asserting that man is free, he contradicts himself by claiming that man is dependent on, and determined by, natural necessity. A similar contradiction takes place in the speeches of the carnival Barker, Kobel writes, in that he first discounts nature and praises art and education for making something proper out of it, then praises the unideal nature of the horse for behaving naturally. (It is not clear from the manuscripts whether both speeches cited by Kobel are actually spoken by the same person.) The Doctor and the Barker are both charlatans in their defense of freedom. Their arguments are as unreliable and ridiculous as the opposite thesis Valerio defends in his description of Leonce and Lena as automatons. Büchner does not reject the possibility of freedom, but he does mock the desire for freedom based on idealistic assumptions (1974, 289, 292–93).

To assume that Woyzeck is mad is to accept the Doctor's evaluation. In Kobel's view, Woyzeck is not mentally disturbed, and the murder is deliberate. Büchner does not write his play to exonerate Woyzeck. Nor does he consider him to be the victim of social circumstances. There is no causal nexus between Woyzeck's diet of peas and his mental state. The grievous state of the social conditions is not a cause but rather an expression of human misery. The times are out of joint, which is a theme in all of Büchner's works, according to Kobel. Woyzeck is a poor counterpart to the princely Leonce. To his question: "What is it in us that lies, steals, murders," Büchner's answer is "melancholy due to transitoriness, despair over the fact that the eternal does not exist and that everything is therefore meaningless" (278–87, 306).

In separate studies of Büchner's use of the Biblical passages cited by Krause, John M. Grandin and Cornelie Ueding reach conclusions quite different from Krause's. According to Grandin, Büchner's use of apocalyptic language and references to Sodom and Gomorrah and the Last Judgment create "a mood of wrath and condemnation rather than of love and forgiveness," and its purpose is to demonstrate the fixation in Woyzeck's mind that leads to the murder, not, as Krause claims, to remorse and Christian reconciliation. Grandin bases his interpretation both on the occurrence in the Biblical passages of motifs that recur throughout the play and refer to guilt, sin, and punishment, namely, heat, fire, flame, blood, wrath, and the color red, and on the increasing importance Büchner places during the course of composition on the fiery images of Judgment Day (1977–78, 175–78).

Cornelie Ueding has different reasons for disagreeing with Krause's interpretation of the apocalyptic content of the Biblical passages. In her view, the connection of the apocalyptic threat with the motif of Marie's infidelity contributes little to the elucidation of the specific Biblical references used by Woyzeck. Rather than being related to their concrete Biblical context, these passages serve as a means for the uneducated and inarticulate Woyzeck to express his own experiences, his own situation, and his own fears and suffering in a language and context that is realistic and familiar to the people of his social class. Furthermore, the Biblical language and references, which carry the implication of authority, are intended to increase the credibility and validity of the experience he attempts to describe, but in fact, Ueding claims, they do not, either within the play or with the public, as early criticism reveals (67–68).

The Biblical references of the first scene, for example, are not meant to suggest the judgment of sinful cities, destruction of the world, or apocalyptic visions, according to Ueding. Rather, they represent the subjective expression of a diffusely but strongly felt threat which corresponds objectively to Woyzeck's exposed and endangered state, and they reveal his fear and suffering. Büchner portrays Woyzeck's mental state before showing its causes in social conditions. Furthermore, Woyzeck does not use Biblical language and imagery unconsciously, as Krause claims; "he knows very exactly what he is referring to." He has recourse to it again in attempting to explain to Marie and the Doctor what he himself is not able to comprehend, but they consider him to be mentally disturbed (68–69). Finally, Woyzeck makes use of apocalyptic motifs when he sees Marie dancing with the Drum Major, not, as Krause writes, because Marie's disloyalty becomes an apocalyptic event for Woyzeck, but, Ueding maintains, because destruction and self-destruction lose their threat for Woyzeck in this moment (71).

Following a lead by Hans Mayer, Terry Otten looks in a 1978 article to Shakespeare's *Othello* as a possible source and inspiration, to which *Woyzeck* "likely owes more . . . than to any contemporary play in Büchner's age." Both plays stretch the idea of tragedy and flirt with melodrama in the creation of plot, character, and action. Both heroes "suffer the most modern of ills, alienation. Both struggle to exist amid strangers; both seek in vain for refuge in society, the cosmos and the self." Their inability to heal the breach between themselves and the communal forces of the state, family, and God make them suspect as tragic heroes (124–25). Otten considers the morally loose and poor

Marie to be an ironic, inverted parallel to the aristocratic, morally up-right Desdemona. And though Woyzeck completely lacks Othello's so-cial and personal stature, he shares his tragic circumstances and, no less than Othello, "places his total burden of selfhood on his lover, and he suffers similar consequences." Both act against themselves in killing the woman they love in an attempt to restore justice to the universe (128–29, 131).

In both plays the concept of man as beast and lecher is of central importance. In *Othello* it is Iago who serves as the voice of Othello's in-security and brings him to believe in Desdemona's betrayal and in the fallen state of all men. In *Woyzeck* the animalistic nature of man is pre-sented by the Doctor, the Barker, and the Drum Major. "Having made their lovers the guardians of their identities and their sole contacts with the spiritual powers that protect them from total derangement, Othello and Woyzeck must either accept their meaningless lives or recover their lost innocence" (131–32).

While Otten compares *Woyzeck* to *Othello*, Alfred Schwarz, in his article from the same year, compares it to *King Lear*. Like Lear, Woyzeck experiences a disintegration of personality and a progressive alienation from the world. Their personal affliction becomes a night-mare world, as both men "reach the least common denominator of human existence." The scenes on the heath that constitute the nadir of Lear's pilgrimage "stand in suggestive relation to Woyzeck's whole world." The contrast between the state of nature and the ordered moral life is at the heart of both plays, Schwarz writes, but for the man from the lowest level of society, the latter is an impossibility. Woyzeck's tenuous hold on civil life is broken by his feverish inner confusion and by each encounter with the social world around him. Woyzeck knows that he has nothing, and during the course of events depicted in the play he also becomes aware that he *is* nothing (1978, 104–6).

In an interpretation that has attracted attention and considerable dismissive criticism for its contrarian approach, Wolfgang Wittkowski claims that Büchner scholarship has been morally uncritical of Woyzeck in its tendency to sympathize more with Woyzeck than with his victim. "The human and scientific need for rational unequivocalness resists the basic tragic demand to sympathize with the hero and at the same time to condemn him" (1978, 270). In his view, Woyzeck is responsible for his action, which is carried out in cold blood with clear and deliberate intent (280). From the standpoint of psychological accountability, Woyzeck comes off better than the Doctor and the Captain, who are "less well endowed by God" yet more severely condemned morally: seen metaphysically, Wittkowski claims, Woyzeck is the favored one, of whom the demand is made that he resist the drive to evil, but he does not have the strength to fulfill that demand. The conflict here is not between freedom and determinism but between drive and counter-drive, whereby the stronger one prevails (277). It is a question of weakness which one does not master, cannot master, indeed, cannot even want to master, and still must be responsible for. Büchner is an exponent of a higher justice, indeed, an absolute, transcendent juris-diction (280).

Of central importance for Wittkowski's interpretation of all Büch-ner's works is the quotation that appears in Büchner's letter on fatalism and again in *Dantons Tod*: "Offenses must come, but woe to that man by whom the offense comes" (Matthew 18: 7). Wittkowski mentions the offense taken by the Doctor at Woyzeck's failure to abide by his contract and preserve his urine for the Doctor's experiments. The Doctor tries to resist being upset, but he is as much subject to the "must," the "offense," and the "woe" as Woyzeck is. The Captain is offended by his own eyes when the sight of women's legs arouses his lust, or, as he calls it, love. Like Woyzeck, he too is of "flesh and blood" and subject to their demands. He is also offended and confused by Woyzeck's lack of morality and his attempt to defend himself by citing the words of Christ: "Suffer little children to come unto me" (Luke 18:16). Similar words appear in the book of Matthew in close proximity to the passage on the offenses that must come: "Take heed that ye despise not one of these little ones . . . ," and: "But whoso shall offend one of these little ones which believe in me, it were better for him that a millstone were hanged about his neck, and that he were drowned in the depth of the sea" (18: 10, 6). In German the word for "these little ones" is "die Geringsten," which can also mean "lowliest" and can therefore be applied to Woyzeck as well as to the little children referred to by Christ. In the context of these Biblical passages, Wittkowski concludes, the Captain and the Doctor are clearly con-demned (302–3). But because Wittkowski's interpretation is partially based on words and passages not actually included or directly referred to in the text, it is indeed of questionable validity.

Wittkowski also bases his view of Woyzeck as a cold-blooded and calculating murderer and his attempt to see in Woyzeck the "chance to imitate Christ, his potential proximity to Christ" on Biblical passages that do not appear in Büchner's text. One such passage follows imme-diately upon the line quoted by Marie in H4,16 ("neither was guile found in his mouth" [1 Peter 2:23]), namely: "Who his own self bare our sins in his own body on the tree, that we, being dead to sins, should live unto righteousness: by whose stripes ye were healed"

(1 Peter 2:24). Also related to Marie's quotation is a passage from Isaiah 53:3–4: "He is despised and rejected of men; a man of sorrows, and acquainted with grief . . . and we esteemed him not. 4. Surely he hath borne our griefs, and carried our sorrows: yet we did esteem him stricken, smitten of God, and afflicted." The passages Marie reads in the Bible refer to Christ but, according to Wittkowski, also to Woyzeck, who should treat the "adulteress" the same way Christ does, telling her: "Neither do I condemn thee; go, and sin no more!" (John 8:11). Likewise, Marie's despairing outcry: "Savior, Savior, I would like to anoint Your feet" expresses her desire to give herself to Christ but supposedly also to Woyzeck: "For Marie everything depends on his [Woyzeck's] coming like Christ and forgiving her. And we feel that he should do it, that he should imitate Christ" (316–19).

In the testament scene, which immediately follows Marie's reading in the Bible and which Wittkowski considers no less a "point of integration" than the Grandmother's tale, Woyzeck receives the call to follow Christ in forgiveness. According to Wittkowski's interpretation, the puzzling line: "Mei Mutter fühlt nur noch, wenn ihr die Sonn auf die Händ scheint" [My mother only feels now when the sun shines on her hands] refers also to Woyzeck: the sun, God's light, shines on him but does not shine into him. He gives to Andres with indifference the cross that was his sister's and the picture of a Saint that was in his mother's Bible. Furthermore, the same religious song that deeply moves Büchner's Lenz, causing him to experience a *unio mystica*, is read laconically by Woyzeck, as if it means nothing to him.

> Leiden sey all mein Gewinst,
> Leiden sey mein Gottesdienst.
> Herr, wie dein Leib war roth und wund
> So laß mein Herz seyn aller Stund
>
> [Let suffering be my reward,
> Through suffering I praise the Lord.
> As your body, Lord, was red and sore,
> Let my heart be for evermore.]

This verse is another call to Woyzeck to take all suffering upon himself as Christ did. But Woyzeck does not understand. Wittkowski sees other evidence for this interpretation in Woyzeck's age, which is the same as that traditionally assumed for Christ when he took up the cross, and in the sacred numbers seven and twelve: "Today I am thirty years, seven months, and twelve days old" (320–22).

Given Marie's desire to be forgiven, it would be easy for Woyzeck to win her, Wittkowski concludes, but he doesn't go to her ("Franz hasn't come! Not yesterday, not today" [H4,6]). With reference to the Fool's words in the same scene: "This one has the golden crown — His Majesty, the King. Tomorrow I'm going to fetch the Queen's child," Wittkowski writes that Woyzeck is the "king" to the "queen," whose child the Fool is going to fetch. "He [Woyzeck] 'has the golden crown,' the innermost possibility of imitating Christ." Woyzeck quotes Christ's words: "Suffer little children to come unto me," but instead of imitating Christ, he emulates King Herod, who is mentioned in the scene in which Woyzeck comes to take Marie to her death: King Herod had his wife executed for adultery and ordered the slaughter of children in Bethlehem (322). As noted above, Wittkowski's fanciful interpretation has attracted considerable attention, but it has not found much acceptance.

In an enlightening discussion of Büchner's aesthetics published in 1979, Friedrich Gaede cites Hans Mayer's claim that "the final root of Büchner's aesthetics is atheism" and adds that such a connection between an author's aesthetics and his view of God is not uncommon. In Büchner's case, his aesthetics, "and with that his atheism," are expressed concretely in the relationship of his figures to nature, society, and history. His demand for life in art is less a call for realistic concreteness than a critical expression of an irreconcilable dualism of mind or spirit (*Geist*) and nature. Gaede considers this dualism to be a fundamental principle of realistic literature. He refers to the attempt by Büchner's Lenz to reconcile lifeless nature and spirit by attempting to bring a dead girl back to life, the failure of which results in his being seized by atheism, whose form of expression is boredom, that is, suffering caused by the absence of meaning or spirit in the world and life. And Lenz's fate is symptomatic for the critical situation of literature in the nineteenth century (43).

The irreconcilability of nature and spirit is the "rent" (*Riß*) in the world or creation of which Danton and Lenz complain. It results in isolation and hence also in hopelessness and loss of faith in the future. This sense of loss and metaphysical homelessness is summed up in a line in which Büchner describes Lenz's situation: "he felt an urge in him; he looked for something as if for lost dreams, but he found nothing" (I.79). According to Gaede, this sentence indicates that realism cannot be defined on the basis of form alone, since it also involves questions of substance. Attempts to define realism based on an unexplained concept of reality culminate in the nineteenth century's postulates of similarity or imitation and are the product of the "post-idealistic loss of substance." Therefore, they do not constitute an explanation of realism but are themselves a manifestation of it (44–45).

Gaede finds the Archimedian point for understanding Büchner's realistic position in his lecture "Über Schädelnerven" (Concerning the Cranial Nerves), in which Büchner notes the chasm between dogmatic, idealistic speculation on the one side and nature and scientific observation on the other, a chasm which has not been and undoubtedly will not be bridged. In his scientific writing Büchner disparages idealist philosophy and its distance from life and nature, but in his poetic works he presents the natural world as being in an equally deplorable and hopeless situation (45).

Whereas Viëtor and others have seen a similarity between Büchner's scientific thinking and Goethe's, Gaede discovers a fundamental difference. For Goethe, reason and nature are not divided by a chasm; they form a unity. Whereas Goethe seeks a general unity or image that is higher than, and realized in, its various manifestations, Büchner attempts to trace all forms back to the most simple primitive type. "The unity that Büchner seeks in the manifold is for him not general but concrete and particular; it is a question of the 'simplest and most definite type.'" This is not an ideal type but is understood concretely. Thus it can only be a beginning type, a kernel from which the subsequent forms develop. But since it remains definite and dominant, it casts doubt on the idea of evolution. The "primitive type" is not only "the original and absolutely necessary," it also persists and is ever present, since for Büchner all complex, higher forms of nature, including man as the "most developed form," are only modifications of the primitive type in a higher power. The brain, for example, is simply a metamorphosis of the spinal column (46–47).

The primitive type is not only the biological root of man, it also determines his substance, a conclusion that, according to Gaede, provides a key to Büchner's aesthetics and literary texts and explains his realism as a counterposition to idealism's concept of reason. To understand human reason as the result of the final modification of the most simple type means to attribute to it a peripheral role, as Büchner does in his letters and works ("Der Verstand nun gar ist nur eine sehr geringe Seite unseres geistigen Wesens . . ." [Reason is only a very small part of our intellectual being: II.422]). From this view derives the pessimism and resignation of Büchner's literary figures and their reduction to the level of animals. The reduction of man to the animal or bestial is one of the expressions of the loss or irrelevance of reason and therefore also of God in Büchner's works and in much of the literature of the period. The self-realization of the human mind degenerates into a natural event as described by Büchner in his letter on fatalism. The only figures in Büchner's works who can be complacent and at one with themselves are those, like Marion in *Dantons*

*Tod* and to a lesser degree Marie in *Woyzeck*, who follow nature and are unconcerned about how destructive this may be for others (47–49).

Büchner's criticism of idealism is based on a misunderstanding or lack of knowledge of philosophical idealism, Gaede maintains, for "no philosophical-literary epoch thought through the problematics of abstract thinking and construction and, connected with that, the question of totality with such intensity as did the idealistic." And Büchner himself is following its lead when he criticizes the cold, distanced observation of nature exhibited by the painter David in his representation of corpses, and when he demands that one overcome the chasm between object and subject through love: "Man muss die Menschheit lieben . . ." [One must love mankind . . .]. Büchner contradicts his own program, Gaede claims, in his representation of people as marionettes or automatons, just as Lenz does in expressing the wish to be the head of Medusa so that he can turn beautiful but transitory images to stone. In what may be a too-literal interpretation of Lenz's metaphor, Gaede writes: "Where Lenz seeks and thinks he has found living beauty, he wants to turn it to stone, in order to capture it artistically, to make 'dead nature' from nature" (50–51).

Gaede compares Lenz's desired result to still-life painting, which has been referred to as "natura morta," and claims that Lenz becomes a victim of contradiction in his search for life, just as Büchner does. Gaede notes that Hegel defines life or living as the contradiction between ideal unity and real separation. As opposed to a lifeless, material being, each part of which can exist on its own, every part of a living body lives only from the union of all its parts. As matter, every part of a living organism exists on its own, but it also lacks independence, since it is part of and dependent upon a whole. Thus a living organism is always a contradictory simultaneity of ideal unity and concrete externality. Life itself is the ideal unity of the organism, ideal because it is the nonsensual bond that holds the material parts together. As a natural *and* social being, man experiences the opposition of mind and nature. Only in art can the contradictory relationship between ideal unity or spirit and concrete externality or nature be reconciled. Büchner was denied this possibility, however, according to Gaede, because he was not able to comprehend the living as a contradictory simultaneity of ideal unity and concrete externality. He identified the living only with the latter (51). One might question Gaede's identification of Lenz's frozen moments with "dead nature," since those moments do not exist in isolation but as part of a larger unity, much as the individual scenes of *Woyzeck* coalesce to form a whole or what might be considered an "ideal unity" consistent with what Büchner describes in his lecture on cranial nerves as a "law of beauty that brings forth the highest and purest forms according to the simplest designs and lines. Everything, form and matter, is . . . bound to this law" (II.292).

# Works Cited

Abutille, Mario Carlo. *Angst und Zynismus bei Georg Büchner.* Basler Studien zur deutschen Sprache und Literatur 40. Bern: Francke, 1969.

Benn, Maurice B. *The Drama of Revolt: A Critical Study of Georg Büchner.* London, New York, Melbourne: Cambridge UP, 1976.

Emrich, Wilhelm. "Georg Büchner und die moderne Literatur." In Emrich's *Polemic*, 131–72. Frankfurt: Athenäum, 1968.

Gaede, Friedrich. "Büchner's Widerspruch — Zur Funktion des 'type primitif.'" *Jahrbuch der internationalen Germanistik* 11 (1979): 42–52.

Grandin, John M. "Woyzeck and the Last Judgment." *German Life and Letters* 31 (1977–78): 175–79.

Hauser, Ronald. *Georg Büchner.* Twayne World Authors Series. New York: Twayne Publishers, 1974.

Henze, Eberhard. "Mensch oder Marionette? Gedanken zu Kleist und Büchner." *Merkur* 21 (1967): 1144–54.

Kobel, Erwin. *Georg Büchner: Das dichterische Werk.* Berlin: Walter de Gruyter, 1974.

Lamberechts, Luc. "Zur Struktur von Büchners 'Woyzeck.' Mit einer Darstellung des dramaturgischen Verhältnisses Büchner-Brecht." *Amsterdamer Beiträge zur neueren Germanistik* 1 (1972): 119–48.

Lindenberger, Herbert Samuel. *Georg Büchner.* Carbondale: Southern Illinois UP, 1964.

Müller-Seidel, Walter. "Natur und Naturwisssenschaft im Werk Georg Büchners." In *Festschrift für Klaus Ziegler*, ed. E. Catholy and Winifried Hellmann, 205–32. Tübingen: Niemeyer, 1968.

Otten, Terry. "*Woyzeck* and *Othello*: The Dimension of Melodrama." *Comparative Drama* 12 (1978): 123–36.

Richards, David G. *Georg Büchner and the Birth of the Modern Drama.* Albany: State U of New York P, 1977.

Schwarz, Alfred. *From Büchner to Beckett: Dramatic Theory and the Modes of Tragic Drama.* Athens, OH: Ohio UP, 1978.

Ueding, Cornelie. *Denken, Sprechen, Handeln: Aufklärung und Aufklärungskritik im Werk Georg Büchners.* Bern, Frankfurt: Herbert Lang, 1976.

Ullman, Bo. "Der unpolitische Büchner. Zum Büchner-Bild der Forschung, unter Berücksichtigung der 'Woyzeck'-Interpretation." *Stockholm Studies in Modern Philology* N.S. 4 (1972): 86–130.

————. *Die sozialkritische Problematik im Werk Georg Büchners und ihre Entfaltung im "Woyzeck," mit einigen Bemerkungen zu der Oper Alban Bergs.* Stockholmer Germanistische Forschungen 10. Stockholm: Almqvist & Wiksell, 1972.

Völker, Ludwig. "Woyzeck und die Natur." *Revue des langues vivantes* 32 (1966): 611–323.

Wiese, Benno von. "Der 'arme' Woyzeck. Ein Beitrag zur Umwertung des Heldenideals im 19. Jahrhundert." In *Texte und Kontexte: Studien zur deutschen und vergleichenden Literaturwissenschaft. Festschrift für Norbert Fuerst,* ed. Manfred Durzak, 309–26. Bern, Munich: Francke, 1973.

————. *Die deutsche Tragödie von Lessing bis Hebbel.* Hamburg: Hoffmann und Campe, 1948.

Wittkowski, Wolfgang. *Georg Büchner. Persönlichkeit. Weltbild. Werk.* Heidelberg: Winter, 1978.

# 5: Recent Criticism: 1980–1999

TWO EVENTS MARK THE BEGINNING of a new period in Büchner scholarship: the founding of the Georg Büchner Gesellschaft in May 1979 and Gerhard Schmid's publication of a facsimile edition of *Woyzeck* in 1981. Also in 1981, in a second special volume of *Text und Kritik* devoted to Georg Büchner, Thomas Michael Mayer, a founder of the Georg Büchner Society, announced in a review entitled "Some New Tendencies of Büchner-Scholarship" that the society's annual publication, the *Georg Büchner Jahrbuch,* would "serve as an organ for taking stock of the current state of scholarship and for new contributions, for reflection and debate, for the documentation of sources, the rapid mediation of controversy and communication of new findings," and would be comprehensive in its inclusion of debate and the results of research (265).

In a study published in 1980, Albert Meier summarizes and continues the trend of the politically oriented seventies to emphasize the socially critical content of *Woyzeck.* Meier sees the play not as a fragment but as an analytical model of a historically determined situation as it relates to an individual. In his view, it is a politically and dramaturgically radical attempt to "represent the historical totality" of Büchner's time (16).

In a brief discussion of the manuscripts Meier concludes that Büchner changed his conception of the play after writing the first sequence of scenes, nearly all of which relate to jealousy and murder. Only the carnival scene and some lines spoken by a barber go beyond this basic plot. With the exception of the figures appearing in the last scene (H1,21), all the figures in this version are from the same social class. The second group of scenes introduces representatives from other social levels, and the various relationships of the figures to each other make possible the "very exact placement of each one into a social system of coordinates." In this context Woyzeck's abnormal behavior no longer appears to be the result of his "sickly exaggerated jealousy" but rather of his social situation, the forces of which do not allow him any autonomy and compel him to work constantly to support his family (24–27).

Whether H2 represents a change in conception or a filling of the gaps does not seem particularly relevant for Meier's interpretation, since he considers H4 to be a synthesis of H1 and H2. In this final version Büchner presents Marie's infidelity, intensifies Woyzeck's jealousy, and at the same time develops their social conditions. Appearing for the first time in this version, Meier claims, is a psychologically accurate connection between unhealthy jealousy and the social situation. Meier finds support for this interpretation in scene H4,4, in which Marie admires her new earrings for the effect they have on her appearance and for their intrinsic value. Woyzeck loses her for two reasons: he cannot acquire social recognition for her, and his work prevents him from being able to spend time with her. He can meet neither her material nor her physical demands. According to Meier, Woyzeck's thought of killing Marie derives not merely from jealousy but also from the social causes of his jealousy and from his ever-increasing isolation. Marie's infidelity undermines his social position and subjects him even more to the ridicule and abuse of his social superiors (30–31).

Also contained in scene H4,4 is Marie's use of "psycho-terror" on her son, by which Meier means her reference to the sandman, which is meant to force the child to self-discipline by creating fear of supernatural punishment. To escape this danger, the child must continually control himself, thus internalizing the supernatural force and becoming accustomed to being controlled by it. This supposedly hinders his ability to resist real danger. Marie thus contributes to the continuation of oppression of her own class; to get her own pleasure she must deprive others of theirs (36).

Furthermore, Meier argues, in possessing something of value, the earrings, Marie becomes isolated; she behaves malevolently toward her child and Woyzeck. Because of their poverty, Marie and Woyzeck find it difficult to maintain a relationship of trust toward each other. Marie feels guilty for possessing earrings, and he believes that her attempt to hide them from him reveals that she has gained them dishonestly. Woyzeck understands the situation immediately and lets her know that he understands, but he does not blame her. In order to forestall his reprimand, she expresses what she knows he is thinking: "Am I a whore?" To avoid direct conflict and preserve their relationship, Woyzeck avoids answering this aggressively stated question, and the issue remains unresolved (37).

Although Woyzeck and Marie are in the same situation, Meier writes, there is no solidarity between them. Both are forced to carry out unwanted and self-destructive acts. Since they do not understand that the contradiction between their way of life and their needs has been forced upon them, their aggression is directed against each other rather than against their oppressors and the social structure. Because of the opposition between rich and poor, Woyzeck is forced to work in order to support Marie and his child, but, Meier claims, work is alienating and self-destructive: it forces Woyzeck to renounce life, and it disturbs his relationship with Marie and the relationship between Marie and her child. Marie suffers its indirect consequence in the disturbance of her inner equilibrium: following Woyzeck's departure she admits to herself: "I really am a whore. I could stab myself" (37–39).

Meier deals in his interpretation only with the scenes that support his thesis, namely, H4,4, H4,14, and the scenes in which the Doctor and the Captain appear. H4,14 is the only scene in which Woyzeck and the Drum Major come directly into conflict. The Drum Major does not stand much higher in the military hierarchy than Woyzeck. Since his function is representational, he wears fine uniforms to make a good impression on the public, a role that alienates him from his "individual, subjective being," according to Meier. Only in the manifestation and recognition of his superiority, which he asserts through aggression and violence, does he experience self-affirmation. The social conflict that runs through the entire play is repeated here: even people belonging to the same class reproduce the social hierarchy in their relations to each other. The bystanders in the inn show no sympathy for one of their own and make no effort to help him. The oppression that one receives is passed on, from one soldier to another, from husband to wife, from parents to children (40–41).

In contrast to most earlier interpreters, who consider the Captain and the Doctor to be representatives of the aristocracy Büchner despised, Meier sees them as representatives, almost allegories, of different socio-political conditions, namely, feudalism and the bourgeoisie, that are in competition with each other. Feudalism obtains its social legitimization from religion, he writes, and in Büchner's day had to rely for support on the material power of the military, since its theological justification had lost much of its effectiveness during the period of Enlightenment. Nevertheless, "irrational thinking based on religious categories and concepts remained the decisive factors in the feudal Weltanschauung." In the Captain's fear of fast, restless motion, Meier sees a representation of feudalism's fear of progress and its desire to preserve the status quo. The Captain's melancholy relationship to time and eternity supposedly expresses feudalism's presentiment of its lack of social function and of the unbearable emptiness that result from the lack of any motion or progress (42–43).

Just as feudalism requires everyone's agreement and cooperation, even if it must be forced, Meier continues, so the Captain needs Woyzeck's agreement and cooperation. He projects his fears, which are socially determined, onto Woyzeck by interpreting his seemingly unhealthy haste as a moral deficiency. The Captain cannot understand the true reason for Woyzeck's condition, which for him must have its source in the conflict of conscience and self-blame that comes from moral guilt. Meier equates the Captain's admonition of Woyzeck to be moral with feudalism's attempt to save itself by imposing its principles on society (42–45).

Whereas the Captain is supposedly an aristocrat and defender of feudalism, the Doctor represents the new order, the bourgeoisie and capitalism. His desire to revolutionize science is the manifestation of a fundamental principle of capitalism, namely, competition. Whereas Woyzeck is subject to the Captain by class and rank, he is subject to the Doctor by contract. In not keeping to his contractual agreement, Woyzeck threatens the whole social system and the Doctor's position in it, according to Meier, since the Doctor's experiment and, indeed, the social order, rely on such contracts. Woyzeck is worse off even than the proletariat, since he is selling his body and not just his labor. Because of his nature, however, he is not completely successful in prostituting himself, which alienates him from ordered society and also from himself, since he wants to fulfill society's demands on him but cannot (47–48). Furthermore, his claim that he cannot resist the demands of nature contradicts the bourgeois faith in reason and free will. As his person is split into body and reason, so nature appears to him "doubled": it seems to be attempting to speak to him in order to save him, but he cannot understand its language. Paradoxically, the illness that is destroying him makes him valuable for the Doctor (48–49).

Like Albert Meier, Bo Ullman, and others, Heinz Wetzel analyzes the different stages of composition in order to determine whether the play is "to be understood as a social drama, which provides insight into the mechanism and the effects of social dependence, or as a representation of the human condition and an inquiry into the meaning of our existence" (1980, 375). In Wetzel's view, each of the major sequences of scenes ends with a scene suggesting that Büchner gained new insight that demanded a change in the conception of the play. The first version resembles a murder ballad (*Mordballade*) in its presentation of a murder committed by a man from the lowest level of society, whose poverty and low social status result in the loss of his beloved. The play ends with the cold-blooded determination by public officials that the murder of Marie was as "beautiful as one can expect." Büchner may have been aware that the theater public could be constituted of a mix of people similar to the one on the stage. It would be witnessing Marie's corpse on the stage, and, since the public is accustomed to judging dramatic conflicts aesthetically, it could view the representation of the murder with the same aesthetic delight as the Court Clerk does. It may then have occurred to Büchner, Wetzel speculates, that the continuation of the murder and court scenes would evoke inappropriate interest on the part of the public. He therefore immediately discontinued the work on this version, realizing that it required greater changes than could be made through simple revision, and began the second version on the same page (377–78, 391–92).

That Woyzeck has changed in the second version is indicated by the change of name from Louis to Woyzeck, Wetzel writes. His response to the supernatural events he experiences now reveals a deeper metaphysical aspect of his fate. His social status takes on much greater importance through the introduction of the Doctor, to whom he is bound by contract, and the Captain, who is superior to him in rank and upon whom he is economically dependent. He needs the money he earns from both to buy Marie's loyalty. Like the first version, this one too breaks off in the middle of a scene, that is, following the mere suggestion of what the scene was to contain, namely, Louisel (=Marie) in prayer. New here is Marie's awareness that she is responsible for Woyzeck's suffering and her expression of Christian morality. Wetzel interprets Büchner's doodling and sketches drawn around the title of the scene as an indication that he again reached a point where he could not continue without making major revisions. Like H1,21, this scene, too, points in a new direction (378–79, 392).

Wetzel sees a tendency to resignation and to suicide in the final version. Since elements from both earlier versions are retained in H4, the image of Woyzeck is now contradictory, he claims. The introduction of Biblical images in connection with Woyzeck's hallucinations indicates a shift from "the unique criminalistic and pathological case of Woyzeck to the case of a man who is not only a plaything of the powerful people of this world but who also recognizes a transcendental power against which he cannot defend himself." According to Wetzel, uncertainty about Marie's infidelity is lacking, since Woyzeck gains certain knowledge of it when he sees her with the earrings (H4,4). He supposedly understands and sympathizes with her because of his insight into the determining force of nature. This explains for Wetzel why Woyzeck's appearance in H4,9 was eliminated: the Captain's reference to Marie's infidelity no longer has any force (379–80). Wetzel's interpretation does not account for the powerful impact on Woyzeck of his discovery of Marie dancing with the Drum Major in the inn scene, a discovery that sets the murder plot in motion.

Woyzeck's resignation, which is especially prominent in the new scenes of H4, calls greater attention to the suicide, which, in Wetzel's view, was the implied conclusion of H2. The Jew from whom Woyzeck buys a knife assumes and thus suggests to the spectator that it is to be used for suicide, though evidence in the play, Wetzel adds, also points to the murder. According to Wetzel, however, Woyzeck's questioning of the voices in H4,12 ("Shall I? Must I?") implies an attempt to resist. Whether Woyzeck commits murder, takes his own life, or both is not as important, Wetzel claims, as the fact that Woyzeck is destroyed by his insight that he cannot resist the forces that determine him. The inner breakdown depicted in the testament scene is so complete that a violent attempt by Woyzeck to resist his fate would no longer be believable. Following this scene, Wetzel writes, "the representation of the possible murder or of the possible suicide would appear trivial." Such an outcome would provide theatrical effect, but it would obscure the social and metaphysical tragedy. Büchner may again have gained an insight that called for another revision of the play (381–82, 395–96).

Given his political and philosophical position, Büchner did not attract the kind of attention one might expect from critics and scholars in the former German Democratic Republic. An exception is Henri Poschmann, who has edited Büchner's texts and dealt with them in books and articles notable for the lack of the polemical and dogmatic tone that is characteristic of many studies by GDR critics. Indeed, his approach is far less obviously Marxist than is Albert Meier's, for example, and that of other scholars from the Federal Republic of Germany. Referring to the ambivalence toward Büchner in the German Democratic Republic, Poschmann writes that he was appreciated for his social revolutionary position, but that his modernity as an artist placed him at odds with the officially-sanctioned Weimar classicism and nineteenth-century realism. Not until the 1980s were critics in the GDR able to consider his politics and aesthetics as a unity (1989, 85–86).

In the wake of the severe criticism of Franzos and his edition of *Woyzeck* that was elicited by the new editions, Poschmann joins those who come to Franzos's defense and recognize the pivotal importance of his contribution to the preservation and transmission of Büchner's works in general and of *Woyzeck* in particular. (Based on the evidence of the testament scene, Poschmann does disagree with Franzos's addition of a stage instruction indicating that Woyzeck drowns. In his view, this scene indicates that Woyzeck anticipates his arrest and execution [1983, 247].) In Poschmann's opinion, the new editions have not included changes of such magnitude as to render earlier interpretations invalid. Indeed, he thinks the text is in danger of disappearing behind the expanding mass of complicated discussions and the scholarly apparatuses dealing with the obscure relationship of the manuscripts and the various text constructions based on them. In Poschmann's view, this problem reaches its extreme in Egon Krause's argument against constructing a playable text and the practice of Bornscheuer and others of leaving it to readers and theater directors to construct their own texts, which begs the issue of a valid text and opens the door to all manner of arbitrarily constructed texts, a temptation directors find hard to resist in any event (1983, 241, 243–4).

Poschmann's own interpretation does not deviate significantly from its predecessors. He sees Woyzeck as belonging to the class of poor people from which the proletariat was recruited: "In a strict social-economic sense he belongs to the semi-proletariat, the latent factory proletariat." Comparison of Büchner's figure with the historical source reveals that the author omitted the elements in the historical Woyzeck which connect him as a deprived craftsman to the petite bourgeoisie and that he developed his character's proletarian attributes as much as possible (252).

In keeping with his materialist perspective, Poschmann does not recognize the existence of a moral conflict in Woyzeck or Marie that derives from their Christian faith. In his view, both figures experience a collision between their natural right to live as and for themselves with alienating and destructive social forces that compel them to actions against others and thereby also against themselves, a clash with a power that Büchner considers to be a fateful reality but not a higher necessity. Marie's so-called prayer scene is misnamed, according to Poschmann, since her attempt to pray fails. She finds no escape into transcendence, no comfort from a merciful, helpful God. She has no religious sense of guilt and sin, Poschmann argues, but secular pangs of conscience. Since she does not accept a value outside of life that is more important to her than life itself, she has no appreciation or taste for self-denial. She cannot "go her way and sin no more" (253–55).

The "inviolable holiness of law," referred to by Clarus in his report, and the holiness of religion and morality lose the appearance of being absolute when confronted with the reality of poor peoples' experience; law and morality reveal their true source, as both Woyzeck and Marie realize, in class difference and the structure of society. If they had money, Woyzeck could be moral and Marie could hold her own in competition with the grand ladies. Through his plebeian figures Büchner reveals the shortcomings of bourgeois society and the need for change, but he does not offer a solution (256–58, 264).

Ingrid Oesterle claims in a 1984 article that *Woyzeck* is related to, but not a pure example of, "Schauerliteratur" (thriller or Gothic literature) and the tragedy of fate. Büchner found inspiration and sources in the works of Ludwig Tieck, E. T. A. Hoffmann, and other romantic writers. Characteristic of this genre is the shift from dominance of vision and the eye to involvement of all the senses: hearing, smelling, touching, and the awareness of temperature and physical pain. Since the source of suffering and anxiety is obscure, mysterious, and incomprehensible, dialogue and communication decrease in importance and language is simplified and loses its literary quality (1984, 169–74, 186–87). From her analysis of the play's first scene, Oesterle demonstrates that *Woyzeck* shares the following structural elements and motifs with Gothic literature: disagreeable and fateful places, bewitched nature (ghostly light phenomena and optical illusions with deadly consequences), the terror of seemingly unnatural appearances and forces such as the Freemasons, terrible stillness, and the sudden change from deathly silence to deafening noise and from darkness to visionary brightness (189–96).

In another article published in 1984, Heinz-Dieter Kittsteiner and Helmut Lethen object to interpretations that seek a "hidden center" and that fill the "empty spaces" beneath the "semblance of a plot," as do Wolfgang Wittkowski (by supplying a Christian content) and Albert Meier (by applying Ingarden's aesthetics). Kittsteiner and Lethen intend, on the other hand, to heed Mercier's advice from *Dantons Tod* and "to follow the phrases to the point they become embodied," that is, to look at what actually is, rather than at what supposedly lies hidden. In their view, Büchner's accomplishment was to "destroy linguistically the meaning-centers around which the thinking of his time circled," an accomplishment that is itself a product of his time, in which thought patterns that were common in the eighteenth century were losing their validity. Büchner rejects the thinking and theories of the Enlightenment and idealism in favor of an "anthropological materialism" (240–42).

In comparison with the historical Woyzeck, who belonged to and wanted to be a part of bourgeois society but was incapable of internalizing bourgeois morality, Büchner has deprived his figure of many of Woyzeck's bourgeois attributes, write Kittsteiner and Lethen. Thus, in disagreement with those interpreters who identify a conflict of conscience in Woyzeck, Kittsteiner and Lethen argue that Woyzeck does not reflect upon his situation and on what is right or wrong; rather, he responds to inner voices and their projection onto the outside world. Büchner agrees with the Romantics in their devaluation of the moral influence of conscience on action and in their recognition of angst as internalized conscience. In depriving Woyzeck of his bourgeois attributes, Büchner does not portray Woyzeck's supposed madness as medical pathology but as a mode of perceiving and understanding the world. The revolutionary implications disappear from this "magical-apocalyptic world view": Woyzeck does not experience a call to rebellion but simply the command to kill (249–52).

According to Kittsteiner and Lethen, the bourgeois ego, which Woyzeck does not possess, views its actions from a moral-philosophical perspective, according to which the world must be thought of as a system of goals in the pursuit of which there is no insurmountable gap between nature and freedom. The world as history is a place for the future realization of morality. History is linear, goal-oriented, and progressive. Büchner appears to adapt an earlier view of history as cyclical. Or perhaps more accurately, his thinking about history is paradoxical, in that, as Maurice Benn and Reinhold Grimm have claimed, he considers it to be both linear and cyclical. The Doctor and the Captain in *Woyzeck* represent these opposing views (255–57).

The Captain suffers from the cyclical nature of time, the eternal and hopeless repetition of the same or similar actions as represented for him by the turning of the mill wheel. He has a "feudal" relationship to time but, seen existentially, he is also modern in his melancholic reaction to the passing of time and in his awareness of the absurdity of life. As indicated by his attempts to slow down Woyzeck and the Doctor, he wants to reduce or escape from the consequences of passing time (258–64). The Doctor, in contrast, is always in a hurry. He wants to move with time and to contribute to the progress of time and history. In the Doctor's view, the Captain and Woyzeck are anachronisms (265–66). According to Kittsteiner and Lethen, the representation of the restive motion of Woyzeck's body shows the conflict in him of the cyclical and linear orientations to time and his lack of an inner regulator that could reconcile the opposing tendencies (266–67).

In a study of accountability in works by E. T. A. Hoffmann and Büchner published in 1985, Georg Reuchlein views *Woyzeck* as a reaction against the fundamental assumptions of restoration psychology and justice upon which Dr. Clarus's evaluations are based, especially the belief that, except in certain extreme cases, people are able through reason and free will to determine their fate and control their actions. Whereas the judicial system in the eighteenth century had tried to separate morality and religion from the administration of justice, lawyers and psychiatrists in the 1920s criticized the separation of moral and juridical judgments. Woyzeck's case provided grist for the mills on both sides of the question. A year after their publication in 1824, Clarus's conclusions were attacked by the Bamberg court physician Dr. Carl Moritz Marc and defended against Marc's attack by Dr. Johann Christian August Heinroth, who, like Clarus, considers the loss of reason to be the consequence of sin and therefore punishable. By caricaturing and criticizing morality, religion, and indeterminism, Büchner discredits and disqualifies the philosophical, ideological foundation of Clarus's and Heinroth's juridical and medical assumptions ( 55–57).

It can be determined from Büchner's play that Woyzeck is not sane and accountable for his violent action, Reuchlein writes, but the actual state of his mind cannot be determined. In the first stage of composition, the signs of Woyzeck's madness follow his discovery of Marie's infidelity and could be considered products of his passion. In H2 and H4, which Reuchlein sees as belonging together in the second stage of composition, these signs precede the discovery and are therefore pathological, a fact that is of such importance that it becomes the focus of the beginning scene of the second version (H2) and, in revised form, of the final one as well. Like the Doctor, Marie and Andres, too, note Woyzeck's disturbed mental state. If Woyzeck is not actually mad, he is at least, as Kanzog writes, psychically stigmatized. In either case, he is not as Clarus sees him. On the other hand, Büchner's depiction of him also departs from the historical facts. Unlike the historical Woyzeck, Büchner's obtains a knife only after he hears voices commanding him to kill Marie, and Büchner's Woyzeck hears the command repeatedly, whereas the historical Woyzeck heard voices only once. Büchner thus emphasizes the compulsive element of the murder (61–63). Because he makes his Woyzeck more moral than the historical murderer, Büchner's text could not have changed the official judgment of Woyzeck, Reuchlein concludes, but it could have had an impact on the public, which was unfamiliar with the factual details. Furthermore, Büchner raises questions about causes, which he finds not only in the individual but also in social relationships. While definite causal relationships cannot be determined — we don't know, for example, what the effect of Woyzeck's diet of peas is — it is clear that blame lies, or also lies, with the social order (69–71, 74–75).

The primary goal of John Guthrie's 1984 study of the dramatic form of plays by Lenz and Büchner is to demonstrate that these playwrights do not have as much in common as has generally been assumed and that Büchner's plays do not fulfill the theoretical demands of the open form of drama as defined by Krapp, Klotz, and others. Guthrie considers it ironic that the theories of the open form of drama, which have influenced subsequent editors and interpreters of the text, were based on Bergemann's edition, whose editorial principles, according to his critics, were based on the closed form of drama. While it is true that Bergemann's edition has been criticized for the contaminations undertaken to strengthen causal connections, this in itself does not result in a text representative of the closed form of drama. Nor should it be assumed, as Guthrie does, that all editors and critics who "assign the play as a whole to the category of the open form" place theory ahead of analysis (121).

At issue here is not the assignment of the play "as a whole" to a particular category, but the identification and analysis of the characteristics peculiar to different and in some ways opposing traditions and forms of drama, namely, the classical and the Shakespearean, the closed and open form, the linear and episodic, or whatever designations one might choose to give them. Klotz does not presume to prescribe what characteristics the forms *must have*: rather, on the basis of his analysis of a number of plays of each type, he identifies characteristics he considers peculiar to each form. Klotz's procedure certainly has greater methodological validity than the one proposed by Guthrie, which is based on his "conviction that theories such as that of the open form do not substantially contribute to an understanding of the play's real, that is to say, dramatic structure" (121).

In opposition to presumed implications of the theory of the open form of drama, Guthrie argues that *Woyzeck* does not consist of a sequence of static images or independent and autonomous scenes that can be rearranged at will without affecting the meaning of the whole (121). But Klotz does not claim that scenes can be rearranged at will. As noted above, those who advocate the arbitrary rearrangement of scenes tend to represent the standpoint of theatrical production and directorial creativity. Likewise, the argument for the play's open ending does not mean, as Guthrie implies, "that a number of endings are possible and can be supported by internal evidence" (121). It means, rather, that no ending is given and none unequivocally foreshadowed by internal evidence. The play ends as it begins: *in medias res*. There are a number of possibilities for what could follow the break in the action, but none of these is specified by the author.

In a scene-by-scene analysis, Guthrie attempts to demonstrate that the plot follows a clear line of development, with each scene having its proper and foreordained place, and that the play therefore belongs to the closed form of drama. "It is argued," he writes, "that because the open form of drama knows no exposition," because scenes are supposedly interchangeable, and because each scene anticipates the conclusion in the same way, it is possible to begin the play "with any, or at least a large number of scenes," an argument that supposedly has been used to justify beginning the play with H4,5, in which Woyzeck shaves the Captain. But Guthrie's assumptions about the implications of the open form are not accurate and the explanation he offers apodictically for the placement of H4,1 is based on subjective criteria: "if one looks carefully at the justification for using H4,1, apart from its authorization in the manuscripts, one finds that it is justified not at all from the point of view of a theory but because it is the best scene to commence with in every conceivable way." And: "In view of the scenes Büchner has left us, however incomplete, this one cannot be bettered as exposition" (122).

In his discussion of the fair scene, Guthrie identifies the middle section between the Barker's speech outside the booth and the Showman's performance inside, that is, the moment in which contact is made between Marie and the Drum Major, as the "most important part of the scene" and "its real body," because it is significant for the development of the plot. "The actual content of the 'Marktschreier's' ranting does not matter as much as this does." Compared to the "serious foreground action," Guthrie claims, the meaning of the Barker's words comparing Woyzeck to a monkey (words actually spoken by the "Ausrufer" rather than the "Marktschreier") "cannot conceivably be evident to an audience at this stage, for the simple reason that we have not seen enough of the main character." The impact of the speeches in this "quasi-episodic element in the plot" differs in nature from that of the rest of the scene, Guthrie claims. "One may suggest that it is a less intense impact, analogous to comic relief in Shakespeare, preparing us for the main point of the scene" (128–29).

Here and elsewhere, Guthrie appears to contradict his own argument by acknowledging the existence of episodic elements in the play, that is, elements peculiar to the open form as defined by Klotz. He identifies H4,9 (Captain. Doctor), for example, as a "pendant-like scene" that "does not forward the plot in the most direct way possible" (134). Likewise, some of scene H1,14 (Margret [= Marie] with Girls in Front of the House) is "not, strictly speaking, part of the development of the plot" (146). Furthermore, some of Guthrie's assumptions regarding the forms of drama are not accurate: he argues, for example, that the scenes are not independent and autonomous because there are manifold connections between them (126), but such interconnection is described by Klotz and others as not only typical of, but essential for the open form of drama, since such connections — Klotz's "metaphorische Verklammerung," and the recurrence of various types of motifs — help create dramatic unity where some of the unifying devices of the closed form of drama are lacking.

More convincing is Guthrie's opposition to the claim that the play's end is implied in every scene or that the structure of the play is circular.

As he, and more recently Burghard Dedner have demonstrated, the plot is characterized by a tight linear and chronological development.

Burghard Dedner joins Guthrie in arguing against the commonly accepted view that *Woyzeck* is an example of the open form of drama and in deploring what he considers to be attempts by editors to make their editions comply with this form. Dedner acknowledges that Büchner follows Shakespeare rather than the classical drama, but with the retention of linear plot development and the strict and condensed sequence of scenes that is characteristic of the latter. Taking exception to the comparison of the structure of *Woyzeck* to the form of a ballad, which he attributes especially to Viëtor, but which, in fact, was quite common in criticism before Viëtor, Dedner claims that the play is not non-linear and does not progress through stations or separate episodes, and that the scenes were not written "helter skelter" (*bunt durcheinander*), as Viëtor maintains, but in sequence. "If the open drama has no continual, uninterrupted plot development," he argues, then the form of *Woyzeck* is closed (1988/89, 163–165). However, by admitting to the inclusion of remnants of folk life such as folk songs and some of the events involving children, and of a number of "interior scenes" such as H4,2, in which Marie observes the Drum Major, H4,3, in which she observes the Barker, and H4,17, in which Woyzeck surveys his life and possessions, Dedner, like Guthrie, undermines his own argument (169). And to his examples could be added others such as the Grandmother's tale and the banter of the journeymen.

Dedner bases his argument on conclusions drawn from what he considers to be a complete manuscript: in his view, the plot as contained in H4 and H1,14–21 — with the possible inclusion of H3,2 — is complete as it stands and does not require further supplementation from earlier drafts (147). In H1 he sees a causally connected sequence of scenes with some passages left open, whether intentionally or not. This manuscript consists of a closed sequence of scenes focusing on the murder and its aftermath and connected by two principles he identifies as "haste" (Hetze) and a "tendency to simultaneity" (Tendenz zur Simultaneität). The scenes are connected by Woyzeck's scurrying from one activity to the next and by an increase in the tempo toward the end. Simultaneity or near simultaneity can be found in several instances where scenes overlap or appear to be taking place at the same time: for example, after Marie has been stabbed in H1,15, her dying sounds are heard by the people coming in H1,16; and scene H1,18 with the children may be taking place at the same time as the inn scene, H1,17. In Dedner's view, both of these "connecting principles" are more developed in H2 and H4, though he admits that some are actually eliminated in the revision of earlier scenes for inclusion in H4 (147–51).

According to Dedner's calculations, the action of the play takes place in as little as forty-eight hours and in no more than three days, which is in keeping with the unity of time of the classical drama. He argues against the transposition of H1,18, which was introduced by Franzos, retained by Lehmann and Poschmann, and defended by Kanzog. In his response to Lehmann's argument that the children would not be up at such a late hour, Dedner echoes an observation made by Patterson in a 1978 study of the play's duration, which Patterson estimates to be four days, namely, that it "depends on a rather middle-class view of bringing up children" (Patterson 1978, 120). Not all children are so disciplined as to be in bed two hours after dark, Dedner argues, and that would be especially true on an evening in which the news of a murder would spread quickly through crowded quarters, creating a special situation in which the children would likely share the excitement and desire to witness the murder scene. As indicated above, H1,18 could be taking place at the same time as H1,17, and it establishes a connection between H1,16 (the arrival of people at the pond and discovery of the murder) and H1,19, in which people responding to the news of the murder arrive at the pond and scare off Woyzeck, who has returned to the scene of the crime. Furthermore, Dedner continues, H1,18 reflects the immediate, sensational reaction to the murder, which would have diminished somewhat by the following morning, and it gives Woyzeck time to get from the inn to the pond (Dedner 155–57).

As for other problematic passages, Dedner notes that even though the Captain's reference to Marie's infidelity in H2,7 is represented in H4,6, he still thinks it probable that Büchner would have added Woyzeck's appearance in H4,9, but he would have had to change it to agree with the new situation in which Woyzeck has already seen the Drum Major with Marie or leaving her house (154–60). Dedner seems to agree with Poschmann that H3, or at least H3,2 (The Idiot. The Child. Woyzeck) was written after H4, that H3,2 authorizes the murder sequence H1,14–21, and that it corresponds to an increasing tendency on Büchner's part to "individualize figures from the folk." In Dedner's view, H3,2 should follow H1,20, Woyzeck's entry into the pond, to which the Idiot supposedly refers with his finger-counting game. With respect to H3,1, The Doctor's Courtyard, Dedner agrees with Müller-Seidel, Paulus, and Richards that this scene cannot be placed before the end of H4, where it no longer has any purpose. Since the comic content of H3,1 is on a lower level than that of H4, it appears that H3,1 precedes H4 and was superseded by it (161–63).

In a paper presented at a 1987 colloquium at the University of Aalborg, Denmark, and published in 1988, Swend Erik Larsen identifies three components in the phenomenon of power and powerlessness in *Woyzeck* and *Lenz*:

> — the concrete *event* in which power and powerlessness meet and where the strength of power is tested,
>
> — the *structures* that determine the forms of confrontation,
>
> — consciousness which the parties or persons involved possess of the connection between structure and event. (1988, 176; author's emphasis)

Larsen claims that reflection about oppression and the abuse of power emanates from every sentence in the play. The event he chooses to analyze in detail is the scene in which Woyzeck shaves the Captain (H4,5). In this scene Woyzeck is clearly inferior and subordinate to the Captain, who demonstrates his superiority in various ways: he gives orders, comments on Woyzeck's private life, makes fun of him, and instructs him. During the course of the scene, however, Woyzeck gains the upper hand, which distresses and confuses the Captain. His replies to the Captain, which are at first short and automatic, become longer, and his participation in the dialog becomes more active. He gives an unexpected twist to the Captain's religious allusions, for example, and raises the issue of money in relation to morality (176–77).

The Captain's loss of ground is manifest also in the use of personal pronouns. He begins addressing Woyzeck in the third person singular "Er" rather than with the "Du" or "Sie" that would be used with a person of similar status. Accepting his inferior role, Woyzeck avoids the use of pronouns in addressing the Captain: to refer to the Captain as "Sie" would presuppose considering himself as an "ich," Larsen claims, as a person with a right to speak. Only when Woyzeck begins to seize the initiative in the conversation does he address the Captain as "Sie" and begin, tentatively at first, to assert his own individuality: after first speaking about poor people in general and using the plural pronoun "wir" and the impersonal "man," he finally speaks in the first person singular. The scene ends with the Captain apparently accepting the "partial identity" between himself and Woyzeck, both of whom are "good men." Thus the hierarchy breaks down on the verbal level, according to Larsen, and, because his power stands on shaky feet, the Captain identifies with Woyzeck. Woyzeck does not take advantage of the Captain's weakness in order to undermine his power, however, but to define his own difference and in a subjective way to confirm the hierarchy of power. Woyzeck is conscious of and accepts his position in the power-structure (177–78).

Because of their cynical arbitrariness, writes Larsen, the representatives of power are dangerous, and because of their neurotic narrowmindedness, they are also ridiculous. They possess real power, but it is power they have not earned and do not deserve. It is a "perverse-routinized extension" of a power that may once have served a useful purpose but has now lost its meaning and function in a new and different social context, where it continues to function for its own sake. When power is no longer part of a total structure and no longer contains any vision, Larsen writes, those who exercise that power live in a "partial universe" that only includes themselves and not the totality. Hence we experience them in the "here and now" where they are threatened by that which they would dominate, the Captain by Woyzeck and his craftiness, the Doctor by nature and arbitrariness. For his part, Woyzeck also identifies with the Captain, Larsen maintains, and behaves like him as the master in his own partial world. And just as the Doctor views Woyzeck as his property, so Woyzeck views Marie as his. When Marie asserts her independence, Woyzeck's identification with the other persons of power moves him to kill her (179–81).

Conclusions similar to Larsen's are reached by Richard T. Gray, who, borrowing a phrase from Max Horkheimer and Theodor Adorno, analyzes the "dialectic of enlightenment" in Woyzeck. While the Enlightenment purports "to provide the means for the emancipation of humanity from the obscurity of myth," according to Horkheimer and Adorno, it "ultimately reveals itself to be a more insidious manifestation of myth itself" (1988, 79). Büchner had similar insight, Gray maintains, and this manifests itself in his skepticism toward the transition from a holistic science to the purposive-rational approach that was coming into prominence in his time. He finds confirmation for his "worst suspicions about the potential inimicality of reason to life" in Clarus's report on Woyzeck, which was not only the source of Büchner's play but the "true impetus behind the entire conception of the work." Büchner is less interested in Woyzeck himself than in the way Clarus portrays him. The aim of Büchner's fragments, Gray writes, "is to reflect critically on the 'dogmatism of reason' as manifest in the Clarus report with the goal of bringing enlightenment to reflect on itself" (80–81).

In his diagnosis of Woyzeck's motivation to commit murder, Clarus asserts the dominance of reason over emotion in the same absolute manner as Büchner's Doctor, a caricature of Clarus. Like the Doctor in *Woyzeck*, Clarus valorizes "freedom of will" and "the free use of reason" without ever questioning the appropriateness of these values for the uneducated and underprivileged Woyzeck; he condemns Woyzeck based on Enlightenment conceptions about human beings. Clarus assumes that Woyzeck is capable of reasonable thinking and that his will is free, but that he misuses his reason in a perverse manner. Whereas pure insanity, the complete absence of reason, may be accepted, the hybrid between reason and unreason, the "confusion of subjective feelings with objective conceptions," in the words of Clarus, undermines the integrity of reason itself and threatens to overturn the relationship between subject and object on which scientistic reason is based (81–82).

Clarus's position, Gray argues, "can be read as an unwitting condemnation of the socioeconomic order responsible for Woyzeck's 'limited means.'" Clarus objects to Woyzeck's "inherently underprivileged status in society, his lack of formal education, his poverty, his 'moralische Verwilderung' [moral degeneration]." According to Gray, Clarus reveals in his report that he is possessed of the very qualities he condemns in Woyzeck, namely, a specific set of prejudices, false judgments, and errors. Consequently, when he passes judgment on Woyzeck as a curious hybrid of reason and unreason, he is also passing judgment on himself. He exemplifies the "merging of myth and enlightenment, or the reversion of enlightenment to myth" that is the central thesis of Horkheimer's and Adorno's critique of enlightenment (82–83).

Gray suggests that Büchner's reading of Clarus's report was similar to his own reading based on theories of Horkheimer and Adorno. In *Woyzeck* Clarus's pedagogical and scrutinizing gaze is itself subjected to a scrutinizing gaze, "the gaze of dramatic spectatorship." Büchner's drama "assumes the spectatorial gaze of enlightened reason only in order to turn it against this reason itself." In this regard the carnival scenes are of central importance. Carnival inherently involves inversion and destabilization of authoritative values, and it possesses revolutionary potential. In his carnival scenes Büchner introduces dominant societal values in a context that mocks and overturns them. Clarus's idealized vision of rational human beings is mocked by the grotesque hybridization of reason and unreason as represented by a variety of trained animals. The Barker's ironic praise of reason in this scene is simultaneously its denunciation. This figure therefore embodies the "dialectic of enlightenment" in the same way Clarus does and provides skeptical comment on the attitudes he represents. The "self-ironization and self-condemnation of reason is put on display" in this scene, and the audience is "invited to witness this event in all its grotesqueness." The Captain and the Doctor are noncarnivalesque counterparts of the

Barker and represent in stylized exaggeration the enlightened bourgeois values of Clarus (84–85).

When we critically overturn Clarus's metaphysical privileging of reason in the classical duality of reason and unreason, free will and necessity, "then Woyzeck's hybridization ceases to signify the failure of enlightenment and instead indicates its incipient and insidious victory." Woyzeck's murder of Marie does not indicate the failure of reason to control passion, Gray argues, but becomes an expression of the enlightened will to mastery. Woyzeck thus represents the "attempted coming to enlightenment of myth." Following a different line of argument, Gray reaches a conclusion similar to Larsen's: in reaction to his exploitation and oppression Woyzeck appropriates the "same structures of mastery and control under which he suffers as a strategy for his own liberation." Marie's behavior toward her child constitutes a similar attempt at mastery and control. It is behavior characteristic of most of the figures in the play: the oppressed become the oppressors (88–90, 94).

An increasing tendency among critics who emphasize the play's socially critical content has been to identify Dr. Clarus as a callous, inhumane, and morally rigid practitioner of medicine and as a servant of the state and the people with power who stand to benefit from keeping the common people poor and powerless. In the extreme, this criticism has considered the Doctor in *Woyzeck*, and by implication the historical figures he caricatures — the anatomist Johann Bernhard Wilbrand and the chemist Justus Liebig, both of whom were professors at the University of Giessen when Büchner was a student there, as well as Clarus himself, who was also a university professor — as precursors of the doctors who carried out grotesquely inhumane experiments on people in Nazi concentration camps. Dorothy James places this matter in the proper perspective in a 1990 essay by considering Clarus's judgment and the positions represented by him and by Büchner's Doctor in the context of the time in which Büchner was writing. While the play's form belongs more to the twentieth century than to Büchner's time, she writes, it contains "real and documentable threads" that connect it to both time periods (119), a claim she supports with ample documentation.

Woyzeck was indeed an "interesting case" in his own time, James argues, a time in which the nature of man and his behavior was the topic of considerable disagreement and debate. On one side of the issue was Dr. J. C. A. Heinroth, a supporter of Dr. Clarus's conclusions, who was convinced that man stands above the animals because he has reason and can choose to be free. Consciousness and reason can lead him to God; if he does not take this path, it is his own fault and a sin. Heinroth considers illness to be the result of sin, which agrees with Clarus's conclusion that Woyzeck's dissolute life led to his downfall. When he committed the murder, Woyzeck was not controlled by a "necessary blind and instinctual drive," that upset his "free use of reason," Clarus concluded. He therefore exercised free will and was responsible for his action (113–14).

Clarus and Heinroth represented a minority position even in their own time, according to James, who cites Professor Johann Christian August Grohmann as a leading proponent of the opposing side of a heated debate. Grohmann maintained that the human being is not "essentially free" or "essentially rational." He may have raised himself above the animals by virtue of his intellect and reason, but he has not eliminated the animal forces in himself. His animal nature is particularly evident in the various drives aimed at the survival of the species. The will is influenced by physical as well as intellectual needs: circumstances can brutalize men and incline them to the bestial side of human nature. In such circumstances, the human being no longer exercises free will but is rather the victim of sickness that attacks not only the body but also the spirit and the will, upon which it has a brutalizing effect. "Is the death penalty possible in such circumstances as punishment," he asks, "or is the animal simply to be sacrificed?" Grohmann disagreed with Clarus's verdict on Woyzeck, and he certainly opposed the punishment, which was described by J. B. Friedrich, a contemporary authority on criminal justice, as "a terrible judicial murder" (115–16).

James notes that the diagnosis of Woyzeck provided by Büchner's Doctor is not unreasonable in the context of contemporary systems of classifying mental disease, though his "outspoken relish in pronouncing his diagnosis to the disturbed man himself" is unreasonable, even grotesque. "Fixed ideas" were considered at the time to be partial mental disturbances or madness. Particularly in the early part of the nineteenth century they were associated with melancholy, which was defined by the French authority Dr. Philippe Pinel as a "delirium attached to an object." As James writes, fixed ideas "involved a confusion of the subjective and the objective, the subject being convinced that a given fantasy attached to an object was literally true. It was much debated whether a person's derangement could really be limited to one area or object." If so, could a person be considered sane in all other aspects of his life? If a person suffered from partial or periodic insanity associated with fixed ideas, he presumably could not be held accountable for acts committed when in that state, but what about behavior during the periods in which the person's behavior appeared to be normal and responsible? Clarus addressed this point in his report and concluded that Woyzeck's reason was never overpowered by "an incorrect or overwrought concept of the objects of the physical or transcendental world or by the conditions of his own physical and moral personality" such that the "free perspective for other conditions was distorted and the proper assessment of them obscured." In other words, he did not suffer from fixed ideas and was therefore accountable for his actions. Had Clarus's diagnosis agreed with that of Büchner's Doctor, Woyzeck's life would have been spared, which is not to say that Büchner is not mocking the Doctor and his disregard for the well-being and humanity of his fellow men (105–107).

James proposes an additional model for Büchner's Doctor, the one he was closest to and knew best: his own father, who also functioned as a court doctor and wrote expert opinions for the court, some of which were published (109–110).

Finally, James discusses the debate taking place in Büchner's time concerning the nature of animals, in particular the seemingly human attributes of animals that perform tricks, as do the animals in Büchner's carnival scene. Do animals have souls, imagination, feeling, free will, a form of language, or are they simply machines? This debate connects to the emerging evolutionary theory that appalled defenders of free will such as Heinroth and Clarus (117). "It is not a coincidence," James writes,

> that Grohmann, who viewed Woyzeck as a victim of social and environmental circumstances and of physiological determination, was "evolutionary" in his thinking, rejecting as early as 1820 teleological explanations of evolution which Büchner later mocked in his *Woyzeck*, and which he seriously combatted in his lecture "Über die Schädelnerven." (118)

As a number of critics have pointed out, the focus on Woyzeck given by the play's title is an editorial construct, since there is no mention of a title in the manuscripts or any of Büchner's letters. It is conceivable that Büchner's title for the play would have included Marie's name along with Woyzeck's, as is the case with *Leonce und Lena*. And while Woyzeck has certainly been at the center of most criticism, a number of critics have recognized the tragic dimension of Marie's fate and have exonerated her and placed the blame on Woyzeck and society, which has instilled in him the notion of erotic possessiveness (e.g. Ullman 1972, 80; cf. Larsen and Gray above). Those efforts have not been enough for feminist critics, however, who consider criticism of the play to be unbalanced in favor of Woyzeck and a patriarchal view of the world, and who turn their attention to Marie.

Taking her cue from a performance of the play in Sydney, Australia in which the actor playing Woyzeck rammed his knife up between

Marie's legs and later commented in an interview that "it felt good to kill Marie in this manner because he, Woyzeck, had been dependent on Marie's sexuality for too long" (294), Kerry Dunne sets out in an article published in 1990 to demonstrate that Marie is as much a victim as Woyzeck. In her sexuality Marie is subject to the demands of her nature just as Woyzeck is when he pisses on the wall or when he creates a child without the blessings of the church. In addition, she is also a victim of her sexual attractiveness and desirability. In Dunne's view, Büchner's aim is to rehabilitate sexuality as a meaningful and natural part of human existence, but to do so would have required that Woyzeck be brought to trial and sentenced, which would have repudiated the so-- cietal values upon which the murder was based, namely, the assumption that women are men's possessions (294, 304–7).

Noting the recent attention given to love and sex in Büchner's works and to the female figures as those most clearly linked with love and the depiction of sexuality, Dunne intends to fill what she considers to be the need for a more detailed study of the play's sexual imagery. She considers Marie to be a parallel figure to the Drum Major and the Sergeant: each uses animal imagery and refers to parts of the body in responding to the physical appeal and animal vitality of the other. Marie's reference to the Drum Major's beard, for example, has symbolic associations with male virility and pubic hair, Dunne maintains, which betray the erotic nature of her interest. The Sergeant's comment about her heavy dark hair shows he is "responding to her sensual appearance and his statement that its weight could pull her down, indicates not only the abundance of hair, but is also perhaps an indirect expression of his desire to see her lying beneath him." The Sergeant's stress on the blackness of Marie's eyes suggests "the physiological response of enlarged pupils during sexual arousal," Dunne interprets rather fancifully. The reference to her hair dragging her down also implies that her sexuality could be her downfall, and the reference to her black eyes introduces the notion of death (296–97).

The Drum Major amplifies on his colleague's implied innuendoes when he compares looking into her eyes with looking into a chimney or a well, "images which suggest an underlying image of the vagina." Also having vaginal connotations, according to Dunne, are references to Marie's mouth and lips. As he is about to kill her, Woyzeck refers to her hot lips and the attraction they still have for him. Earlier, when he begins to suspect her, he refers to her red mouth and looks at her lips for a blister that would be evidence of her infidelity. "Blisters are traditionally a symbol of deceit," Dunne writes, but could also be an allusion to a lesion from a sexually transmitted disease. In killing Marie,

Woyzeck is not inflicting punishment for sin — he says he would forgo heaven in exchange for kissing her — he is acting out of sexual jealousy, as is indicated by his repeated stabbing of her body with the knife, which also suggests to Dunne "the phallic revenge on female sexuality that has castrated the owner (by preferring another lover)" (296–99, 304).

Most of these images point to a positive view of sexuality, Dunne writes. Since the imagery used in connection with Marie is similar to that used for the Drum Major, one cannot say that Marie or women are denigrated in Büchner's portrayal. His view of Marie and her fate is also indicated by his choice of her name, which refers both to Mary Magdalene and to the Virgin Mary. The choice of this name "suggests an authorial caution to the reader/viewer against the division of women into the pure and the carnal." It has been suggested that Marie exploits her attractiveness and sexuality, the only bargaining power a poor woman has in a class-ridden, patriarchal society, to gain financial support from Woyzeck and to better her social standing through the Drum Major. But while Marie has indeed exploited her sexuality to obtain financial support from Woyzeck, Dunne argues, the images she uses to describe the Drum Major indicate that her involvement with him is not motivated merely by a desire to better herself but also by her sexual needs (298–99).

Dunne identifies two different types of cultural knowledge that determine the moral views of the play's characters: one derived from folksongs, in which the existence of female sexuality is acknowledged and in part celebrated, and which reflect "the existence and power of sexuality in a relatively playful, non-judgmental manner," and one derived from Christianity, which regards female sexuality as threatening and evil. It is the latter that prevents Büchner from rehabilitating the physical and sexual. Woyzeck and the Drum Major share the Christian view: the Drum Major asks whether the devil is in her, and Woyzeck views her as a sinner. Licentiousness, evil, and destruction are linked in Woyzeck's vision of Sodom and Gomorrah in the beginning scene, in his reaction to seeing Marie and the Drum Major dancing, and in his linkage of female sexuality with the devil in the final inn scene. The reason Woyzeck kills Marie rather than the Drum Major, Dunne writes, is that he acts not merely out of jealousy but as the instrument of punishment in a patriarchal society that considers female sexuality to be especially sinful and threatening and in which women are regarded as possessions. Even Marie herself is unable to embrace her sexuality in an unfettered way, as Marion does in *Dantons Tod*. Following her conflict with Margret, her neighbor, she accepts society's attitude toward her in referring to her child as a "whore's child," and following Woyzeck's discovery of her with the earrings she calls herself a whore (*ein schlecht Mensch*). And when she cannot resist the Drum Major's advances, she longs in vain to be able to follow the example of the repentant Mary Magdalene (295, 300, 302–6).

Countering the devaluation of the physical and sexual within society is the admonition by the Barker to accept our animal nature. Woyzeck is torn between the two views: in defending himself against the Captain and the Doctor, he considers his poverty and the demands of his nature to be excuses for his "immoral" behavior, but he accepts the views of society as represented by his oppressors when he punishes and takes revenge on Marie for her sin. Without explaining how or why, Dunne claims that if Woyzeck were to have been "brought to trial and sentenced, then not only would the overall importance of societal values be different but Woyzeck would be punished," an outcome resulting in a view of sexuality more in accordance with that represented by Marion (302–306).

Writing in the same year as Dunne, Elisabeth Boa, too, notes the incongruity between Woyzeck's appeal to nature in defense of his performance of bodily functions and his inability to see Marie's transgression in the same light, namely, as nature "in revolt against a life denuded of pleasure," but Boa places greater blame on class structure and social conditions. In her view, both Marie and Woyzeck are subject to brutal assertions of power by those who treat them as instruments to be exploited: the power of knowledge and science represented by the Doctor and the power of a repressive morality represented by the Captain. Another contributing factor is the "antithetical structuring of masculinity and femininity," which includes the sexual division of labor in which Woyzeck and Marie are caught up — he to provide for his family, she to mother their child — and the sexual antagonism that is created by this division. In a patriarchal society, men have exclusive right of ownership of the female body, and mothers are not supposed to feel sexual desire. The allocation of power to men provokes Marie's reaction and her willingness to use her sexuality as a vehicle of power, though internalized religious teachings make her feel guilty. Furthermore, Boa writes, the sexually active woman in a patriarchal society provokes a violent reassertion of male dominance and the barbaric reassertion of his masculinity, as is the case when Woyzeck murders Marie. As long as the sexes remain divided, social justice is impossible (1990, 174–77).

Contrary to Dunne's reading of the folk songs as an affirmation of sexuality, Laura Martin sees them in an article published in 1997 as representing an ideology according to which loose women represent a social problem. Martin claims that Marie's sexual promiscuity "indicates her belief in herself as a free agent," which goes against patriarchy's ownership of women. Woyzeck is not destabilized by his diet of peas or the other abuse he suffers as a poor man but by Marie's refusal to be controlled by him, or by "her ignorance that she is to be considered his property, his chattel" (436). The contribution of Christianity is not different from that of the folk songs, according to Martin, though it is less light-hearted, and it introduces the concept of sin and retribution. In applying the Biblical concepts, Woyzeck becomes "the prophet of the apocalypse" (436–37).

With reference to René Girard's book *Violence and the Sacred*, Martin considers Marie to be an example of the scapegoat whose sacrifice Girard considers to be the foundation of every religion. The scapegoat must be similar to the real or potential perpetrators of violence in order to substitute for them, but it must also be different enough not to threaten the commonality. "What better victim, then, than a woman?" Martin asks. "A woman is the same, but different, other." The scapegoat must be sufficiently other for its sacrifice not to require revenge, a demand fulfilled, Martin claims, by the loose woman. The "sacrificial crisis" preceding the act of sacrifice is a communal situation in which distinctions have been erased, according to Girard. Martin finds such a loss of distinctions in the play's repeated equation of animal and human, and in the supposed loss, or at least confusion, of class distinctions that occurs here in the false application of bourgeois morality to a member of the proletariat. The Doctor's and Captain's "nagging" of Woyzeck is inappropriate and misplaced, Martin maintains, "for it assumes a sameness of outlook and lifestyle between these two classes which simply does not exist." In fact, Marie and Woyzeck have no need to be as "moral" as the Doctor and the Captain, since "Kantian moral free will is . . . contingent on class and upbringing." Finally, distinction between the sexes also begins to blur: Marie is "uncharacteristically active for a woman character." She is closer to Faust than to Gretchen in her masculine will to experience pleasure. Woyzeck, on the other hand, is passive, lacking in will power, and effeminate. He is easily victimized by the real men in what Martin calls their "thirst for violence" (437–38, 441).

Martin weakens her argument by pointing out that the act of sacrifice in Girard's sense is a communal activity, whereas Woyzeck acts alone. "The Girardian sacrificial crisis cannot ever be resolved in the play, for there is no unanimity in the choice of the victim: at times it appears to be Woyzeck himself, yet he chooses his own victim in the

form of Marie." Thus the choice of Marie as scapegoat, which Martin
has considered so obvious, is

> not unproblematic, and it is in fact on this paradox that the play turns.
> Only if all those involved were to agree on the necessity of her death
> could the play be a tragedy in the ancient sense of that word. All the
> evils threatening the social order would be heaped upon Marie's
> shoulders and Woyzeck would be the hero for ridding society of the
> unclean thing. (439)

But of course Woyzeck himself is an outcast whose deed is not celebrated by society but condemned and punished. In our time of "objective justice," the sacrifice of an ignorant and unstable fool like Woyzeck
can no longer be accepted as a legitimate means of eliminating violence
from society. Thus, neither Woyzeck nor Marie can serve as a proper
scapegoat. The conclusion, then, with respect to Girard's theory is that
it is impossible to find the perfect victim in a society that lacks "consen-
sus and a community of faith" (439).

Martin nevertheless tries to defend her hypothesis by claiming that
Marie succeeds in her role as victim. She is the only one of Woyzeck's
tormentors to accept any guilt for the effect her actions have on him,
and in saying that she could stab herself, she reveals a readiness for self-
sacrifice. Readers and audiences seem willing to recognize her suitabil-
ity as a sacrificial victim: "violence against a woman is disapproved of,
yet understood, and therefore actually effectively condoned." The
community that condemns Woyzeck is the same one that spurred him
on to the deed. Marie's spilt blood becomes a purifying libation to the
gods. She becomes "the scapegoat for crimes not committed by her,
but by her supposed social superiors, if anyone. *Woyzeck* then is not so
much about the victimization of the hero as it is the portrait of the development of the violent criminal — or of the accession to manhood in
our rotten society" (439–40, 442).

In a study of Woyzeck published in 1991, Edward McInnes comes
closer to Boa than to Dunne in the emphasis he places on the social
dimension of Marie's attraction to the Drum Major. With his fine
clothing and ability to give her a valuable gift — she thinks the earrings
could be gold — he represents for her a higher social standing and af-
firms her view of herself as equal to the grand ladies. According to
McInnes, the Drum Major senses from the beginning a strong impulse
of revolt in Marie's responses to him, and he is able to exploit it for his
own ends. In strutting before her and referring to the Prince's admira-
tion of his manliness, he impresses on her that he is socially sophisti-
cated and successful and that he is at ease in all strata of society. The
gift of the earrings confirms his status as a man of some means. In se-

ducing her, he is able to take advantage of her dissatisfaction with her social status and her frustration with her narrow and demeaned existence. In yielding to his seduction, McInnes argues, Marie not only expresses her strong sensuality, she also reveals a strong impulse of social rebellion and revolt (1991, 21–23).

As opposed to his emphasis on the social dimension of Marie's situation, McInnes considers the murder to be an entirely personal matter concerning Woyzeck and Marie alone, and he downplays the importance of the Captain and the Doctor as vehicles of social protest. They may be seen to "embody a strong socially enforced authority," he writes, but "both are in reality anguished men, each in his own way ravaged by a deep sense of existential horror and apprehension." They are "torn by feelings of inner emptiness and of their estrangement from a world in which they can see no ultimate sustaining meaning." Büchner seeks through them "to lay bare a disabling sense of metaphysical desolation which neither can fully articulate much less confront" (31, 47).

In his 1994 *Georg Büchner: The Shattered Whole*, the first book-length study of Büchner published in English since the 1970s, John Reddick follows a trend of recent scholarship to establish more fully and accurately the intellectual, cultural, social, and political contexts that provide a background for evaluating and interpreting Büchner's works. Reddick discusses in four introductory chapters some of the primary elements of Büchner's thought and art. Although Büchner's artistic vision is disjunctive with its insistence on fragments and particles, he believed in the fundamental unity and wholeness of nature, and this, Reddick claims, locates him in the German tradition of *Naturphilosophie*, which was already outdated at the time (9). Consequently, Reddick considers Büchner to be "hopelessly remote from the prevailing spirit of his time" in his "reliance on idealist, poetical, mystical notions" and his rejection of rationalist philosophy and mechanistic science (39–40). The manner of his writing is "inexorably un- and anti-classical," but "the faith and vision that underlies it is classical almost to the point of anachronism" (13). Reddick considers Büchner to be involved in a "Rearguard Action," as his second chapter is entitled, and dismisses Büchner's often-quoted pronouncement on fatalism as "the sonorous trumpeting of a transient mood" (29), a reading that is based not on evidence from the text but on the fact that Büchner did not cease his political activity after supposedly gaining this shattering insight. He identifies a similar contradiction or paradox in the discrepancy between Büchner's scornful dismissal of intellect and learning and his relentless pursuit of knowledge. Reddick finds similar inconsistencies in the main figures of Büchner's works; they appear to be part of the fullness and quickness of life Büchner wants to capture in his art and that he opposes to the marionettes of idealist art, whose mechanistic obsessions and behavior he caricatures in such figures as King Peter in *Leonce und Lena* and the Doctor and the Captain in *Woyzeck* (50).

Fundamental to Büchner's thought, Reddick writes, is his affirmation of life and his emphasis on the individual, each of which is a valuable manifestation of a primal law and exists in and of itself. ("Everything that exists, exists for its own sake" [II.292].) He is antagonistic to every kind of anti-life force or process. King Peter in *Leonce und Lena* is satirized for his anti-life philosophizing, the Doctor, Büchner's "most savagely satirical stooge," for his "anti-life scientizing" (43, 46). The Doctor sacrifices his patients to an excess of science. He is not interested in helping suffering individuals but rather in promoting his own self-interest. At the same time, he is also a laughable victim, who is demented by his own version of the fixed idea he diagnoses in Woyzeck. In speaking of freedom of will to the man he has enslaved, he contradicts and refutes his own theories, as he does also in praising individuality while denying the existence of individuals, who for him are reduced to the status of specimens or cases (46–49).

The Captain represents a variant on the comic model of power, according to Reddick. He plays a role similar to King Peter's: both figures occupy the supreme power position within their respective plays, Reddick writes, "but in comic contrast to the might and mantle of their positions, both of them are puny and petrified, and utterly dwarfed by their ostensible victims." Both are easily thrown into confusion, and they share a sense of fear, which is at once existential and the product of thinking. As has been frequently pointed out, the Captain is more complex and interesting than the Doctor, since he is "stricken by glimpses of an abyss that in varying forms critically affects the destinies of all Büchner's central characters." Because he fears infinitude and eternity, time appears monstrous to him. As opposed to Woyzeck, he behaves as an abject coward in his avoidance of the abyss and in his attempts to seek refuge in artificial constructs such as specious morality and a measured routine of unhurried activity (50–52).

Reddick cautions against taking any particular speech or argument as the play's ultimate truth. The statements by Woyzeck and Marie relating to poverty, for example, are not sufficient, in his view, to characterize the play as a social drama. In fact, Büchner's Woyzeck is much better off than his historical counterpart: he has some income, a place to stay, and a familial relationship with Marie and their child, none of which was true for the historical Woyzeck. The first draft of the play contains no sign of poverty, the second, not much more. In H4 Büchner thematizes poverty and projects it in class terms, but it is not a central issue. Furthermore, Reddick continues, Woyzeck contradicts himself no less than does the Doctor: in defending himself against the Captain for his illegitimate child and against the Doctor for his inability to control his bladder, he cites the demands of nature, but, as the feminist critics point out, he condemns and punishes Marie for yielding to the demands of her nature. Likewise, the words of the Barker relating to the animal nature of man and the words of the Journeyman concerning the teleological view of life are not meant to be swallowed whole. At issue in the play, according to Reddick, are "questions of civilization as against nature; moral choice as against animal compulsion; responsibility and accountability; crime and punishment; sin and retribution." Büchner conjures up a context that "challenges the very idea of humanity, society, civilization" (304–308).

Büchner's concern is with the nature of man; the whole play can be seen as a kind of "*Ecce homo.*" According to Reddick's count, the word "Mensch" (man, mankind), which, apart from proper nouns and titles, is the most frequently used noun in all Büchner's poetic writings, appears 78 times in *Woyzeck*, which is considerably more than in *Dantons Tod* (29 times) and *Leonce und Lena* (34 times). The personae are not presented as "quirky individuals caught up in the specificity of their particular personality and history, but emblematically, as archetypes" (336). (Reddick sees the interspersion of song fragments as a device that encourages us to see the story in archetypal terms [337–44].) Woyzeck's story can be understood in the terms of the child's questions in the Grandmother's tale as to the what and the why of man. He is more profoundly tormented than any other of Büchner's protagonists by the gulf "between thinking and knowing, between subject and object, between the lonely, errant, solipsistic mind and the objective reality of the world outside" (350).

It is not surprising, given Büchner's background and the direction of his study, that illness, especially psychological illness, appears in all his works and is of primary importance in *Lenz* and *Woyzeck*. Analysis of the illnesses he portrays and their treatment, or lack of it, and the relationship of Büchner's position to the medical knowledge and practice of his time has been the object of two published dissertations in the nineties: Sabine Kubik's *Krankheit und Medizin im literarischen Werk Georg Büchners* (Sickness and Medicine in the Literary Works of Georg Büchner) was written as a dissertation at the Ludwig-Maximilians University of Munich in 1990 and published in 1991; and *Büchner and Madness: Schizophrenia in Georg Büchner's Lenz and Woyzeck* by James

Crighton, a retired medical doctor, was presented as a dissertation at the University of Leicester in 1994 and published in 1998.

Kubik agrees with Dorothy James that Büchner's play was not written merely as a counterargument to Clarus but also and even more as a critique of the scientific view of medicine and the scientific method of investigation that were becoming predominant at the time. According to Kubik, Woyzeck is not presented unequivocally as organically sick or as a psychopathic murderer. The play contains no explicit diagnosis of Woyzeck's condition, and the question of his accountability remains open. In his awareness of the complexity of human behavior, determined as it is by hereditary and social factors, Büchner does not consider a clear judgment to be possible, and he is therefore critical of the unequivocalness that is a central postulate of forensic and juridical discourse. Emphasizing the inadequacy of the means of evaluation in those fields, he begins his investigation or presentation where medicine and justice reach their limits (167–70).

Kubik finds support for her argument in her study of the sequence of manuscripts, from which she concludes that Büchner gives greater emphasis in the second stage of the play's composition (H2) to Woyzeck's pathology and the origins of his illness. Through the introduction of the Captain and especially the Doctor, Büchner establishes a causal connection between Woyzeck's illness, the severity of which is increased in H2, and the socially superior figures who exploit and abuse him. The Doctor's interest in Woyzeck is limited to his diagnosis of Woyzeck's illness and to the contribution he may be able to make to the progress of science. He makes no attempt to treat or heal him. On the contrary, his experiments contribute significantly to Woyzeck's destabilization, Kubik assumes. Unfortunately, Kubik relies for most of her evidence on two scenes whose inclusion in the final version is questionable, namely, H2,7, in which the Doctor makes Woyzeck the victim of his scientific observations, and H3,1, in which Woyzeck is treated no better than an animal, and in which his symptoms can "undoubtedly" be attributed to the diet of peas the Doctor has subjected him to (64–71).

In his lack of humanity and medical ethics, the Doctor represents a type of scientist that was not uncommon in an era when positivistic, empirical scientific investigation was replacing the romantic, speculative *Naturphilosophie* as the dominant mode of discovery and in which science was becoming less human. Kubik refers to the similarity between Justus Liebig's nutritional experiments on soldiers and the Doctor's experiment on Woyzeck, and she also cites the example of doctors who dissected their own relations, including one Philip Meckel who dis-

sected three of his own deceased children and used his eight-year-old
nephew as his assistant (181–83, 189).

Though Büchner is seen by many critics as a precursor of modern
literature, and though his influence on writers in the twentieth century
has indeed been widespread and profound, Büchner belonged very
much to his own time in dealing with actual problems of the new positivistic science, according to Kubik. His doctor is the first in German
literature to be oriented to the natural sciences, and he is the only one
in the century to be treated critically, Kubik claims: the other doctor
figures in this period are heroized and idealized in keeping with the
new faith in the progress of science. Not until the expressionists in the
twentieth century were doctors again seen with a similarly critical eye
(250–58).

James Crighton's study is similar to Kubik's in its historical review
of philosophical and medical theories of madness and of the occurrence
of madness in works of literature. In keeping with his medical background and his diagnosis of Woyzeck, however, he gives greater emphasis to the symptoms and medical descriptions of what later became
known as schizophrenia. Unlike Kubik, he does not consider the Doctor, who is but one part of Woyzeck's threatening and unfathomable
world, to be responsible for Woyzeck's breakdown. According to
Crighton, the roots of Woyzeck's madness lie in his "resistance (defiance would be too strong a word) to the relentless forces which have
shaped the world he lives in and which have condemned him to subjection." Andres and Marie inhabit the same world, but they are pro-
tected by their passivity. Woyzeck attempts to understand the world
and to cling to the woman who gives his life meaning and stability. In
his attempt to find meaning in life and in nature, he is driven ever
deeper into unreason. Finally he sees only chaos in the world and he
sees himself devoid of all freedom. In what he calls "double nature"
Woyzeck perceives an unbridgeable gap between appearances and reality, most painfully in the person of Marie. His suffering is "caught in
this gulf between the essence of things and their appearance," a gulf
also evident in his relationship to Marie, his mate and the mother of his
child, in whom he discovers a whore (284, 275–76).

# Works Cited

Boa, Elizabeth. "Whores and Hetairas. Sexual Politics in the Works of Büchner and Wedekind." In *Tradition and Innovation: 14 Essays*, ed. Ken Mills and Brian Keith-Smith, 161–81. Bristol: U of Bristol P, 1990.

Crighton, James. *Büchner and Madness: Schizophrenia in Georg Büchner's Lenz and Woyzeck.* Bristol German Publications, Vol. 9. Lewiston, NY: The Edwin Mellen Press, 1998.

Dedner, Burghard. "Die Handlung des Woyzeck: wechselnde Orte — geschlossene Form." *Georg Büchner Jahrbuch* 7 (1988/89): 144–70.

Dunne, Kerry. "Woyzeck's Marie 'Ein schlecht Mensch'?: The Construction of Feminine Sexuality in Büchner's *Woyzeck*" *Seminar* 26 (1990): 294–308.

Gray, Richard T. "The Dialectic of Enlightenment in Büchner's *Woyzeck.*" *The German Quarterly* 61 (1988): 78–96.

Guthrie, John. *Lenz and Büchner: Studies in Dramatic Form.* Frankfurt: Lang, 1984.

James, Dorothy. "The 'Interesting Case' of Büchner's Woyzeck." In *Patterns of Change: German Drama and the European Tradition: Essays in Honour of Ronald Peacock.* Ed. Dorothy James and Sylvia Ranawake, 103–19. New York: Peter Lang, 1990.

Kittsteiner, Heinz-Dieter and Helmut Lethen. "Ich-Losigkeit, Entbürgerlichung und Zeiterfahrung. Über die Gleichgültigkeit zur 'Geschichte' in Büchner's *Woyzeck.*" *Georg Büchner Jahrbuch* 3 (1983): 240–269.

Kubik, S. *Krankheit und Medizin im literarischen Werk Georg Büchners.* Stuttgart: M. & P. Verlag für Wissenschaft und Forschung, 1991.

Larsen, Svend Erik. "Die Macht der Machtlosen. Über Lenz und Woyzeck." In *Georg Büchner im interkulturellen Dialog.* Eds. Klaus Bohnen and Ernst-Ulrich Pinkert, 176–94. Copenhagen: Verlag Text und Kontext; Munich: Fink, 1988.

Martin, Laura. "'Schlechtes Mensch/gutes Opfer': The Role of Marie in Georg Büchner's *Woyzeck.*" *German Life and Letters* 50 (1997): 427–44.

Mayer, Thomas Michael. "Zu einigen neueren Tendenzen der Büchner Forschung. Ein kritischer Literaturbericht (Teil II: Editionen)." In *Georg Büchner III.* Special issue in the series *Text und Kritik*, ed. Heinz Ludwig, 265–311. Munich: edition text + kritik, 1981.

McInnes, Edward. *Büchner, Woyzeck.* Glasgow: U. of Glasgow French and German Publications, 1991.

Meier, Albert. *Georg Büchner: "Woyzeck".* Munich: Fink, 1980.

Oesterle, Ingrid. "Verbale Präsenz und poetische Rücknahme des literarischen Schauers. Nachweise zur ästhetischen Vermitteltheit des Fatalismusproblems in Georg Büchners *Woyzeck.*" *Georg Büchner Jahrbuch* 3 (1983): 168–99.

Patterson, Michael. "Contradictions Concerning Time in Büchner's 'Woyzeck.'" *German Life and Letters* 32 (1978–79): 115–21.

Poschmann, Henri. *Georg Büchner: Dichtung der Revolution und Revolution der Dichtung.* Berlin, Weimar: Aufbau Verlag, 1983.

———. "Büchner ein Klassiker?" In *Büchner. Zeit, Geist, Zeit-Genossen*, 73–88. Darmstadt: Technische Hochschule Darmstadt, 1989.

Reddick, John. *Georg Büchner: The Shattered Whole.* Oxford: Clarendon Press, 1994.

Reuchlein, Georg. *Das Problem der Zurechnungsfähigkeit bei E. T. A. Hoffmann und Georg Büchner: Zum Verhältnis von Literatur, Psychiatrie und Justiz im frühen 19. Jahrhundert.* Frankfurt: Lang, 1985.

Wetzel, Heinz. "Die Entwicklung Woyzecks in Büchners Entwurfen." *Euphorion* 74 (1980): 375–96.

# Conclusion

T HE HISTORY OF THE CRITICISM OF WOYZECK is unique in that it is inseparable from the history of editions of the unfinished manuscripts and the constructions of a reading and acting text, a fact that has not always been obvious to the critics themselves. *Woyzeck* first became known in 1879 as *Wozzeck* in the poorly edited and badly contaminated edition by Karl Emil Franzos. The first critically sound edition was published in 1922 by Fritz Bergemann, but Bergemann changed the text in subsequent editions, which provided the model for other editors and therefore also the text used by scholars and critics until the publication of Werner R. Lehmann's edition in 1967 and Egon Krause's of 1969. Other editions followed, but the next substantial progress came with the publication by Gerhart Schmid in 1981 of a facsimile edition, which makes it possible to study the manuscripts without traveling to Weimar.

The problems faced by editors are twofold. On the one hand is the task of deciphering Büchner's handwriting and of determining the sequence of drafts and of scenes within the drafts, the task, in other words, of trying to determine as accurately as possible the actual text of the scenes, the sequence in which they were written, and how they relate to each other. On the other hand is the challenge of constructing a reading and acting text that comes as close as possible to what the author may have intended for a play that, from the evidence of his letters, he considered nearly ready for publication.

The facsimile edition does not put an end to the debate on editorial problems and especially on the task of constructing a reading and acting text from the various drafts, a debate that has been in progress since the mid-sixties, but it does give further support to what by now has become almost unanimous agreement on the sequence of the manuscripts and of the scenes within manuscripts. Schmid has determined the readings of some disputed words and phrases with a reasonable degree of probability, but others remain the object of controversy and most likely will never be resolved with certainty. Likewise, the construction of a reading and acting text will never be, and cannot be, determined with certainty: since no authorized text ever existed, every attempt to construct one requires some contamination, and every contamination is controversial.

Most scholars now agree that H4, Büchner's last working of the material, constitutes an authorized sequence of scenes. The order of

scenes in this manuscript should not be changed, nor should the sequence be disrupted by the interpolation of scenes from other drafts.
Only the minimal number of contaminations required for the construction of a reading and acting text should be introduced. These include above all the addition of a conclusion to H4 from H1. Further
contamination is necessary if one chooses to construct a fair scene to fill
the gap Büchner left for it in H4. At issue here is whether to rely entirely on the last version of the material in H2 or whether also to include the segment of the scene that takes place outside the booth but is
contained only in H1. The contamination of H4,9 by the addition of
material from H2,7 that includes Woyzeck's appearance is now considered by a majority of scholars to be inappropriate and unjustified.

Especially problematic is the disposition of the two scenes of H3.
Most scholars now agree that H3,1 (The Professor's Courtyard) precedes and was replaced by H4,8 and should not be included in a construction. On the other hand, nearly all editors and interpreters
advocate the inclusion of the scene H3,2 (The Idiot. The Child.
Woyzeck), but its placement remains controversial. The question is
whether it should follow H1,20, where it imposes an ending on the
play, namely, that Woyzeck is still on the loose and faces arrest and
trial, or whether it should be interpolated some place in the sequence
of scenes in H1 preceding Woyzeck's return to the pond, in which case
the possibility of drowning is not excluded.

It is not surprising that efforts to edit Büchner's manuscripts and
attempts to construct a minimally contaminated working text grew out
of and coincide with New Critical or *werkimmanent* studies of the
play's language, form, and structure. With a few exceptions, most of
the criticism before the fifties was not closely bound to the text. Positivistic, biographical, and historical studies dealt with content independent of form and treated such matters as influences on Büchner, his
connections to other literary movements, especially Romanticism, the
documentary material he used as his source, and the relationship between his figure and the historical Woyzeck. Likewise, language and
style had little relevance for the scholars who looked for mythological
motifs in literature and considered Woyzeck to be an embodiment of
Dionysian myth, the myth of the "Volk," or of the Christian Passion.
Although Büchner's political ideology and social thought were diamet-
rically opposed to the ideology and program of the National Socialists,
a few conservative or "pre-fascist" critics and those active during the
Third Reich were able to continue writing about Büchner by focusing
on the supposed appearance in his works of mythological, demonic, or
nationalistic elements, for example, his love of and concern for the

Volk, or by identifying the pessimistic and nihilistic consequences of his determinism as a symptom of the cultural disease that was in need of the Nazi cure.

Because of the importance in Büchner's life and works of his radical political activity and thought, criticism of his works has often had a political bias. The conflict of political ideologies was apparent in the criticism preceding the Third Reich and again in the postwar appearance of books by the Marxist Hans Mayer and the conservative Karl Viëtor. Political tendencies even had an impact on constructions of the text, as Fritz Bergemann, Werner R. Lehmann, and other editors admitted: by undertaking certain contaminations in their constructions, these editors were attempting to enhance what they considered to be the legitimate political and social-critical content of the play. Büchner's modern view of political and social forces and circumstances contributed, in turn, to his growing recognition in the politically oriented sixties and seventies and was the subject matter of numerous investigations and considerable controversy.

At the same time Büchner scholarship was becoming more politicized than ever before, it was also focusing on the style of his works more than at any time since Hans Winkler's pioneering dissertation (1925), which anticipated the New Critical analysis of the play's structure, language, imagery, and motifs, and Erwin Scheuer's 1929 study of the open form of drama. By the sixties Büchner had finally taken his place in the pantheon of classical or canonical German writers and had begun to attract the critical attention of literary scholars and historians outside of Germany. The first full-length study of Büchner and his works in America was published in 1964 by Herbert Lindenberger and was followed in the mid-seventies by three comprehensive studies in English and by numerous articles and dissertations. Critics outside Germany joined their German counterparts in the continuing exploration of, and controversy over, problems and issues identified by early critics such as the conflicts between determinism and freedom, man and nature, the individual and society, atheism or nihilism and Christian faith. In several studies of Büchner's aesthetics, renewed attempts were made to define his realism in opposition to idealism and to better characterize his use of the open form of drama, or, indeed, to argue that the form of his plays is not open at all.

The series of modernist and postmodernist methodologies beginning with structuralism have had relatively little impact on Büchner scholarship. The wave of feminist criticism, on the other hand, has yielded several essays on *Woyzeck*: feminist critics give more attention to Marie's tragedy and her role in the play as a representative of oppressed women in a patriarchal society, and they take pre-feminist criticism to task for its patriarchal perspective and its failure to give Marie her due. The novelty of this criticism lies more in emphasis and perspective than in its findings and interpretations, which do not differ substantially from those offered by some earlier writers.

Finally, following several decades of fundamental work on the text, recent criticism has focused on the historical Woyzeck and the social conditions in which he lived; on Clarus's medical reports evaluating his mental state, the controversy they gave rise to, and the psychological, medical, and juridical context in which this controversy took place; and on the identification of new motifs and motif complexes and the exploration in greater depth of themes, motifs, images, and other elements identified by earlier scholars. Considering how much has been written about this short play, one might think that little or nothing remains to be said, but given the resourcefulness of scholars and the inevitable development of new approaches to the analysis of texts, the ongoing process of discovery will surely continue.

# Appendix: The Manuscripts of *Woyzeck*

AFTER DECADES OF STUDY AND DEBATE, editors of *Woyzeck* now agree that the manuscripts consist of (1) five gray folio sheets containing two sequences or groups of scenes (H1 and H2) (2) a single quarto sheet with two scenes (H3) and (3) six folded quarto sheets with seventeen scenes that appear to represent the fair copy of a final version (H4). Although there is still some disagreement on the sequence of scenes in H1, the following order of scenes has now become generally accepted.

## H1

1. Buden. Volk (Fair Booths. People)

2. Das Innere der Bude (Inside the Booth)

3. Margreth allein (Margret [=Marie] alone)

4. Der Casernenhof (Barracks)

5. Wirtshaus (Inn)

6. Freies Feld (Open Field)

7. Ein Zimmer (A Room)

8. Casernenhof (Barracks)

9. Der Officier. Louis (Officer. Louis [=Woyzeck])

10. Ein Wirtshaus (An Inn)

11. Das Wirtshaus (The Inn)

12. Freies Feld (Open Field)

13. Nacht. Mondschein (Night. Moonlight)

14. Margreth mit Mädchen vor der Hausthür (Margret with Girls in front of the House Door)

15. Margreth und Louis (Margret and Louis)

16. Es kommen Leute (People approach)

17. Das Wirtshaus (The Inn)

18. Kinder (Children)

19. Louis allein (Louis alone)

20. Louis an einem Teich (Louis by a Pond)

21. Gerichtsdiener. Barbier. Arzt. Richter (Court Clerk. Barber. Doctor. Judge)

## H2

1. Freies Feld. Die Stadt in der Ferne (Open Field. The City in the Distance)

2. Die Stadt (The City)

3. Öffentlicher Platz. Buden. Lichter (Public Place. Booths. Lights)

4. Handwerkburschen (Journeymen)

5. Unterofficier. Tambourmajor (Sergeant. Drum Major)

6. Woyzeck. Doctor (Woyzeck. Doctor)

7. Strasse (Street)

8. Woyzeck. Louisel (Woyzeck. Louise [=Marie])

9. Louisel allein. Gebet (Louise alone. Prayer)

## H3

1. Der Hof des Professors (The Professor's Courtyard)

2. Der Idiot. Das Kind. Woyzeck (The Idiot. The Child. Woyzeck)

## H4

1. Freies Feld. Die Stadt in der Ferne (Open Field. The City in the Distance)

2. Marie mit ihrem Kind am Fenster. Margreth (Marie with her Child at the Window. Margret)

3. Buden. Lichter. Volk (Booths. Lights. People) (Consists only of a title followed by a page and one-half left blank)

4. Marie sizt, ihr Kind auf dem Schoos, ein Stückchen Spiegel in der Hand (Marie Sits, her Child in her Lap, a Piece of Mirror in her Hand)

5. Der Hauptmann. Woyzeck (The Captain. Woyzeck)

6. Marie. Tambour-Major (Marie. Drum Major)

7. Marie. Woyzeck (Marie. Woyzeck)

8. Woyzeck. Der Doctor (Woyzeck. The Doctor)

9. Hauptmann. Doctor (Captain. Doctor)

10. Die Wachtstube. (The Guardhouse)

11. Wirtshaus (Inn)

12. Freies Feld (Open Field)

13. Nacht (Night)

14. Wirtshaus (Inn)

15. Woyzeck. Der Jude (Woyzeck. The Jew)

16. Marie. Der Narr (Marie. The Fool)

17. Caserne (Barracks)

# Works by Georg Büchner

1834. *Der hessische Landbote*. Privately printed.

1835. *Dantons Tod*. Frankfurt: J. D. Sauerländer.

1835. *Leonce und Lena*. Published 1838 in *Telegraph für Deutschland*.

1835–37. Work on *Lenz*. Published 1839 in *Telegraph für Deutschland*.

1836–37. Work on *Woyzeck*. Published 1879 in *Sämmtliche Werke und handschriftlicher Nachlaß*, ed. Karl Emil Franzos. Frankfurt: J. D. Sauerländer.

# Works Cited

Franzos, Karl Emil, ed. 1879. *Georg Büchner's Sämmtliche Werke und hand-schriftlicher Nachlaß: Erste kritische Gesammt-Ausgabe.* Frankfurt: J. D. Sauerländer.

Landau, Paul. 1909. *Georg Büchners Gesammelte Schriften.* 2 vols. Berlin: Paul Cassirer.

Majut, Rudolf. 1912. "Farbe und Licht im Kunstgefühl Büchners." Ph.D. diss., Greifswald.

Bieber, Hugo. 1914. "Wozzeck und Woyzeck." *Das Literarische Echo* 17: 1188–91.

Zobel von Zabeltitz, Max. 1915. *Georg Büchner, sein Leben und sein Schaffen.* Berlin: G. Grote.

Hausenstein, Wilhelm. 1916. *Georg Büchner: Gesammelte Werke, nebst einer Auswahl seiner Briefe.* Leipzig: Insel.

Witkowski, Georg. 1919–20. "Büchners 'Woyzeck.'" *Inselschiff* 1: 20–30.

Bergemann, Fritz. 1920. "Der Fall Woyzeck in Wahrheit und Dichtung." *Inselschiff* 1: 242–49.

Kupsch, Walter. 1920. "'Wozzeck.' Ein Beitrag zum Schaffen Georg Büchners (1813–1837)." *Germanische Studien* 4. Berlin: Emil Ebering.

Bergemann, Fritz. 1922. *Georg Büchners Sämtliche Werke und Briefe.* Leipzig: Insel.

Hoyer, Walter. 1922. "Stoff und Gestalt bei Georg Büchner." Ph.D. diss., Leipzig.

Lipmann, Heinz. 1923. *Georg Büchner und die Romantik.* Munich: Hueber Verlag.

Renker, Armin. 1924. *Georg Büchner und das Lustspiel der Romantik: Eine Studie über "Leonce und Lena."* Berlin: Emil Ebering.

Winkler, Hans. 1925. *Büchners 'Woyzeck.'* Greifswald: Ratsbuchhandlung L. Bamberg.

Scheuer, Erwin. 1929. *Akt und Szene in der offenen Form des Dramas, darge-stellt an den Dramen Georg Büchners.* Berlin: Emil Ebering.

Gundolf, Friedrich. 1930. "Georg Büchner." Chap. in *Romantiker*, 375–95. Berlin-Wilmersdorf: H. Keller. Also in Martens, ed., 1965, 82–97.

Viëtor, Karl. 1936. "Woyzeck." *Das innere Reich* 3: 182–205. Also in Martens, ed., 1965, 151–77.

Schmid, Peter. 1940. *Büchner: Versuch über die tragische Existenz.* Bern: Verlag Paul Haupt.

Diem, Eugen. 1946. *Georg Büchners Leben und Werk.* Heidelberg: Meister.

Mayer, Hans. 1946. *Georg Büchner und seine Zeit.* Wiesbaden: Limes Verlag. 2nd ed., 1959.

Büttner, Ludwig. 1948. *Georg Büchner: Revolutionär und Pessimist. Ein Beitrag zur Geistesgeschichte des 19. Jahrhunderts.* Nuremberg: Verlag Hans Carl.

Wiese, Benno von. 1948. *Die deutsche Tragödie von Lessing bis Hebbel.* Hamburg: Hoffmann und Campe.

Viëtor, Karl. 1949. *Georg Büchner: Politik, Dichtung, Wissenschaft.* Bern: Francke.

Knight, Arthur H. J. 1951. *Georg Büchner.* Oxford: Blackwell.

Martens, Wolfgang. 1957–58. "Zum Menschenbild Georg Büchners. 'Woyzeck' und die Marionszene in 'Dantons Tod.'" *Wirkendes Wort* 8: 13–20. Also in Martens, ed., 1965, 373–85.

Höllerer, Walter. 1958. "Georg Büchner." In Höllerer, *Zwischen Klassik und Moderne: Lachen und Weinen in der Dichtung einer Übergangszeit,* 100–142. Stuttgart: Ernst Klett Verlag.

Johann, Ernst. 1958. *Georg Büchner in Selbstzeugnissen und Bilddokumenten.* Hamburg: Rowohlt.

Krapp, Helmut. 1958. *Der Dialog bei Georg Büchner.* Literatur als Kunst. Darmstadt: Gentner. (Since 1959: Munich: Hanser.)

Martens, Wolfgang. 1958. "Zur Karikatur in der Dichtung Büchners. (Woyzecks Hauptmann)." *Germanisch-Romanische Monatsschrift* 39, New series 8: 64–71.

Klotz, Volker. 1960. *Geschlossene und offene Form im Drama.* Literatur als Kunst. Munich: Hanser.

Martens, Wolfgang. 1960. "Der Barbier in Büchners 'Woyzeck'. (Zugleich ein Beitrag zur Motivgeschichte der Barbierfigur)." *Zeitschrift für deutsche Philologie 79: 361–83.*

Fink, Gonthier-Louis. 1961. "Volkslied und Verseinlage in den Dramen Georg Büchners." *Deutsche Vierteljahrsschrift* 35: 558–93. Also in Martens, ed., 1965, 443–87.

Mautner, Franz Heinrich. 1961. "Wortgewebe, Sinngefüge und 'Idee' in Büchners 'Woyzeck.'" *Deutsche Vierteljahrsschrift* 35: 521–557. Also in Martens, ed., 1965, 507–54.

Weiss, Walter. 1962. "Georg Büchner." In Weiss, *Enttäuschter Pantheismus: Zur Weltgestaltung der Dichtung in der Restaurationszeit*, 247–301. Dornbirn: Voralberger Verlagsanstalt.

Lehmann, Werner R. 1963. "Prolegomena zu einer historisch-kritischen Büchner Ausgabe." In *Gratulatio: Festschrift für Christian Wegner zum 70. Geburtstag*. Ed. Maria Honeit and Matthias Wegner, 190–225. Hamburg: Christian Wegner Verlag.

Meinerts, Jürgen, ed. 1963. *Georg Büchner: Sämtliche Werke nebst Briefen und anderen Dokumenten*. Gütersloh: S. Mohn.

Steiner, George. 1963. *The Death of Tragedy*. New York: Hill and Wang.

Lindenberger, Herbert Samuel. 1964. *Georg Büchner*. Carbondale: Southern Illinois UP.

Müller-Seidel, Walter, ed. 1964. "Georg Büchner, Woyzeck." In *Klassische Deutsche Dichtung*, vol. 15: *Bürgerliches Trauerspiel und soziales Drama*. Ed. Fritz Martini and Walter Müller-Seidel. Freiburg, Basel, Vienna: Herder.

Paulus, Ursula. 1964. "Georg Büchners 'Woyzeck.' Eine kritische Betrachtung zu der Edition Fritz Bergemanns." *Jahrbuch der deutschen Schiller-Gesellschaft* 8: 226–46.

Elema, J. 1965. "Der verstümmelte 'Woyzeck.'" *Neophilologus* 49: 131–56.

Martens, Wolfgang, ed. 1965. *Georg Büchner*. Darmstadt: Wissenschaftliche Buchgesellschaft.

Völker, Ludwig. 1966. "Woyzeck und die Natur." *Revue des langues vivantes* 32: 611–32.

Büttner, Ludwig. 1967. *Büchners Bild vom Menschen*. Nuremberg: Verlag Hans Carl.

Henze, Eberhard. 1967. "Mensch oder Marionette? Gedanken zu Kleist und Büchner." *Merkur* 21: 1144–54.

Lehmann, Werner R. 1967. *Georg Büchner: Sämtliche Werke und Briefe*. Vol. 1, *Dichtungen und Übersetzungen mit Dokumentation zur Stoffgeschichte*. Hamburg: Christian Wegner Verlag.

———. 1967. *Textkritische Noten: Prolegomena zur Hamburger Büchner-Ausgabe*. Hamburg: Christian Wegner Verlag.

Emrich, Wilhelm. 1968. "Georg Büchner und die moderne Literatur." In Emrich, *Polemic*, 131–72. Frankfurt: Athenäum.

Müller-Seidel, Walter. 1968. "Natur und Naturwisssenschaft im Werk Georg Büchners." In *Festschrift für Klaus Ziegler*. Ed. E. Catholy and Winifried Hellmann, 205–32. Tübingen: Niemeyer.

Schlick, Werner. 1968. *Das Georg Büchner-Schrifttum bis 1965: Eine Internationale Bibliographie*. Hildesheim: Georg Olms Verlagsbuchhandlung.

Abutille, Mario Carlo. 1969. *Angst und Zynismus bei Georg Büchner.* Basler Studien zur deutschen Sprache und Literatur 40. Bern: Francke.

Krause, Egon, ed. 1969. *Woyzeck: Texte und Dokumente.* Frankfurt: Insel.

Pongs, Hermann. 1969. "Büchners 'Woyzeck.'" In Pongs, *Das Bild in der Dichtung.* Vol. 3, 618–63. Marburg: N. G. Elwert'sche Verlagsbuchhandlung.

Schmidt, Henry J., trans. 1969. *Georg Büchner: Woyzeck.* New York: Avon.

Buch, Wilfried. 1970. *Woyzeck: Fassungen und Wandlungen.* Dortmund: Crüwell.

Lehmann, Werner R. 1971. *Georg Büchner: Sämtliche Werke und Briefe.* Vol. 2, *Vermischte Schriften und Briefe.* Hamburg: Christian Wegner Verlag.

———. 1971. "Repliken: Beiträge zu einem Streitgespräch über den *Woyzeck.*" *Euphorion* 65: 58–83.

Richards, David G. 1971. "Zur Textgestaltung von Georg Büchners *Woyzeck*: Anmerkungen zur Hamburger Büchner-Ausgabe, den *Woyzeck* betreffend." *Euphorion* 65: 49–57.

Bornscheuer, Lothar. 1972. *Erläuterungen und Dokumente: Georg Büchner: Woyzeck.* Stuttgart: Reclam.

———. 1972. *Woyzeck: Kritische Lese- und Arbeitsausgabe.* Stuttgart: Reclam.

Lamberechts, Luc. 1972. "Zur Struktur von Büchners 'Woyzeck.' Mit einer Darstellung des dramaturgischen Verhältnisses Büchner-Brecht." *Amsterdamer Beiträge zur neueren Germanistik* 1: 119–48.

Ullman, Bo. 1972. *Die sozialkritische Problematik im Werk Georg Büchners und ihre Entfaltung im "Woyzeck," mit einigen Bemerkungen zu der Oper Alban Bergs.* Stockholmer Germanistische Forschungen 10. Stockholm: Almqvist & Wiksell.

———. 1972. "Der unpolitische Büchner. Zum Büchner-Bild der Forschung, unter Berücksichtigung der 'Woyzeck'-Interpretation." *Stockholm Studies in Modern Philology,* N.S. 4: 86–130.

Kanzog, Klaus. 1973. "Wozzeck, Woyzeck und kein Ende: Zur Standortbestimmung der Editionsphilologie." *Deutsche Vierteljahrsschrift* 47: 420–42.

Wiese, Benno von. 1973. "Der 'arme' Woyzeck. Ein Beitrag zur Umwertung des Heldenideals im 19. Jahrhundert." In *Texte und Kontexte: Studien zur deutschen und vergleichenden Literaturwissenschaft. Festschrift für Norbert Fuerst.* Ed. Manfred Durzak, 309–26. Bern, Munich: Francke.

Hauser, Ronald. 1974. *Georg Büchner.* Twayne World Authors Series. New York: Twayne Publishers.

Kobel, Erwin. 1974. *Georg Büchner: Das dichterische Werk.* Berlin: Walter de Gruyter.

Knapp, Gerhard P. 1975. *Georg Büchner: Eine kritische Einführung in die Forschung.* Frankfurt: Fischer Athenäum Taschenbücher.

Mori, Mitsuaki. 1975. "Der Barbier und die Bogenanordung der WOYZECK-Handschriften." In *Memoirs of the Faculty of General Education. Kamamoto University. Series of the Humanities* 10: 157–71.

Richards, David G. 1975. *Georg Büchners Woyzeck: Textgestaltung und Interpretation.* Bonn: H. Bouvier Verlag.

Benn, Maurice B. 1976. *The Drama of Revolt: A Critical Study of Georg Büchner.* London, New York, Melbourne: Cambridge UP.

Ueding, Cornelie. 1976. *Denken, Sprechen, Handeln: Aufklärung und Auflkärungskritik im Werk Georg Büchners.* Bern, Frankfurt: Herbert Lang.

Knapp, Gerhard P. 1977. *Georg Büchner.* Stuttgart: Sammlung Metzler. 2nd revised edition, 1984.

Richards, David G. 1977. *Georg Büchner and the Birth of the Modern Drama.* Albany: State U of New York P.

Schmidt, Henry J., ed. and trans. 1977. *Georg Büchner: The Complete Collected Works.* New York: Avon.

Grandin, John M. 1977–78. "Woyzeck and the Last Judgment." *German Life and Letters* 31: 175–79.

Otten, Terry. 1978. "*Woyzeck* and *Othello*: The Dimension of Melodrama." *Comparative Drama* 12: 123–36.

Schwarz, Alfred. 1978. *From Büchner to Beckett: Dramatic Theory and the Modes of Tragic Drama.* Athens, OH: Ohio UP.

Wittkowski, Wolfgang. 1978. *Georg Büchner. Persönlichkeit. Weltbild. Werk.* Heidelberg: Winter.

Patterson, Michael. 1978–79. "Contradictions Concerning Time in Büchner's 'Woyzeck.'" *German Life and Letters* 32: 115–21.

Gaede, Friedrich. 1979. "Büchner's Widerspruch — Zur Funktion des 'type primitif.'" *Jahrbuch der internationalen Germanistik* 11: 42–52.

Meier, Albert. 1980. *Georg Büchner: "Woyzeck."* Munich: Fink.

Wetzel, Heinz. 1980. "Die Entwicklung Woyzecks in Büchner's Entwürfen." *Euphorion* 74: 375–96.

Mayer, Thomas Michael. 1981. "Zu einigen neueren Tendenzen der Büchner Forschung. Ein kritischer Literaturbericht (Teil II: Editionen)." In *Georg Büchner III.* Special issue in the series *Text und Kritik.* Ed. Heinz Ludwig, 265–311. Munich: edition text + kritik.

Schmid, Gerhard, ed. 1981. *Georg Büchner: Woyzeck. Faksimileausgabe der Handschriften.* Leipzig: Edition Leipzig; Wiesbaden: Dr. Ludwig Reichert Verlag.

Kittsteiner, Heinz-Dieter, and Helmut Lethen. 1983. "Ich-Losigkeit, Entbürgerlichung und Zeiterfahrung. Über die Gleichgültigkeit zur 'Geschichte' in Büchner's *Woyzeck*." *Georg Büchner Jahrbuch* 3: 240–269.

Oesterle, Ingrid. 1983. "Verbale Präsenz und poetische Rücknahme des literarischen Schauers. Nachweise zur ästhetischen Vermitteltheit des Fatalismusproblems in Georg Büchners *Woyzeck*." *Georg Büchner Jahrbuch* 3: 168–99.

Poschmann, Henri. 1983. *Georg Büchner: Dichtung der Revolution und Revolution der Dichtung*. Berlin, Weimar: Aufbau Verlag.

———. 1984. *Georg Büchner. Woyzeck. Nach den Handschriften neu hergestellt und kommentiert*. Leipzig, Insel.

Guthrie, John. 1984. *Lenz and Büchner: Studies in Dramatic Form*. Frankfurt, Bern, New York: Lang.

Knapp, Gerhard P. 1984. *Georg Büchner*. 2nd ed. Stuttgart: Metzler.

Reuchlein, Georg. 1985. *Das Problem der Zurechnungsfähigkeit bei E. T. A. Hoffmann und Georg Büchner: Zum Verhältnis von Literatur, Psychiatrie und Justiz im frühen 19. Jahrhundert*. Frankfurt: Lang.

Gray, Richard T. 1988. "The Dialectic of Enlightenment in Büchner's *Woyzeck*." *The German Quarterly* 61: 78–96.

Hartung, Günther. 1988. "Woyzeck's Wahn." *Weimarer Beiträge* 34: 1102–17.

Larsen, Svend Erik. 1988. "Die Macht der Machtlosen. Über Lenz und Woyzeck." In *Georg Büchner im interkulturellen Dialog*. Eds. Klaus Bohnen and Ernst-Ulrich Pinkert, 176–94. Copenhagen: Verlag Text und Kontext; Munich: Fink.

Schmid, Gerhard. 1988. "Probleme der Textkonstituierung bei Büchners 'Woyzeck.'" In *Studien zu Georg Büchner*. Ed. Hans-Georg Werner, 207–226, 331–34. Berlin: Aufbau-Verlag.

Dedner, Burghard. 1988–89. "Die Handlung des Woyzeck: wechselnde Orte — geschlossene Form." *Georg Büchner Jahrbuch* 7: 144–70.

Poschmann, Henri. 1989. "Büchner ein Klassiker?" In Poschmann, *Büchner: Zeit, Geist, Zeit-Genossen*, 73–88. Darmstadt: Technische Hochschule Darmstadt.

Boa, Elizabeth. 1990. "Whores and Hetairas. Sexual Politics in the Works of Büchner and Wedekind." In *Tradition and Innovation: 14 Essays*. Ed. Ken Mills and Brian Keith-Smith, 161–81. Bristol: U of Bristol P.

Dunne, Kerry. 1990. "Woyzeck's Marie 'Ein schlecht Mensch'?: The Construction of Feminine Sexuality in Büchner's *Woyzeck*." *Seminar* 26: 294–308.

Goltschnigg, Dietmar, ed. 1990. *Büchner im "Dritten Reich": Mystifikation, Gleichschaltung, Exil; eine Dokumentation*. Bielefeld: Aisthesis-Verlag.

James, Dorothy. 1990. "The 'Interesting Case' of Büchner's Woyzeck." In *Patterns of Change: German Drama and the European Tradition: Essays in Honour of Ronald Peacock*. Ed. Dorothy James and Sylvia Ranawake, 103–19. New York: Peter Lang.

Kubik, Sabine. 1991. *Krankheit und Medizin im literarischen Werk Georg Büchners*. Stuttgart: M. & P. Verlag für Wissenschaft und Forschung.

McInnes, Edward. 1991. *Büchner, Woyzeck*. Glasgow: U. of Glasgow French and German Publications.

Poschmann, Henri. 1992. *Georg Büchner: Sämtliche Werke, Briefe und Dokumente*. Frankfurt: Deutscher Klassiker Verlag.

Reddick, John. 1994. *Georg Büchner: The Shattered Whole*. Oxford: Clarendon Press.

Martin, Laura. 1997. "'Schlechtes Mensch/gutes Opfer': The Role of Marie in Georg Büchner's *Woyzeck*." *German Life and Letters* 50: 427–44.

Crighton, James. 1998. *Büchner and Madness: Schizophrenia in Georg Büchner's* Lenz *and* Woyzeck. Bristol German Publications, Vol. 9. Lewiston, NY: The Edwin Mellen Press.

# Index